Irish Sign Language

Irish Sign Language

A Cognitive Linguistic Account

LORRAINE LEESON AND JOHN I. SAEED

EDINBURGH
University Press

Edinburgh University Press Ltd
22 George Square, Edinburgh

www.euppublishing.com

Typeset in 10/12 Times New Roman
by Servis Filmsetting Ltd, Stockport, Cheshire, and
printed and bound in Great Britain by
CPI Group (UK) Ltd, Croydon, CR0 4YY

A CIP record for this book is available from the British Library

ISBN 978 0 7486 3823 9 (hardback)
ISBN 978 0 7486 5629 5 (webready PDF)
ISBN 978 0 7486 5650 9 (epub)
ISBN 978 0 7486 5630 1 (Amazon ebook)

Contents

Figures and Tables

Figures

Table

Preface

This book seeks to provide a description of Irish Sign Language (ISL) based on how the language is used by Deaf ISL users from across Ireland. Irish Sign Language is a visual-gestural language used by some 6,500 Deaf people across the island of Ireland and an estimated 65,000 hearing signers. ISL is quite distinct in its structure and history from its near neighbour, British Sign Language (BSL). The description of ISL is still in its infancy but the authors have had the advantage of drawing on one of the largest multi-modal corpora of a signed language in the world, the Signs of Ireland corpus, described in Chapter 1. Using this corpus we offer a description of the phonetics, phonology, morphology, syntax and discourse that is grounded in a cognitive linguistic account, the first of its kind for Irish Sign Language. This approach promises new insights into the role within ISL of gesture, spatial models, iconicity, metaphor and metonymy. The book's accompanying DVD presents examples used in the discussion in a realistic dynamic form.

We have attempted, as far as space will allow, to set this description against the social and historical context of the language. We trace aspects of the history of the language, outlining some of the influences that other signed and spoken languages have had, and tell the story of how ISL has influenced other signed languages including Australian Sign Language and South African Sign Language. The volume also highlights the link between educational policy and language outcomes for ISL users in historical and contemporary settings.

We would like to thank the following people for their help, support, insights, encouragement and enthusiasm in making this book possible: Mr Robert Adam, Prof. Brita Bergman, Ms Suzanne Bussiere, Br Martin Byrne, Dr John Bosco Conama, Dr Onno Crasborn, Mr Senan Dunne, Ms Angela Fitzgerald, Ms Julianne Gillen, Ms Meryl Glaser, Ms Carmel Grehan, Prof. Terry Janzen, Dr Jeff Kallen, Prof. Jim Kyle, Prof. Barbara LeMaster, Prof. David Little, Ms Teresa Lynch, Mr Patrick Matthews, Dr Patrick McDonnell, Ms Suzanne Militzer (now Mohr), Dr Anna-Lena Nilsson, Dr Brian Nolan, Dr Rosemary Orr, Sr Renee Rossouw, Dr Adam Schembri, Dr Rachel Sutton-Spence, Ms Gudny Thorvaldsdottir, Dr

Myriam Vermeerbergen, Sr Margaret Wall, O.P., Profs Sherman and Phyllis Wilcox, Prof. Erin Wilkinson and Prof. Bencie Woll.

We are indebted to the forty Irish Deaf people who kindly participated in the Signs of Ireland digital corpus project and without whom this book would not be possible: Nicholas Banville, Frankie Berry, Eilish Bradley, Bernadette Costello, Louise Deane, Michael Doran, Fergus Dunne, Noeleen Dunne, Fiona Ennis-Regan, Geraldine Fitzgerald, Orla Grehan, Marion Hayes, Eric Hennessey, Sean Herlighy, James Horan, Mary King, Catherine Landers, Kevin Lynch, Michelle MacLaughlin, Willie John Mariga, Fergus Massey, Linda McLoughlin, Marion Moloney, Sarah-Jane Moloney, Annie Murphy, Peter Murray, Mary O'Connor, Patrick O'Rourke, Rebecca O'Meara, Lianne Quigley, Noreen Ryan, Laurence Stanley, Valerie Stanley, Margaret Sutton, Alice Walsh, Derek Walsh, Michael Walsh, Patrick Whelan, Helen Winters and Caroline Worthington.

We also owe special thanks to the annotators of this data: Deirdre Byrne-Dunne, Cormac Leonard and Alison Macduff for their years of effort. We also thank colleagues at the Max Planck Institute, Nijmegen, for their work in creating and supporting ELAN, which made the SOI project possible. We acknowledge the support of Trinity College Dublin's Arts and Social Sciences Benefaction Fund, which funded the purchase of a video camera and covered some of the costs associated with the SOI data collection and annotation.

We thank those authors, editors and publishers who have supported this publication by giving permission to reproduce illustrations and images in this document:

Example 4.10, from Patrick A. Matthews (1996a), with permission, IRAAL.
Example 5.9, from Patrick A. Matthews, with permission.
Example 5.10, from Patrick McDonnell (1996), with permission.
Example 5.12, from Patrick McDonnell (1996), with permission.
Example 6.8(a), from Leeson and Grehan (2004), with permission.
Example 6.9, from Leeson and Grehan (2004), with permission.
Example 6.10, from Carmel Grehan, with permission.
Example 8.5, Julianne Gillen interview, SIGNALL II project, Leonardo da Vinci (2008–10), from Interesource Group (Ireland) Limited, with permission.
Figure 2.1, from Patrick A. Matthews (1996a), with permission, IRAAL.
Figure 3.2, from Suzanne Bussiere, with permission.
Figure 4.1, from Patrick A. Matthews (2005), with permission, Forest Books.
Figure 4.2F, adapted from Thomas Hanke, Hamburg University, with permission (see <http://www.sign-lang.uni-hamburg.de/projekte/hamnosys/hamnosyserklaerungen/englisch/contents.html>).
Figure 4.3, from Thomas Hanke, Hamburg University, with permission.
Figure 4.4 from Susanne Militzer (2009), with permission.

Figure 4.5 from Susanne Militzer (2009), with permission.
Figure 5.1 from Patrick McDonnell (1996), with permission.

We owe special thanks to Haaris Sheikh (Interesource Group (Ireland) Limited) and Gillian Quinlan for their assistance in preparing photographic data, images and video clips for this volume and accompanying DVD.

John would like to thank Joan Maguire for her support and Carmel Grehan for her skill and patience as a teacher of ISL. Lorraine would like to thank the Leeson clan for their patience, encouragement and support and Prof. Bencie Woll for instigating the desire to learn more about how ISL works. A very special vote of thanks goes to the ever-enthusiastic Haaris. Finally, both authors give thanks to the community of ISL users who help them do this – THANK YOU.

1 Introduction

1.1 Introducing Irish Sign Language

Irish Sign Language (ISL) is the language used by an estimated 5,000 Deaf people in the Republic of Ireland and some 1,500 signers in Northern Ireland. It is neither Irish (Gaeilge) on the hands nor English in manual form. ISL is a natural human language that has evolved over time and is distinct also from the signed languages of other countries that share English as a spoken language, such as Britain, where British Sign Language (BSL) is used, and the United States of America, where American Sign Language (ASL) is used. Irish Sign Language has no formal standing in law in the Republic of Ireland although it has been mentioned in the Education Act 1998. In contrast, Irish Sign Language along with British Sign Language is recognised by the British Government under the auspices of the Good Friday Agreement.[1] As we shall see in Chapter 3, the history of modern Irish Sign Language can be traced back to the early nineteenth century. While we know that some variety of signed language was used before that in Ireland, there is little documentation available to us to support any meaningful recreation of what that language looked like. However, with the establishment of the first schools for the deaf in the early 1800s, communities of Deaf signers formed and documentation began to grow, upon which we can draw in tracing the development of ISL and the influences on it. As we shall see, these influences include BSL, French Sign Language (Langue des Signes Française, LSF), spoken English, French, and cued speech and gesture. While the late-twentieth-century Irish Deaf community made efforts to resist influences from BSL, what we find is that it has in reality been a main source of influence on ISL for at least 200 years.

The link between these varied influences is educational policy: both BSL and LSF were linguistic instruments in the establishment in Ireland of the first Protestant and Catholic schools for the deaf, respectively. These languages, though not recognised as having full linguistic status in the nineteenth century, were modified by educationalists to become carriers for English via a system called signed English. With the suppression of signed language in the twentieth century, a system of teaching through speech called oralism was implemented, which, as we shall see in Chapter 3, had devastating consequences for many. Another result of this was the introduction of English mouth patterns, or mouthings, into ISL. For some students, mostly girls in St Mary's School for Deaf Girls, in Cabra, Dublin, a system called cued speech was introduced and remnants of that system have permeated ISL and have become one element of women's signing.

The fact that ISL was suppressed during the strong oralist period in the mid twentieth century and the fact that more than 90 per cent of Irish deaf children are born to parents who are not deaf has meant that the transmission pathways to acquiring ISL became more complex. In the absence of Deaf adult caregivers who were themselves ISL users, children draw on gesture to bootstrap their language development, sometimes supported by spoken language. Despite this atypical environment for language acquisition and the concurrent lack of institutional status associated with its use, ISL has survived and thrived. It has also been a language of influence in other countries where Irish missionaries and educators travelled alongside the British Empire's civil service. Irish missionaries travelled to British colonies to provide education, medical care and chaplaincy services for the military and civil servants who administered the colonies, as well as embarking on missionary endeavours. As a result, Irish religious orders and some lay teachers engaged in deaf education travelled to Australia and South Africa bringing with them Irish Sign Language, with discernible influences still evident in some varieties of Australian and South African Sign Languages.

1.2 The Signs of Ireland corpus

This book aims to provide a linguistic snapshot of Irish Sign Language as used at the turn of the twenty-first century in the Republic of Ireland. We do this by building on linguistic analysis of the language over the past two decades by a relatively small number of people, and we emphasise that we are still in the early days of understanding the detail of many parts of this linguistic system, particularly at the level of syntax and discourse structure. At the same time, this study of ISL is boosted by the availability of a digital multi-modal corpus of Irish Sign Language called the Signs of Ireland (SOI) corpus. The SOI corpus is part of the Languages of Ireland programme at the School of Linguistic, Speech and Communication Sciences, Trinity College Dublin (TCD). It comprises video data from Deaf users of ISL from across the Republic of Ireland in digital form, and has been annotated using ELAN, a software program developed by the Max Planck Institute, Nijmegen. The corpus is housed at the Centre for Deaf Studies, TCD.

The Signs of Ireland corpus consists of data from forty signers aged between 18 and 65 years, at time of filming, from five locations across the Republic of Ireland: Dublin, Wexford, Waterford, Cork and Galway. It includes male and female signers, all of whom had been educated in schools for the deaf in Dublin, St Mary's School for Deaf Girls and St Joseph's School for Deaf Boys. This allows for comparison between male and female sign variants, insofar as they were captured in the data, as well as gendered generational issues in areas such as mouthing, fingerspelling and lexical choice. In building the corpus, we deliberately decided to include no signed language teachers, other than a first signer who served as a pilot data set. The aim was to avoid the collection of data from signers who had firm notions of correct or pure ISL. Instead, the corpus aims to capture ISL in its authentic form as used by ordinary Deaf people from across the country in order to reveal how the language is really used and help provide students with data that are far removed from the classroom. Users of the corpus can access a range of signing styles, age groups and content type that has not been previously available. While all the informants use ISL as their preferred language, only a minority are native signers from Deaf families. The majority are not native signers, but several have Deaf siblings. All forty signers use ISL as their first or preferred language.

All of the data were collected by a female Deaf researcher, Deirdre Byrne-Dunne, in 2004 and annotated by Ms Byrne along with Cormac Leonard and Alison MacDuff between 2005 and 2007. This allowed for consistency in terms of data elicitation. It also meant that, due to the nature of the Irish Deaf Community, Ms Byrne was known to all of the participants. In the data, this shows up in terms of interaction on-screen between informants and data collector, allowing for some interesting and natural interaction. In addition to SOI data, some images in this book come from SIGNALL II project data. SIGNALL II was a Leonardo da Vinci (European Commission Lifelong Learning) Project which created a large body of digital data in five signed languages including ISL between 2008 and 2010.[2]

Since signed languages are articulated in three-dimensional space, using not only the hands and arms but also the head, shoulders, torso, eyes, eyebrows, nose, mouth and chin to express meaning, analysts are faced with highly complex, multi-linear and potentially dependent tiers that need to be coded and time-aligned. The data are viewable across a multiplicity of tiers in the ELAN system.[3] These tiers are searchable, allowing for the sophisticated collection of data, which better supports analysis of discourse in signed languages and the analysis of the frequency of occurrence of specific features both within single texts and across larger bodies of data. An example of a screen shot from the SOI corpus in ELAN can be seen in Figure 1.1. Figure 1.2 shows the results of a search for the lexical sign DEAF in the SOI corpus.

As with spoken languages, discussion about what is linguistic and what is extra-linguistic in the grammars of various signed languages continues (Engberg-Pedersen 1993; Liddell 2003; Schembri 2003). Further, the influence of gesture on signed languages has begun to be explored (Armstrong et al. 1995; Armstrong and Wilcox 2007; Vermeerbergen and Demey 2007;

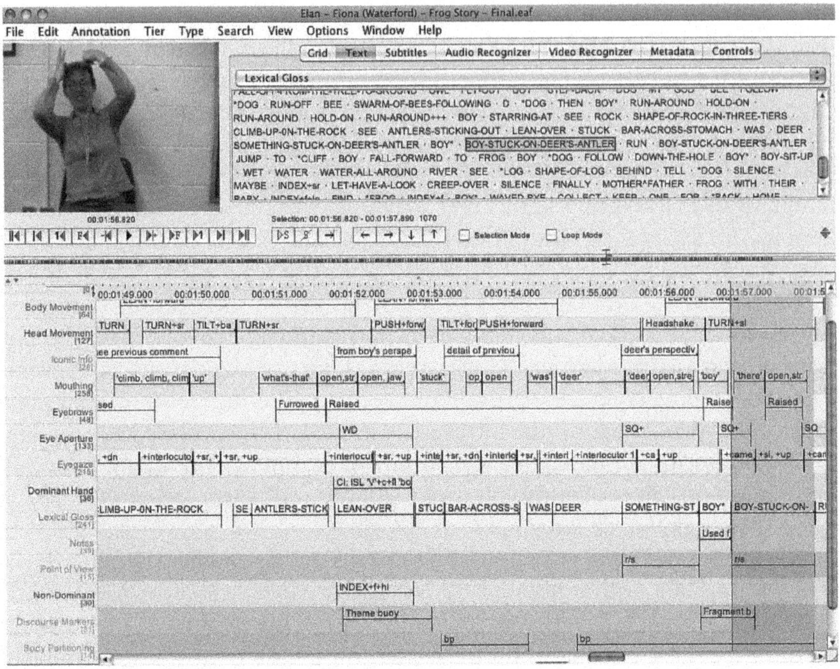

(Fiona (36) Frog Story (Waterford))

Figure 1.1 Screen shot of SOI example in ELAN (Fiona (36) Frog Story (Waterford))

Wilcox 2004b). While these remain theoretical notions at a certain level, decisions regarding their role and function as linguistic or extra-linguistic constituents play an important role when determining what will be included or excluded in an annotated corpus. Such decisions also determine how items are notated, particularly in the absence of a written form for the language being described. In turn, these decisions will determine how user-friendly and how useful the final corpus will be.

1.3 A cognitive perspective on Irish Sign Language

This book is aimed at a broad audience: teachers and learners of ISL, linguists, interpreters, parents, Deaf and hearing signers of ISL, and readers interested in signed languages in general. With this in mind, we attempt to offer a comprehensive presentation of discussion on ISL, though we emphasise that for some parts of the analysis of this language we are still at an early stage. This is particularly true for the analysis of syntactic and discourse structures. Throughout this book our discussion is underpinned by a theor-

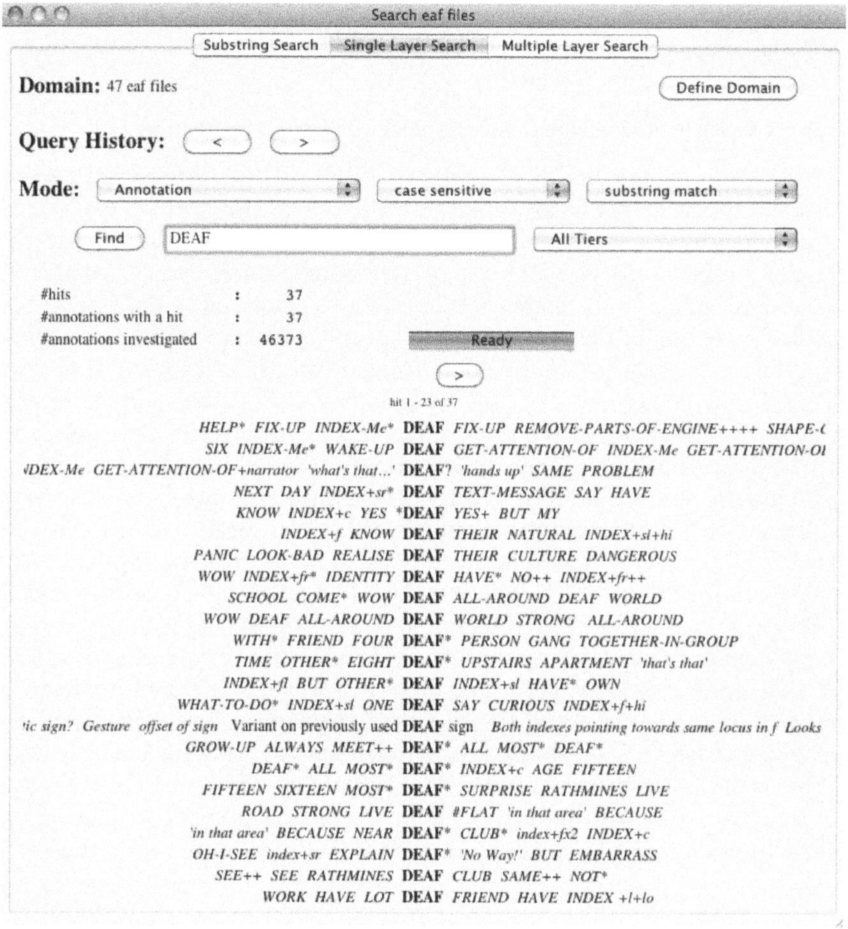

Figure 1.2 Results of search for the lexical sign DEAF across forty-seven narratives in the SOI corpus

etical perspective on language known as cognitive linguistics. This approach has several principles which we believe allow for an elegant description of many of the features found in signed languages. These principles allow for discussion of topics such as iconicity, gesture, metaphor, metonymy, the construction of lexical meaning, the use of mental models of space for semantic relations, and the partitioning of signing space and the signer's body to represent multiple referents simultaneously. We raise specific aspects of this approach throughout the book and bring these to a summary discussion in Chapter 9. For now, we can identify some key notions that will underpin our analysis by condensing them into four claims: that linguistic knowledge is encyclopaedic and non-autonomous; that linguistic meaning is perspectival;

that linguistic meaning is dynamic and flexible; and that linguistic knowledge is based on usage and experience.

1.3.1 Linguistic knowledge is encyclopaedic and non-autonomous

This is the view that meaning constructed through a language reflects our overall experience as human beings. It involves knowledge of the world, and this is integrated with other cognitive capacities. Embodiment is a key concept here (Johnson 1987). The principle of embodiment suggests that our organic nature as humans with bodies influences our experience of the world. For example, we talk of the positions of things in the world with respect to how they relate to us: in front of, behind, facing towards, facing away from, etc. That is, our bodies and our gaze have natural orientations and we project this onto other entities like houses and natural features in the landscape. Embodiment underpins language because of a second important cognitivist assumption: that semantic structure incorporates and transmits conceptual structure. We show examples of this in ISL when we discuss the classifier system in Chapter 5 and when we discuss how lexical meaning is created from a range of sources, linguistic and non-linguistic, in Chapters 6 and 9. Further, human beings are cultural and social entities, and language reveals these identities by embodying the historical and cultural experiences of groups of speakers and of individuals. This feature of language allows us to identify, for example, the influence of French Sign Language on Irish Sign Language, mapping the historical cultural link between Irish and French Catholic Deaf Schools in the 1840s, or to trace certain lexical items back to Ireland's status as a colony of the British Empire via the use of British Sign Language in the early nineteenth century, perhaps from the first schools for the deaf circa 1816.

1.3.2 Linguistic meaning is perspectival

In this view meaning is not an objective reflection of the outside world; instead, meaning is a way of shaping the world (Geeraerts 2006). Linguistic meaning embodies a perspective on the world. For example, we can present information about an event in a number of ways. We can say that 'the tree is in front of the house' or that 'the house is behind the tree'. The crux of the matter lies both in the speaker's or signer's position vis-à-vis the house and the tree and the chosen perspective. As we shall see, ISL has a number of ways to encode for perspective, including the use of the non-dominant hand in simultaneous constructions. Another, which is common to other signed languages, is the movement of the signer's body to another position in signing space to present another referent's view 'through their eyes', so to speak. This strategy has been given a number of labels, including shifted reference and surrogacy constructed action; we discuss its use in discourse in Chapter 8. Perspective is one aspect of the subjectivity of language by which the signers' beliefs and attitudes find expression in the form and meaning of their language, as discussed by Brisard (2006) and De Smet and Verstraete (2006).

1.3.3 Linguistic meaning is dynamic and flexible

Meaning has to do with shaping our world. Given this, language is dynamic and meanings change over time. Geeraerts (2006: 4) writes that 'New experiences and changes in our environment require that we adapt our semantic categories to transformations of the circumstances, and that we leave room for nuances and slightly deviant cases.' As we shall see in Chapters 5 and 6, ISL is a language that has changed over time and there are many influences that have left their mark on the lexicon of contemporary ISL. ISL is also a language that is dynamic, changing to incorporate the types of talk and the topics of talk that modern ISL users wish to discuss, for example new technologies. We can also trace parts of the history of ISL in the contemporary lexicon, and if we have access to documentation of older ISL, we can extrapolate the pathways to language change and to grammaticalisation. Thus language is dynamic and flexible, with meanings shaped over time and subject to change.

1.3.4 Linguistic knowledge is based on usage and experience

Cognitive linguists adopt a usage-based view of language. This means that linguistic analysis begins as far as is possible with the utterance, that is language use that is situated in a context of communication, rather than with abstracted sentences. In this view knowledge of a language derives from experience of its use. Consequently, the investigation of language must be rooted in real instances of linguistic interaction. Such a view of language requires analysts to integrate their investigation with the study of historical change and the processes by which language is acquired since both impact on current linguistic behaviour.

1.3.5 How does this link to our discussion of ISL?

Throughout this volume, we draw heavily on the Signs of Ireland corpus to provide examples of how language is used in practice, rather than depending on sample sentences created to illustrate grammatical points. Our analysis is framed by the four principles outlined in section 1.3 and these are drawn on at various points in our discussion. A key point to make is that our aim is not prescriptive. That is, we are not saying how ISL should be, nor are we outlining a grammar of 'proper' language usage. We describe the language as we find it used, and we try to provide a solid analysis of some of the phenomena that present. We do not assume that contemporary ISL arises in a vacuum. Instead, the historical and social influences on ISL are considered and outlined in the first part of this book in order to ground our understanding of how contemporary ISL has been shaped. We also avoid looking at structures in isolation, as instances of disembodied, non-contextualised language use. Instead, we have drawn all data that form the basis for our discussion of ISL from the Signs of Ireland corpus, or report on examples of ISL that draws on authentic, extended language use in context, for example the body of data referred to by Leeson (2001) . We also draw on previous descriptions of ISL, particularly the work of Barbara LeMaster (1990, 1999–2000, 2002) and her work with O'Dwyer (1991); Patrick McDonnell (1996, 2004); and Dónall Ó Baoill and Patrick A. Matthews (2000).

1.4 The structure of this book

Chapter 2 sets the scene by considering the properties of human language and situating signed languages, and particularly Irish Sign Language, in that context. Chapter 3 situates Irish Sign Language in its social and historical context. We look at the evolution of the modern Irish Deaf community and its language, considering the impact that educational policy has had on language form and function since the early nineteenth century. We also consider the influence of ISL on other signed languages including Australian and South African Sign Languages. We discuss the pathways to language acquisition for Irish deaf children and consider how state policy can improve or impede access to ISL, education through ISL and general participation in society by Deaf ISL users.

In Chapter 4 we consider the basic building blocks of ISL. We look at the phonetic and phonological basis for word formation. In Chapter 5 we explore aspects of the morphology of this language. We consider inflectional and derivational aspects of morphology, looking at verb classes, aspectual modification, the use of signing space and the allocation of referents to loci within the signing space. We also examine plural marking, number and compound formation processes. Chapter 6 builds on this, introducing a discussion of the lexicon in ISL. We consider the role of what has been referred to as the 'established' and the 'productive' lexicons, suggesting that this two-way distinction is rather limiting when one considers the dynamic nature of lexical development in the language. We highlight the influences of other languages, including English, French, French Sign Language and British Sign Language, on contemporary ISL, and discuss the role that gesture plays as a substrate for lexical development. We also explore the metaphoric and metonymic underpinnings of much of the lexicon.

Chapter 7 considers some aspects of the syntax of ISL, beginning with a consideration of grammatical categories and how they present in this language. We then progress to consider sentence types, including discussion of statements, questions, imperatives, negation, the marking of time, constituent order and the role that simultaneity plays. Chapter 8 brings our discussion to the level of discourse. We consider both the macro, interactional level and the more micro, discourse-internal level issues here, including how participants manage conversational interaction: the signalling of turn-taking, topic maintenance and politeness. We are also concerned with discourse cohesion in shorter and across longer stretches of discourse. In Chapter 9 we draw our discussion to a conclusion, teasing out some of the cognitive linguistics principles that permeate our discussion throughout this book. We discuss the principles of embodiment, the relationship between lexical items and real-world knowledge, the role of metaphor and metonymy, an analysis of mental spaces, and conceptual blending processes.

1.5 Some notes on transcription conventions used in this volume

Throughout this volume we present sample ISL data in several forms. We present some still images captured from the video data that make up the Signs of Ireland corpus, normally accompanied by a gloss of the data, that is a literal representation of the lexical signs, represented with English words, and we use a set of conventions for describing locations in signing space, and handshapes that make up 'classifier' or 'productive' forms, as we shall discuss below. We also indicate where examples from our data are available for viewing on the DVD that accompanies this volume. These are included because we believe that the three-dimensional, dynamic nature of a signed language cannot be adequately captured by two-dimensional still images and glosses alone. Where you see ⊛, you will find the example on the DVD for viewing.

We need to say something further here about glossing data. When annotating a corpus, there is a myth that the annotators are neutral with respect to the data they work with and that they simply write down what they see. While this is untrue for anyone working on a corpus linguistics project, it is doubly untrue for those working on a signed language. As ISL does not have a written form, there is no standard code for recording it. While some established transcription keys exist (HamNoSys, Sign Writing, Stokoe Notation), none of these are compatible with ELAN and none are fully developed with respect to ISL. The other problem with these transcription systems is that they are not shared 'languages', that is in the international sign linguistic communities these transcription codes are not commonplace, and to use one in place of a gloss means limiting the sharing of data to a small group of linguists. However, as Pizzutto and Pietrandrea (2001) point out, glossing data with English 'tags' is problematic too. There are dangers inherent in assuming that a gloss can stand in for an original piece of signed language data; this is another reason why we supply as many stills from the original Signs of Ireland data source as we can. Pizzutto and Pietrandrea note that:

> It is often implicitly or explicitly assumed that the use of glosses in research on signed [languages] is more or less comparable to the use of glosses in research on spoken languages [. . .] this assumption does not take into account, in our view, that there is a crucial difference in the way glosses are used in spoken as compared to signed language description. In descriptions of spoken (or also written) languages, glosses typically fulfill an ancillary role and necessarily require an independent written representation of the sound sequence being glossed. In contrast, in description of signed languages, glosses are the primary and only means of representing in writing the sequence of articulatory movements being glossed. (37)

It is also true that glosses impose potentially unwarranted and highly variable lexical and grammatical information upon the data, depending upon the spoken or written language used for glossing (ibid.: 42). To try and mitigate these problems we have adopted the principle of using what Trevor Johnston (2001) refers to as an ID gloss, that is using a consistent gloss for all variants of a single form. Johnston and de Beuzeville (n.d.) describe an ID-gloss as:

> the (English) word that is consistently used to label a sign within the [Auslan] corpus, regardless of the meaning of that sign in a particular context or whether it has been systematically modified in some way. For example, if a person signs HOUSE (a sign iconically related to the shape of a roof and walls) but actually means *home*, or performs a particularly large and exaggerated form of the sign HOUSE, implying *mansion*, (without that modified form itself being a recognized and distinctive lexeme of the language), the ID-gloss HOUSE is used in both instances to identify the sign in the gloss annotation. (7)

This process ensures that searches across the corpus facilitates identification of all listed variants of the same form. In ISL there are many concepts that are represented by a range of variants, including signs for WHAT and DEAF, as illustrated in Example 1.1. In the ISL corpus, these are also assigned a baseline gloss, or, in Johnston's terms, an ID-gloss.

Finally, we should comment on how we reference examples from the corpus. We are eager to ensure that the participants who gave of their time and contributed to the creation of the Signs of Ireland corpus are acknowledged for their contribution. We are indebted to them. Without them, this work would not be possible. To acknowledge their contribution in some small way, we reference each example to its originator. We hope that this makes the often invisible set of language subjects a living part of the joint process of using and describing ISL.

Example 1.1

(a) WHAT
Derek (28) Personal Stories (Cork)

(b) WHAT (or WHAT-FOR)
Fiona (36) Personal Stories (Waterford)

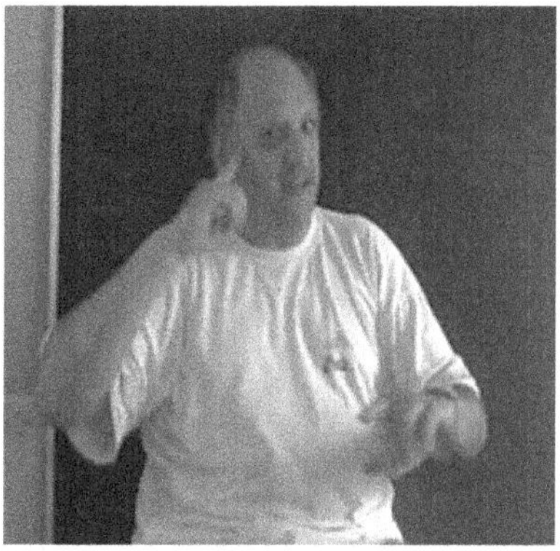

(c) DEAF
Patrick (24) Personal Stories (Wexford)

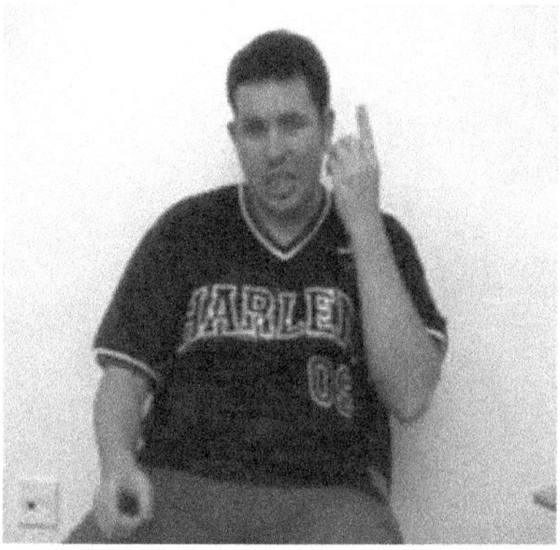

(d) DEAF
Derek (28) Personal Stories (Cork)

(e) DEAF (Part 1)
Noeleen (03) Personal Stories (Dublin)

(e) DEAF (Part 2)
Noeleen (03) Personal Stories (Dublin)

Notes

1. For a description of the political agreement on Northern Ireland known as the Good Friday Agreement, see the Irish Department of Foreign Affairs website, <http://www.dfa.ie/home/index.aspx?id=335> (accessed 25 November 2011).
2. For further details, see <http://www.deafstudies.eu> (accessed 25 November 2011).
3. For further details, see <http://www.lat-mpi.eu/tools/elan/download> (accessed 25 November 2011).

2 What Is a Signed Language?

2.1 Introduction

In this chapter we will introduce the general features of language – spoken or signed. This chapter introduces the notion that language can exist in one of two modalities: oral or gestural. We introduce the design features of language and consider them with respect to signed languages. We discuss the issues which signed linguistics have identified as distinguishing signed languages from spoken languages most radically. Specific topics for consideration include the use of the signer's own body, the ways in which signing space are used, simultaneity and iconicity.

2.2 The design features of language: do they hold for signed languages?

Researchers have identified a list of criteria for defining 'language' as opposed to another system of communication like, for example, Morse code. The criteria should be viewed as a collection of features that have been seen as the necessary and sufficient conditions for a system to be considered a natural language, and we note that the work on signed language research since the mid twentieth century has benefitted the field of linguistics greatly in allowing us to escape from traditional definitions of language and to reconsider some of the features that were formerly considered essential to the definition. A case in point is the use of the vocal-auditory tract. Vocalisation is not in and of itself language. While language typically begins as speech, and speech is dependent on the vocal-auditory channel (see Armstrong 1999), language can also be expressed in the visual-gestural mode. Irish Sign Language, like other signed languages, is expressed using the hands, torso, face, head, shoulders and eyes of the signer. Signs are expressed in the three-dimensional space known as 'signing space', as illustrated in Figure 2.1.

Before we turn to look at the design features in detail, there are a number of preliminary points that we need to consider about signed languages. First, signed languages are often talked about as being 'one-handed' or

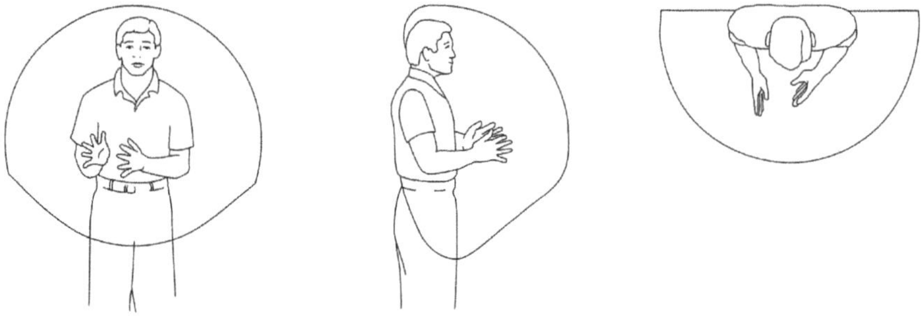

Figure 2.1 Signing space

'two-handed'. This is a misnomer in many ways, as all signed language users make use of two hands in creating signs. The concept of one- or two-handedness relates to the fact that many signed languages make use of a one-handed signed alphabet: that is, the letters of the alphabet are represented on the signer's dominant hand (typically the dominant hand is the hand that one writes with). Irish Sign Language falls into this category. In contrast, British Sign Language (also used in Northern Ireland) makes use of a two-handed alphabet.

Fingerspelling is used to represent the orthographic conventions of written forms of spoken languages and is typically used to spell out proper nouns (names, places), for lexical items in English that have no established lexical equivalent in ISL (for example, g.l.o.b.e.). Fingerspelling may also be used for a lexical item that is 'new' to the language. For example, in the early 1990s, there was no established sign for FAX-MACHINE, and signers fingerspelled f.a.x.

As we shall see in Chapters 5 and 6, items that begin life as fingerspelled items can become lexicalised, as is the case with items like #BANK and #LIMERICK where the entire word is no longer fingerspelled, and cognitively, signers see these 'fingerspelled items' as words in ISL. We also find that in some instances, signers may fingerspell items for which a lexicalised equivalent does exist (for example, one signer in our corpus fingerspells s.n.o.w. when there is a lexical item available meaning SNOW).

We will look at the issue of simultaneity later in this chapter, and will return to consider the possibilities that the expression of language in a visual-gestural modality facilitates throughout this book.

Moving away from fingerspelling, it is also worth noting at the outset that in ISL, some signs are one-handed and others are two-handed. For example, the sign LOVE is typically two-handed, while the sign HOT is one-handed, as in Example 2.1.

Example 2.1

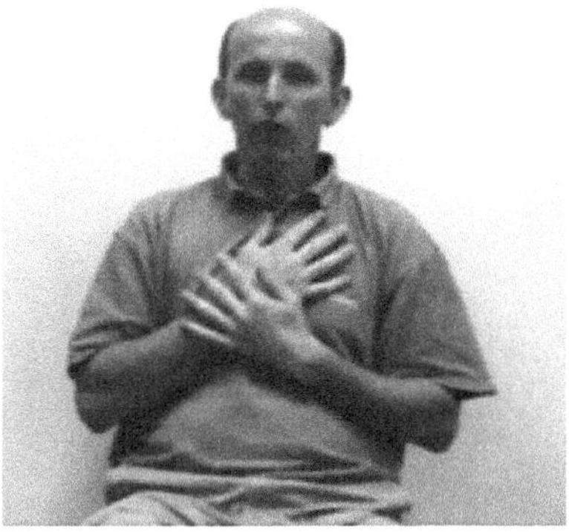

LOVE
Fergus D. (06) Personal Stories (Dublin)

HOT (on signer's right hand)

However, signs that are one-handed can undergo a process called 'doubling'. That is, the non-dominant hand can step in and 'echo' the sign articulated on the dominant hand, even though there is no requirement for this to occur in order for any articulatory constraints to be met. We do find that there may be pragmatic or sociolinguistic factors driving such instances. These include doubling of the hands in a single articulator sign for emphasis, or in formal settings. We talk more about this in Chapter 8.

Conversely, it is also possible for signs that are usually articulated as two-handed signs to be presented as one-handed. There are a range of conditions that allow for this to happen, including discourse management issues (for example, the non-dominant hand may be 'holding' a point while the dominant hand continues to sign), sociolinguistic reasons (informal contexts may see an increase in one-handed production of what are normally two-handed signs) and purely practical reasons (for example, a signer's non-dominant hand may be busy doing something else, like holding a drink or a baby, or the steering wheel of the car). An example of a normally two-handed sign articulated as a one-handed sign can be seen in Example 2.2. Here, the signer articulates the sign ABLE with one hand while, on his non-dominant hand, he holds a fragment of the two-handed sign BUSY, from earlier in the sentence. This fragment is a 'buoy' and we look at the function of a range of buoys in Chapter 8 when we discuss discourse level operations in ISL.

What we can say here is that it is hard to draw hard and fast lines between one- and two-handed signs: what is considered to be a one- or two-handed sign in citation form is not always seen articulated in the same way in discourse.

Moving on to consider the issues which are considered to be universal across languages, we can say that arbitrariness of the sign is a feature that

Example 2.2

AGREE (articulated with one hand)
Fergus D. (06) Personal Stories (Dublin)

receives a lot of attention in the literature. Arbitrariness suggests that there is no necessary link between the word and the object it denotes (for example, a car can also be called *automobile*, *voiture*, *wagon*, etc.). For spoken languages, exceptions to this rule are the English onomatopoeic words like *cuckoo*, *splash* and *slurp*. Onomatopoeia varies from language to language and is not usually taken to be very widespread. However, another view put forward by cognitive linguists such as John Taylor and George Lakoff suggests that language is grounded in meaning and is linked to our experience of being human (Lakoff 1987; Taylor 1995). This is something that we discuss for ISL in greater detail in later chapters. For example, they see the use of metaphor as a core means of expressing ourselves rather than a special feature, used in rare circumstances. They also propose that iconicity occurs even at the level of syntax (Haiman 1998; Taylor 1985). For signed languages, as we shall see, the relationship between form and meaning may be arbitrary, for example as in one of the ISL signs for SCHOOL, as in Example 2.3.

Example 2.3

SCHOOL
Sean (13) Personal Stories (Dublin)

However, another sign for SCHOOL (not found in the SOI corpus) is iconic. The non-dominant hand takes the ISL-L-handshape while the dominant hand takes an ISL-S-handshape. The non-dominant hand represents a page (for example, from a book), while the dominant hand travels from the centre of the non-dominant hand to the forehead. The forehead is associated with concepts of learning and knowledge. The movement path that the dominant hand travels is from the 'paper', the non-dominant hand, to the forehead, the seat of knowledge. That is, the sign represents knowledge moving from an external source to the brain. As we shall see in later chapters, this degree of iconicity, often embedded in conceptual metaphors or associated with metonymic (that is, part-whole relationships such as making reference to a steering wheel as the sign for CAR, a roof as the sign for HOUSE) is pervasive across ISL. Associated with the notion that 'real' words do not have a clearly identifiable relationship with the thing they represent (for example, the word 'cat' doesn't represent the way a cat looks or sounds), arbitrariness of the symbol became a key issue in considering whether signed languages would qualify as meeting the criteria for 'real' languages. As we shall see, this led to two different traditions emerging with respect to how signed languages were described.

2.3 What is unique about signed languages?

In the early days of sign linguistics, the role of iconicity was played down (Vermeerbergen and Leeson 2011; Woll 2003). Vermeerbergen and Leeson (2011) note that in the late twentieth century, two different traditions influenced how signed languages were described. Following Karlsson (1984), we can label these as the 'oral language compatibility view' and the 'sign[ed] language differential view' (see also Woll 2003 for a discussion of modern and post-modern approaches to sign linguistics). Vermeerbergen and Leeson note that:

> The oral language compatibility view presupposes that most of what comprises signed language structure is in line with what is typically described for spoken languages (i.e. oral languages), which means that while signed languages are expressed in a different modality, they have a great deal of structural commonality with spoken languages. The differential view suggests that signed languages are so unique in structure that their description should not be modeled on spoken language analogies. Accordingly, there are two research traditions in Europe, with a minority taking the differential view. The majority have concentrated on the similarities between spoken and signed languages, emphasising their underlying common identity. Characteristics that make signed languages unique were often ignored, minimised, or interpreted as being comparable to certain spoken language mechanisms. (270)

They go on to note that there are many reasons why this approach dominated, the most important of these relating to the contemporaneous questions about the status of signed languages. Researchers stressed points of commonality with spoken languages in a bid to demonstrate that signed languages were natural languages. Since the turn of the twenty-first century, this clear-cut distinction between the two approaches has become blurred, with greater recognition of the unique characteristics that arise from, for example modality differences. We should note that the French researcher, Christian Cuxac, has been a proponent of the differential model and his work has delved into the complexity of the role of iconicity in signed languages in great depth. In the early twenty-first century, cognitive linguistics brought researchers who formerly worked in a general oral language compatibility framework (for example, Liddell 2003) towards a more differentially driven viewpoint.

Iconicity, then, has been a key issue in considering the status of signed language, in identifying the extent of the lexicon in signed languages, and in describing the grammar of signed languages; and as we shall see in Chapter 5, when we come to discuss the morphology of ISL and the structure of the lexicon, there seems to be a lot of 'iconic' or 'isomorphic' vocabulary used in signed languages. Given their pervasiveness in the language, let us take a moment to define these terms.

For signed languages, we can note that early work looked at the role of 'visual motivation' in the creation of lexical items in signed languages. Mandel (1977) categorised signs that might be considered as 'visually motivated' into two groups: (1) signs that show an image of the referent or action, which are 'presentation signs' (that is, signs where we present the referent or the action of the referent in some way); and (2) signs that depict the referent in some way (for example, by outlining the shape of the referent with our hands). Sutton-Spence and Woll (1999) build on this description, and note that all BSL signers use visually motivated signs, although most of the time signers are not aware of the fact that they are including some information in the form of the sign that relates to the referent it represents. This also holds true for ISL, as we shall see, despite the fact that ISL makes much greater use of the manual alphabet in the production of initialised signs than does BSL.

Sutton-Spence and Woll (ibid.) describe the following categories of visually motivated signs:

1. presentable objects
2. presentable actions
3. virtual depiction
4. substitutive depiction.

Presentable objects include referents that are physically present in the signing context – for example, the signer (ME), the interlocutor (YOU), as well as body parts (EAR, NOSE, ELBOW, etc.) – all of which are indicated using the INDEX-handshape in ISL. A bent ISL-L-handshape can be used for items like HEAD, STOMACH, ALL-OF-US. Like BSL, abstract concepts like TIME can be referred to by association in ISL, using the INDEX-handshape to indicate to the wrist, linking to the wearing of a watch, of course.

Presentable actions are referred to by using the body to perform the action that is referred to, and these are often referred to as 'imitative actions' (Sutton-Spence and Woll 1999: 175). Examples from ISL include SWIM, BLOW-NOSE, PUT-HAND-IN-AIR and SCRATCH-HEAD. Other examples include reference to how an item is handled, such as WRITE, FISHING, BRUSH-HAIR, PUT-ON-COAT, RIDE-A-MOTORBIKE and BINOCULARS.

Virtual depiction is expressed when the signer uses his or her hand(s) to trace the outline or extent of a referent, or a part thereof (also known as metonymy). Using an INDEX-handshape, signers may trace, for example, the outline of a table in signing space, or a flat-B-handshape to sign TABLE. Or they may use a C-handshape to trace the extent of an elephant's trunk or to trace the path that a pipe follows on a building site. The relationship between the form of the sign and the referent it refers to is also known as 'iconicity' or 'isomorphism'. We discuss the concept of iconicity in greater detail later in this volume.

Another key feature of human language is 'duality of articulation' or 'dual articulation'. This refers to the organisation of language at two levels: meaningless units and meaningful units. For example, as we shall see in Chapter 3, phonemes are typically meaningless in isolation, but when combined as morphemes they are meaningful. This applies to spoken and signed languages. For example, in English, the sound /b/ is not meaningful in isolation. However, when combined as part of the morpheme [but] it has meaning. Similarly, meaningful signs in ISL must comprise a handshape, a location, a movement and an orientation. Without these combining, we have phonological components of signs, but not meaningful morphemes. Thus, a handshape or a location by itself is simply phonetic in nature. Further, we shall explore the phonological basis of mouthed elements in ISL in Chapter 4.

Semanticity is another of the features considered key to human languages. Semanticity denotes the use of symbols that refer to objects and actions. For example, we use the English word 'tree' to refer to any large woody perennial plant with a distinct trunk and usually having leaves and branches. We also use the word 'tree' to describe concepts such as family tree or shoetree, and we talk about someone being 'at the top of the tree' in terms of having reached the pinnacle of their profession. Here we see the use of the generic term 'tree' (a prototype) and also the use of noun-phrases, compounds and idiomatic expressions. Signed languages also do the same thing. For example, in ISL we have the literal sign BOIL, which is expressed in neutral space, while the idiomatic expression BOIL+c (I'm boiling (angry)), consists of the same manual sign BOIL, with one modification: the place of articulation moves from neutral space to the signer's body (stomach area).

Signed languages are highly complex insofar as there is multi-layering of simultaneously expressed information that occurs both manually and non-manually. Signers make use of multiple articulators (the hands, the mouth, the signer's body) in expressing meaning. Information is typically layered, with meaning created across the articulators (manual and non-manual), and with points in signing space invested with meaning for referents that can then be added to, to further specify or expand a theme (for example, a location in signing space may be co-referential for Dublin, my parents, their home, etc.). This layering of meaning is comprehensible because signers do not make the mistake that learners of a signed language frequently do: they are not simply looking for meaning in the hands of their interlocutor. Instead, they have a gestalt view on information produced. In Example 2.4, we see a relatively simple example from the SOI corpus of simultaneity at work, where the signer is talking about a holiday in Norway. Here, the signer's left hand represents a foot in the snow, while the right hand is captured mid comment, saying that there is 'real (snow) (on the ground where the foot is situated)'.

Example 2.4

REAL SNOW
Mary (33) Personal Stories (Galway)

Another issue for consideration is the creative potential for language. Creativity in a linguistic sense refers to our capacity to produce and understand an indefinite number of sentences, our ability to create from finite means (for example, a limited number of sounds/handshapes that are possible in a language, a finite pattern of rules, etc.) and an infinite number of utterances. Taking a wider view, Valli and Lucas (1995) suggest that language is productive. That is, the number of sentences that can be made in a language is infinite and new messages can be produced at any time about any topic. Irish Sign Language is a language that is evolving, and as such, as new themes become relevant to daily life, signs are developed to express new concepts. Examples include signs relating to information and communication technology (ICT), such as INTERNET, BROADBAND, FACEBOOK, GOOGLE, etc. which simply did not exist in ISL twenty years ago (Matthews 1996b).

We will explore the ways in which ISL is a creative language in further detail when we consider issues such as the creation of new signs and the functionality of the productive lexicon in Chapters 5 and 6, while we will talk further about metaphors in ISL and extended use of language in Chapters 6 and 9. For now, we can say that, like speakers of a language, signers have the capacity to be creative with language and can produce an infinite number of utterances within the confines of the linguistic system. An example is Renga poetry forms in ISL, created by groups of signers who worked together to co-produce short poems.[1]

Valli and Lucas (ibid.) note that languages have mechanisms for introducing new symbols. That is, the lexicon is productive. We noted earlier that ISL has introduced new vocabulary to deal with the developments in ICT. What is also true is that ISL has developed, in rule-governed ways, genre-specific terminology to deal with the broadening range of domains in which ISL users participate. That is, human language can be used for an unrestricted number of domains, and ISL is no exception. An example of this is in the area of linguistics, where, since the 1990s, ISL has developed vocabulary for commonly used terms in linguistics like semantics (MEAN^DEEP), pragmatics (DEPEND^SITUATION), etc. (Leeson and Foley-Cave 2007). Languages change over time. For example, new words are added to a language and others become obsolete. In Chapter 5, we will discuss in more detail issues regarding word formation.

As we shall see, languages can be broken down into component parts, a feature known as 'duality of patterning' or 'duality of articulation'. Equally, more than one meaning can be conveyed by a symbol or a group of symbols. That is, sentences in language can express irony, sarcasm, demands, a request or a statement. At the same time, we can look at the grammatical elements that make up the sentence (nouns, verbs, adverbs, adjectives, etc.). Languages also refer to the past, future and non-immediate situations: they are not restricted to the present and the immediate (we will say more on this when we talk about 'displacement').

Yet another feature of human language is structural dependence: language is arranged in structured chunks, not simple linear sequences. This impacts on word order issues, on the one hand, and how we interpret broader sequences of meaning, on the other (for example, the scope of negation marking or the identification of a topic).

Natural languages show the relationship between symbols. For example, in English, a subject is followed by a verb (for example, I told you), and consequently speakers of English know that the act of telling took place in the past (past tense form of the verb 'to tell') where the person who did the telling was the speaker ('I') and the receiver of the information was the receiver ('you'). Because signed language users express information on the body, in signing space and via specific expressions on the face (non-manual features) as well as on the hands (manual components), the issue of word order is complex. As we shall see in Chapters 7 and 8, signed languages have the potential to employ simultaneous constructions that make use of the face, torso and both hands of the signer. Research shows there are clear preferences for word order in ISL and that these preferences are linked to verb categorisation.

Leeson (2001) reports that plain verbs take overt subjects and objects (for example, I LOVE YOU ('I love you')), while agreement verbs tend to occur in sentences with a topic-comment structure (for example, MAN+f f+EMAIL+c ('The man emailed me')).

Of course, much of what creates meaningful utterances in ISL is non-manual, and the scope of non-manual behaviours is key in our identification of structural dependence. Let us take just two examples here: (1) the scope of negation; and (2) the scope of topic marking.

Irish Sign Language uses a variety of non-manual features (NMFs) to indicate certain types of sentence structures, including negation and in marking for a range of interrogatives. Negation ('n') is marked by an obligatory side-to-side headshake, and a non-obligatory down-turning of the mouth (McDonnell 1996). The 'n' marker co-occurs with appropriate manual signals, as in the following examples.

Example 2.5

          __________n
BOY COME HOME
'The boy did not come home'
(McDonnell 1996: 44)

Example 2.6

          'not interested'
          ____________n
r/s   INTERESTED
'(She) was not interested (in him)'
(Leeson 2001: 39)

While it is typical for 'n' to co-occur with manually articulated lexical signs, in certain contexts, it is possible for NMFs to co-occur with classifier predicates that represent previously established referents in the discourse. Example 2.7 illustrates this point, where 'n' occurs in a segment of discourse where the signer has shifted reference to fill the locus established for the little girl in the story of 'The Bear'. In this segment, she is holding a rabbit that she has been given by her mother to replace a doll that fell into the bear's cavern at the zoo. She is not happy with this replacement for her doll, and in the example below, we see that she looks at the rabbit while crying (expressed via facial expression). The classifier handshape that represents the form of the rabbit is held on the dominant hand while the signer gazes towards the held classifier handshape at the locus established for the rabbit. This is immediately followed by a headshake, before the signer introduces the locative agreement verb c+THROW+f. This final section of discourse co-occurs with the NMF 'th', indicating that the verbal activity was carried out in a clumsy, rather disdainful way.

Example 2.7

________________'crying' 'looks-at-rabbit'; n ______________
R/s 2/h CL-B 'holds rabbit' ____________________ c+THROW+f CL.G.
_________th
'falls-to-floor'
'(The girl) had the rabbit in her hands, looked at him, decided she didn't want him and threw him across the room where he fell to the floor' (Leeson 2001: 39)

In the Signs of Ireland corpus data, we find that negation occurs both manually and non-manually. In Example 2.8 the signer tells how she would never wish to leave her job at St Joseph's School for Deaf Boys. She says that this is because of the affinity she has for the boys, enhanced due to the fact that she too is a Deaf person. She signs (manually): REAL(LY) LIKE MY JOB / NEVER LIKE LEAVE / NO WAY. Non-manually, we see her head tilt to the side-left when she signs NEVER, followed by a negative headshake co-occurring with LIKE LEAVE and continue over the scope of the manually articulated signs, NO WAY. Here, the negative headshake serves to emphasise the manual components.

Example 2.8

Noeleen (03) Personal Stories (Dublin)

We can also take this opportunity to note that while negative manual signs are obligatory in some signed languages, it is the negative non-manual element that seems to be obligatory in ISL. That is, we can have sentences in ISL that, on the basis of the manual signs, do not have a negative reading;

however, the co-occurrence of a negative headshake forces a negative interpretation.

The marking of topics is another domain where non-manual features play a crucial role. Baker-Shenk and Cokely (1980) describe ASL as a topic-comment language, noting that, like speakers of Mandarin Chinese and Tagalog, ASL signers have a tendency to introduce a topic to indicate first the thing they want to talk about and then add a comment to make some statement(s), question(s), etc. about the topic element. Given this tendency, ASL is described as having a 'topic-comment structure'. They note that topic-comment structure can be applied at discourse and at sentential level, and identify several components that comprise topic marking:

> (a) during the signing of the 'topic', the brows are raised, the head is tilted, and the signer maintains fairly constant eye gaze on the addressee (except where directional gaze is needed for establishing or referring to referents in space); (b) the last sign in the topic is held slightly longer than usual, resulting in a pause; (c) then, when the comment is signed, the head position, brows and gaze direction are changed. (157)

For ISL, Ó Baoill and Matthews (2000) report that the main non-manual features associated with the articulation of topic-comment utterances in ISL are the head, which is tilted back slightly, raised eyebrows accompanying the articulation of the topic, followed by a head-nod while maintaining the raised eyebrow position. They propose that the head-nod functions to ensure that the addressee has correctly identified the topic. Further, they report that the eyebrows return to neutral position during the articulation of the comment.

It is interesting to note that Ó Baoill and Matthews present a semi-unified analysis: they consider topics as syntactic elements, but also as pragmatic features that mark for focus. They also explicitly note that there is a difference between syntactic topicality and focus marking. They argue that in some of the examples they consider, the nominals in 'topic' position could be better described as focusing or highlighting particular elements, as the information that is under focus in these utterances is not always a new topic.

Ó Baoill and Matthews suggest that we can think of ISL topics as being similar in structure to cleft sentences found in spoken languages like English and Irish. This involves moving a subject or object to the beginning of a sentence where it is followed by a relative clause, such as 'It is Karen who is having a baby.' In standard English, this process is restricted, with only nominals functioning as clefts. However, in Irish any constituent can reportedly be clefted (ibid.: 189). Ó Baoill and Matthews conclude that:

> the topic/comment sentences in ISL may instead be better described using the linguistic distinction between theme and rheme. Theme represents known information, that is information that is not new to the

receiver. The rheme on the other hand, refers to information that is new. (189)

Leeson (2001) notes a tendency for topics in ISL to be accompanied by raised brows (br) and, frequently, head tilted back (htb). The endpoint of the topic element is often marked by an eyeblink (/eb/), which could be described as an 'intonation break' following Wilbur (1994) and Rosenstein (2000). Leeson notes that while some of the ISL data examined demonstrate overt articulation of a head-nod at offset of the topic element, this does not seem to be obligatory. It may be that the return of the head from its extended position in the backwards tilt to the neutral head position has been interpreted as a head-nod by others commenting on ISL or that head-nodding after topic marking occurs more frequently in some genres and/or amongst certain groups of signers. However, overt head-nodding as a marker of offset of topic was not found to be a frequent occurrence in Leeson's data. Eyeblink seems to be a much more consistent marker of clausal boundaries for this purpose, though she notes that as eyeblinks also mark for offset of non-topic clauses, this delimits the possibility of identifying topic-phrases on the basis of eyeblink alone as a final marker, as in Examples 2.9 and 2.10:

Example 2.9

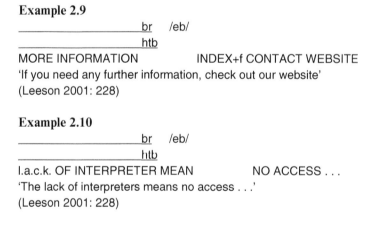

____________________br /eb/
____________________htb
MORE INFORMATION INDEX+f CONTACT WEBSITE
'If you need any further information, check out our website'
(Leeson 2001: 228)

Example 2.10

____________________br /eb/
____________________htb
l.a.c.k. OF INTERPRETER MEAN NO ACCESS . . .
'The lack of interpreters means no access . . .'
(Leeson 2001: 228)

However, eyeblink does not seem to be a compulsory component of the topic-construction, as evidenced by Example 2.11 where brow raise and head tilted back suffice.

Example 2.11

____________________br
____________________htb
BUT PROBLEM WHAT THEIR ATTITUDE
'The problem is their attitude'
(Leeson 2001: 228)

Leeson also notes that the use of the NMF, head-tilted-back also seems to be gender related in ISL. While younger men use the htb NMF to mark for topic, women tend not to. We can see this in Example 2.12b where the male signer is signing LAST MONTH (the topic, setting the temporal scene for the story to follow) and has his head tilted back and eyebrows raised. In contrast, in Example 2.12(a), the signer signs CONDUCTOR, marking this referent as a topic, but her head is in a much more neutral position. Her eyebrows are raised, however, for the duration of the topic.

Example 2.12

(a) ____________ t
CONDUCTOR
Sarah-Jane (09) Personal Stories (Dublin)

(b) ____________ t
LAST MONTH
Sean (13) Personal Stories (Dublin)

Another important feature of language is that it can be used interchangeably: all users of a language can send and receive messages. Irish Sign Language users can therefore produce and understand other signers using ISL, despite gendered, generational and regional variation existing within the language. ISL users, like speakers of spoken languages, also engage in turn-taking behaviours that are rule governed. An understanding of the norms of turn-taking begins at a very early age in humans, well before the onset of speech (for hearing children) or sign (for deaf children). This is an essential part of the framework of interaction that is necessary for language to be acquired. The strategies used for turn-taking by ISL users are signalled visually to make use of the visual-spatial realm and are acquired very early on by deaf infants in Deaf families (Byrne-Dunne 2005). These include making use of eyegaze, with evidence suggesting that deaf infants recognise their mothers, and stop crying when they gain eye contact with their Deaf mothers (ibid.) while adult Deaf interlocutors use eyegaze to 'hear' the message of their interlocutor, and as a strategy for indicating that they wish to take a turn in discourse (Van Herreweghe 2002). Other visual mechanisms for turn-taking include waving to get the attention of an interlocutor, or flashing a light in a room to gain attention from a group. Touch is also used to gain attention, and this too is rule governed. For example, while one may touch a potential interlocutor on the shoulder, the arm or the knee, the back of the head and the chest area are not acceptable points of contact.

Further, language users monitor their use and correct their language output if they think they have made a mistake. Knowledge of Irish Sign Language is not automatic. Even for native signers, who are born to Deaf, ISL-using parents, parts of the system must be learned from other users. Research evidence shows that humans are born with the capacity to acquire a natural language, but it also shows that humans must interact with other speakers or signers of their language in order to acquire it. Further, languages are typically handed down from one generation to the next. For example, a child brought up in isolation does not acquire language. We discuss the issue of language acquisition further in Chapter 3. For now, we can say that the question of cultural transmission is of particular relevance to a discussion of signed languages where only 5–10 per cent of deaf children are reared in Deaf families, with ISL as the primary language. We also know that late acquisition or language deprivation may have a serious effect on cognition, particularly when language is delayed beyond the 'critical period' (0–3 years).

As we shall also see, Irish Sign Language demonstrates gendered-generational variation, and increasingly what seem to be the beginnings of regional variation. Fortunately, another feature of human languages is that language users can learn other variants of the same language: people can learn vocabulary that is used in other geographical locations or by another group of people who share the same language. Language users can also use their language to discuss language: this is referred to as 'metalinguistic' capacity.

2.4 Summary

In this chapter we have looked at the features of natural human language and seen how these apply equally to languages in a visual-gestural modality, acknowledging that one of the key benefits of the 'sign language differential' framework of research is that it has facilitated a greater degree of understanding of the breadth of what constitutes language. We also considered some of the myths that have existed relating to signed languages (concreteness, gesture, damaging for speech, incomplete languages, etc.) and noted that they are just that – myths, although many have been very damaging for deaf children as they strove to acquire and develop language. We talk a little more about this particular context in the next chapter.

Note

1. See 'Fruit' at <http://www.youtube.com/watch?v=l4yXP3Z4gqs> (accessed 25 November 2011).

3 The Historical and Social Context

3.1 Introduction

This chapter discusses the history of ISL and introduces the contemporary context within which it operates. In the first part of the chapter we outline the evolution of ISL, which is inextricably linked to the story of the establishment of deaf education in Ireland, and reveals relationships with Langue des Signes Française (LSF) and British Sign Language (BSL). We also discuss the ways in which ISL has impacted on other languages, again via an educational link: for example, Irish Catholic religious orders established schools for the deaf in Australia, South Africa and the UK, where the language of instruction was Irish Sign Language. In the second part of the chapter we discuss the Deaf community in Ireland today, outlining the population of users, patterns of use of the language, and a range of social issues that impact on language use. These include education, age of onset of deafness and, correlated to this, access to signing models. We discuss the issue of 'home sign' (that is, what deaf children use to communicate when their caregivers are not fluent signers) and its relationship to gesture, leading to consideration of how signers scaffold language acquisition between home sign use and ISL. We then turn to the issue of language variation, examining the variation that has been noted for ISL across genders, generations and, more recently, regions. We outline the range of functions that the language serves today and the legal frameworks that operate to protect the language and language-planning enterprises that have grown up around it. First, we start with the question: 'Where does ISL come from?'

3.2 Did someone 'invent' ISL?

Frequently, people assume that there must have been a hearing person who 'created' or 'invented' ISL, but this assumes that the deaf people who were already in contact with each other before hearing people set up schools for the deaf did not communicate with each other. While there is scant description of what we might call 'Old ISL' looked like, we do know that deaf people used signs to communicate with each other before the establishment of schools for the deaf in 1816.

While there is very little written about the social situation of deaf people and the languages they used before the establishment of the schools, we know that ancient Irish society was cognisant of the existence of deaf people and responded to them in terms of defining their legal status and that of their children. McDonnell (2010: 13) tells us that in ancient Irish society the rearing of children was usually the responsibility of both parents. However, if the mother was deaf or blind, or if she had a mental or physical impairment, the father was required to take full responsibility for the child. A person who was Deaf was regarded as having limited legal capacity or responsibility. In legal cases, a plaintiff had to take the case against the person's guardian rather than against the person him- or herself. Ancient Irish society also thought it necessary to protect deaf people and a heavy fine was levied on anyone who mocked a deaf man. However, deafness rendered an individual ineligible for positions of authority.

McDonnell also notes that there is very strong evidence that ancient Irish society was aware of the possibility of communication through signing; however, this signing may have had no connection with deaf people. The Ogham alphabet was used in writing in Irish from the fourth century CE and perhaps earlier. The basic alphabet consists of twenty characters, divided into four distinct sets of five. In its written form the characters are shown as marks along a central line as illustrated in Figure 3.1.

As in Figure 3.1, most examples of Ogham survive as stone inscriptions where the characters are notched into the edge of the stone. However, we know from the Book of Ballymote (a medieval manuscript published circa 1390) that several different forms of Ogham existed, including signed versions. The three signed versions were known as srón (nose) Ogham, cos (leg) Ogham and bos (palm) Ogham. In these versions the fingers of one hand represented the letters on the nose, the leg or the edge of the palm of the other hand. We might say that Ogham employs two articulators to express each character, much as signers use dominant and subordinate hands to articulate signs. Moreover, McDonnell points out that the letters are grouped in sets of five, not four or three, which suggests that Ogham was structured around the hand.

This leads McDonnell to ask a range of intriguing questions: Which came first, the signed form or the written form? Did the inventors of Ogham get the idea from deaf people? While the answers are lost in the mists of time, we can say that the existence of a signing system in early Irish society shows an awareness that manual signs could be used to express linguistic meaning, though sadly, as McDonnell points out, it tells us nothing of people who used sign as a natural form of communication or of their relations with hearing society.

Figure 3.1 Inscription on the Ogham Stone, St Flannan's Cathedral, Killaloe, Co. Clare. The stone also bears an inscription in runes. The runes read 'Thorgrimr carved this cross', while the Ogham (shown here) reads 'A blessing on Thorgrimr'. (Photo: Lorraine Leeson)

3.3 Schools, policy and language

In modern times, the story of Irish Sign Language is inextricably connected to the story of Deaf education and educational policy. Given this, this section offers some detail about the reasons why schools for the deaf were established in Ireland, the religious and social factors that permeated policy development, and the consequences that these have had for signed language use, its prohibition and consequently, attitudes towards ISL.

3.3.1 The first schools for the deaf in Ireland

The first recorded school for the deaf in Ireland was established in 1816, though it was not until 1889 that the first report on the education of children with disabilities in Ireland and Britain was published by the Royal Commission (McDonnell 1979). McDonnell notes that the issues raised in that report were identical to those raised by deaf educators in the nineteenth century. The report also served to lay down some official guidelines regarding the direction that education should take.

McDonnell outlines three issues that set the scene for the establishment of deaf education in Ireland:

1. The main provisions of the penal code affecting the education of Catholics was repealed in 1782.
2. Grattan's parliament expressed concern about education in Ireland (1787 session) and this concern carried through to the establishment of the Commission of Enquiry into Irish Education in 1806.
3. The activity of Protestant education societies, some of which were overtly proselytising organisations, who, due to funds from parliament and other sources, established schools.

McDonnell argues that the vision of bringing enlightenment through education was the main motivating factor in the establishment of institutions for deaf people in Ireland. For example, the first annual report of the National Institution for the Education of Deaf and Dumb Children of the Poor in Ireland reports that:

> [the] development of the pupil's understanding, great as the benefit must be accounted, is yet subordinate to the farther object of improving his heart and life. To acquaint him with the great truths of Religion; to open to him the pages of the gospel; to enlist him a disciple of Christ are the grand purposes of his Education. (National Institution for the Education of the Deaf and Dumb 1817: 13)

However, it also made economic sense to educate deaf children and prepare them for some kind of 'useful occupation' so that they would no longer be a burden on the public purse (McDonnell 1979). Thus, while moves to establish schools for the deaf evolved from the desire to provide religious and moral education, there were also utilitarian, humanitarian and purely educational factors involved, all of which reflected the tenor of the time. From a Deaf Studies perspective, we can also add that the schools offered an institutional centre where deaf children came together, and based on their shared experiences and their shared language(s), created community.

3.3.2 Protestant schools

Between 1816, when the first school for the deaf was established by Dr Charles Orpen, and 1849, a total of nine institutes for the education of deaf children were established in Ireland, and two of these closed down after short periods of time (McDonnell 1979).[1] These included four institutions in Ulster, a school in Cork, a preparatory day school for the Claremont Institute in Dublin, the Claremont Institute (Dublin) and the Catholic Institution for the Education of the Deaf and Dumb.

Dr Charles Orpen was the most prominent figure in the establishment of the National Institution for the Education of the Deaf in Ireland (the Claremont Institute), which was the first school for deaf children in Ireland.[2] While the school, as we have seen above, had an overt mission to bring the students to God, it also served as

> a school of industry, in agricultural, gardening, mechanical and household occupations [. . .] combined as much as possible with the primary object instruction in the meaning and use of language [. . .] (Orpen 1836: 54)

The school was established in 1816, with an initial enrolment of eight deaf pupils. Over time, the school moved premises and registration increased to forty-three by 1822, and a waiting list of fifty children existed. These children could not be accommodated at the time due to inadequate funding.

The school gradually rose to prominence, with 112 students by 1840. However, from the 1860s onwards the school suffered from declining numbers, with just twenty-seven students enrolled in 1891 (McDonnell 1979). While the Claremont Institute may have lost students to the Catholic Institution, McDonnell notes that it may have lost students to the Ulster Institution too. By 1891, the Ulster Institution had eighty-five students enrolled. As a result, the school, having moved to Monkstown, Co. Dublin, in 1943, finally closed in 1978 (Pollard 2006).

In general, the Irish institutions did not teach the students to speak, and Claremont Institute was no exception in this matter. It was not until 1887 that it reported changing from a manual system to an oral system of instruction. As the original headmaster was educated at Thomas Braidwood's school in Edinburgh, which was established in the 1780s, Woll and Sutton-Spence (2007) point out that he must have known BSL, and we know that up until the twentieth century, graduates of the Claremont Institute used the two-handed BSL alphabet. For some thirty years, the Claremont Institute was the main school for the deaf in Dublin, and even though most of the children registered with the school were Catholic, the school taught a Protestant doctrine (ibid.). However, with the advent of the Catholic institutions, the language used by contemporary nineteenth-century deaf people was about to shift dramatically.

3.3.3 The Catholic response

A small Catholic school was established in Cork in 1822, and as time went on, the Roman Catholic clergy believed that a response to the (as they saw it) proselytising of deaf children was needed. In fact, McDonnell (1979) notes that some of the factors influencing the establishment of the Catholic Institution for the Education of the Deaf and Dumb in 1846 were identical to those that influenced Dr Orpen in 1816. A Vincentian priest, Fr Thomas McNamara, had visited Caen in Normandy, France, and experienced the way that education was being delivered to deaf children at the Le Bon Sauveur school. He returned believing that a similar institution was required in Ireland. McNamara was also aware of the existence of the Claremont Institute and believed that 'wholesale proselytism' was being carried out there (ibid.: 13). At this point, all institutions offering education to deaf children in Ireland were Protestant, with the exception of a school in Cork, St Mary's of the Isle. McDonnell notes that the establishment of the Catholic Institution was, in part, a response to the belief that all Protestant institutions engaged in proselytism. However, arrangements for the establishment of a Catholic Institution were not confirmed until the mid 1840s, with provisional accommodation provided for a small group of girls with the Dominican Sisters in Cabra, Dublin, in 1846. By 1849, new accommodation had been built, allowing the numbers to expand to fifty. The story of the connection to France in the establishment of St Mary's is worth considering here: in establishing St Mary's, it became clear that the Dominican Sisters who would manage and run the school would have to develop a system for teaching deaf children.

To this end, two Dominican nuns travelled with two Deaf girls, Agnes Beedan and Mary Ann Dougherty, aged eight and nine respectively, to Caen to study teaching methods that utilised signed language (Coogan 2003; Crean 1997; Matthews 1996a; McDonnell 1979). The question of why they went to Caen is one worth asking. It is reported that the nuns made initial inquiries with the Braidwoods in the UK regarding the possibility of their studying the Braidwood system, but cost was a factor. It may also have been the case that given the religious backdrop to this story, they wished to avoid a Protestant connection (but this is speculative), and ultimately, they went to the Le Bon Sauveur school, where a form of signed French was used in teaching, though it is fair to speculate that amongst themselves, the children used contemporary French Sign Language (LSF).

The Dominican Sisters adapted the French methodical signing system to one suited to teaching English to those attending St Mary's School for Deaf Girls. What we should bear in mind is that the two deaf girls may have already been in contact with other deaf children before they were brought to France. Even if they were not, we know that there were Irish deaf people educated in the Protestant schools from 1816 onwards, and by this point in time, there would have been many graduates of the system and the probability is that alumni communicated using the language they had acquired and developed at school, which we could for convenience call 'Old ISL'. This will have been influenced by BSL varieties used in the Protestant schools and whatever variants that uneducated deaf people may have used at the time. Given this, we cannot assume that there was a tabula rasa context in existence in terms of language used by Irish Deaf people before the establishment of the Catholic schools, and therefore we assume that the form of 'Modern ISL' that arose as a result of the French connection built on and integrated with 'Old ISL'. We should also bear in mind that as the nuns attempted to modify the form of signed French that they learned to map onto the grammar of English so that they could teach through a form of signed English, there is also an English language influence on the forms of signs, which is noticeable in terms of the extent of initialisation in ISL that remains to this day. Despite this, some LSF signs were borrowed directly. For example, one of the contemporary signs for FRIDAY is articulated with a V-handshape at the chin, maintaining the connection to the French '*vendredi*' (Matthews 1996b).

Yet another issue is that the two Irish deaf girls would have developed a means of communication between themselves, which may have been predicated on home signs (which we discuss later in this chapter), but which were also probably influenced by the LSF they encountered when engaging with their deaf peers in Caen. All of this serves to illustrate that the path to contemporary ISL was not an uncomplicated one.

The committee responsible for the establishment of the Catholic Institution also approached the Christian Brothers regarding the establishment of a school for Deaf boys (Matthews 1996b). The initial offer was turned down by the Christian Brothers and so the committee approached the Carmelite monks for the use of Prospect Seminary in Glasnevin, where there was accommodation for forty pupils. The school opened in 1849 and initially admitted eleven boys. By 1854, overcrowding led to the establishment of a new building and the Committee again approached the Christian Brothers, who, in 1856, agreed to take over the management of the boys' school.

When St Joseph's School for Deaf Boys was established a decade later, the Christian Brothers used the same signing system used by the Dominicans, though alterations were made to the form of many signs. Crean (1997) suggests that the Christian Brothers at St Joseph's School drew on published references to American Sign Language in their preparations for teaching Deaf boys. Folk belief has it that the Christian Brothers wished to make the signs they learned from the Dominican Sisters less feminine and more masculine so as to be appropriate to the teaching of young boys (Leeson and Grehan 2004).

What the deliberate modification of the signing systems used did, coupled with the relative isolation of the girls from the boys, was to create the context for the development of a significant gendered generational variant, which we discuss further below.

An overview of the influences on ISL in the nineteenth century can be seen in Figure 3.2.

In 1857, a total of sixty-eight boys transferred to St Joseph's in Cabra. McDonnell (1979) notes that this was the last major institution for the educa-

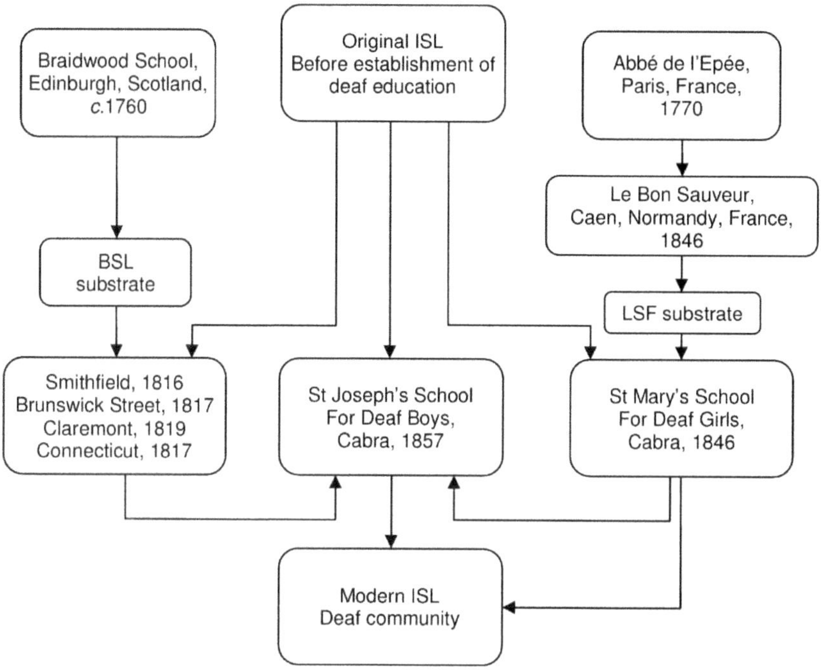

Figure 3.2 Major influences on the development of ISL in the nineteenth century. (After Suzanne Bussiere, personal communication, January 2010)

tion of deaf children established in Ireland in the nineteenth century. By 1891, the Catholic Institution had, between St Mary's and St Joseph's, 421 students enrolled in its schools.

Two further Catholic schools for Deaf girls were established in the nineteenth century, both by the Sisters of Mercy: one in Cork, which opened in 1858 and closed in 1900, and a second in Co. Westmeath, which was established in 1892 and ceased admitting Deaf girls in 1936.

The twentieth century saw the establishment of Mary Immaculate School for Deaf Children. Beechpark School (as it was known) was established in 1956 following from a request by Archbishop Charles McQuaid (Matthews 1996b). The objective was to educate Deaf boys aged 3–10 years in an oral manner. Beechpark was to serve as a preparatory school for St Joseph's School for Deaf Boys in Cabra, and was also specifically geared to serve the parents of Deaf boys living on Dublin's southside (Crean 1997), although it seems that most children were boarders from outside Dublin (John Bosco Conama, personal communication, 6 July 2007). Beechpark School closed in 1998.

The other school established in the twentieth century was the Mid-West School for Hearing Impaired Children (also known as the Limerick School for the Deaf). Established in 1979, the school aims to provide local education for children in the Limerick, Tipperary, Clare and Kerry regions.

Leeson (2007) suggested that the establishment of the Mid-West School opened the way for a variant of ISL to emerge because students no longer had access to the cohorts at St Joseph's and St Mary's, where most deaf people attended school. Conama (2008) found that this was the case in practice: Deaf people interviewed in a review of sign language interpreting provision in the Mid-West reported that they did not always understand what they called 'Dublin signing'.

3.4 Educational policy and sign language

As we have seen, religious instruction was a primary goal of education of deaf children in the nineteenth century, and underpinned the establishment of the schools themselves. However, there was also a strong emphasis on industrial training, with the Census Commissioners of 1851 recommending that the amount of time given to this goal be considerable (McDonnell 1979). However, literacy was also considered key. McDonnell writes that:

> Literary instruction was necessary in order to achieve the religious and vocational aims of the institutions and language was the central subject on the curriculum. The deaf child had not acquired language in the usual manner and so it had to be taught as a subject. The emphasis was on grammar and on the grammatical structure of written patterns. Exercises in identifying the different parts of speech were begun at an early stage. Reading and writing were two other important parts of language instruction. (49)

The focus on language and the issue of how to best educate deaf children is at the heart of the 'oral–manual' debate, which has been ongoing since the eighteenth century (Leeson 2006). Given the focus on teaching language through a signed modality, it comes as no surprise to learn that signed English was the preferred means of delivering education to deaf children. Despite the shift towards oralism in the late 1800s and the infamous resolutions adopted by the Congress of Milan (1880), the Irish schools maintained a steadfast 'manual' approach until the mid twentieth century (Lane et al. 1996).

The Congress had passed a number of resolutions, including the following:

> (1) The Congress, considering the incontestable superiority of speech over signs in restoring the deaf-mute to social life and for giving him greater facility in language, declares that the method of affliction should have preference over that of signs in the instruction and education of the deaf and dumb

(2) Considering that the simultaneous use of signs and speech has the disadvantage of injuring speech, lip reading and the precision of ideas, the Congress declares that the pure oral method ought to be preferred. (Ibid.: 61)

Prior to 1880, in what is often considered the 'enlightened era' for deaf education, the use of signed languages in the education of deaf people in Europe was dominant and many Deaf teachers were employed in schools for the deaf. France was the leading light, with Abbé Charles-Michel de l'Épée's (1712–1789) approach to deaf education studied by educationalists across the world, including, as we have seen, the Irish Dominicans.

By 1880, however, opinion had shifted and the congress delegates, who were mostly hearing educators of the deaf, gathered in Milan, where they voted to exclude overtly the use of signed languages and signed modes in deaf education. An oral approach, focusing on the teaching of speech which had originally been developed by the German teacher of the deaf, Samuel Heinicke (1728–90), was advocated, and had as its aim the 'demutement' of deaf people by the use and adaptation of the oral language of the hearing majority (Heinicke, cited in List et al. 1999). We should emphasise here that oral approaches had been in place in many countries earlier in the nineteenth century, but the Congress gave added weight to the approach and formalised the policy (McDonnell 2010). It is important to stress that while the delegates at the Congress of Milan and many proponents of oralism since have believed that the use of a sign language will in some way 'damage' capacity to learn a spoken language, there is no empirical evidence to support such a claim (Marschark and Spencer 2009).

As a result of the policies advocated by the Congress of Milan, deaf teachers at schools for the deaf were dismissed, signed languages were banned from the classroom and those who could not progress with a speech-based approach were labelled 'oral failures', segregated from the 'oral successes', and frequently stigmatised.[3] Children who used signed languages were seen as 'mentally retarded' in many cases, and in many countries were punished for using a signed language (Leeson 2006).

It was not until 1887 that the Claremont Institute reported changing from a manual system to an oral system of instruction. McDonnell suggests that this late shift to oralism in Ireland resulted from a combination of factors including the scarcity of trained teachers, the large numbers of pupils and the lack of the financial resources required to implement speech training. Instead, the methods reported by Fr John Burke, Chaplain of the Catholic Institution, to the audience at a public examination of students in Carlow were (1) signs: natural and methodical; (2) dactylology; and (3) the analysis of written language (McDonnell 1979). By natural signs, we may assume that Burke meant the signs and gestures used by the children in their communication. 'Methodical signs' refers to a form of signed English, where each individual sign relates to an English word or a part of speech (for example, a sign to mark the *–s* plural form, a sign to mark past tense, a sign to mark the auxiliary *will*, etc.). Dactylology refers to fingerspelling words (that is, where a particular position of the fingers relates to a letter from the English alphabet).

When the Royal Commissioners visited the Ulster Institution in 1887, a small class was being taught orally, though they were educated with their peers who were being taught manually or using the 'combined system' of speech and sign (McDonnell 1979). Thus the learning environment was an impediment to learning orally. A further seventeen students were being taught through a combined oral–manual system (what is called 'Total Communication' or 'Simultaneous Communication'– shortened to 'SimCom'). Another sixty-one pupils were taught manually. Thus all students had access to sign language within the classroom, despite different methods being applied to different cohorts, and, we must assume, outside the classroom too. At that time, teachers reported that the students who were considered most intelligent were those educated via the Total Communication approach. However, in St Joseph's School for Deaf Boys, the pupils were taught through sign and the Commissioners reported that the instruction was '*careful and the results were very good*' (McDonnell 1979: 62, emphasis added). The Catholic Institution was aware of the ongoing debate regarding oral versus manual approaches to education following from the Congress of Milan, but believed that without significant financial resources, it could not abandon the manual approach to education (Catholic Institution for the Deaf and Dumb 1881: 17).

It was not until the mid twentieth century that this shift occurred. St Mary's School for Deaf Girls introduced oralism in 1947, following from Sr Nicholas's time studying in Manchester University under Sir Alexander and Lady Irene Ewing, well-established proponents of oral education. In 1951, following a number of visits to oral schools in Caen (France), Brussels and Ghent (Belgium), and a visit to St Michielsgestel School (Netherlands), Sr Nicholas introduced a policy of highly segregated education for deaf and hard of hearing students at St Mary's, influenced by the St Michielsgestel school, where Van Uden developed the 'maternal reflective method' of oralism, which heavily influenced the work of Sr Griffey, who introduced segregation of 'oral failures' from 'oral successes' in the 1960s (Knoors 1999).[4]

While oralism had been dominant in Europe from 1880, it began to wane in many countries in the 1970s, when research showed the underachievement of deaf children (Vestberg 1999). In many countries, this led to re-evaluation of policy and the introduction of what became known as Total Communication. In turn, many countries moved towards bilingual education for the deaf in the 1980s, and this approach is well established in Scandinavia (Heiling 1999).

The fact that literacy skills were lower for deaf children educated in the UK was known to Sr Nicholas before she introduced an oral policy in St Mary's.

She writes that the written standard of the British deaf children in schools she visited did not match the standard of Cabra, and cites a letter she received from a past pupil working in London, whose niece was about to be admitted to St Mary's:

> You can teach her to speak but be sure that she is able to write down the thoughts of her mind. I meet deaf people here who cannot write what they want to say, or read what is written. (Griffey 1994: 44)

Unfortunately, functional illiteracy followed the introduction of a strict oralist policy in Ireland for the majority of deaf children, affecting deaf children who attended all of the schools for the deaf in Ireland (James et al. 1992). This is also reflected in empirical studies of Deaf adults (Conroy 2006; Matthews 1996a).

It is important to note that St Mary's operated outside of the control of the Department of Education until September 1952. Indeed, Griffey herself, describing the initial shift to oralism in the late 1940s, wrote: 'Since there was no involvement on the part of the Department of Education we were free to make plans for the development of an oral atmosphere in the school' (1994: 47).

As recently as 1952, the Department of Education did not even know where St Mary's school was located and knew very little about the education of deaf children (ibid.: 57). However, if, in 1952, the Department knew little regarding the education of the deaf, it is feasible to surmise that they turned to Sr Nicholas for advice. Despite the fact that she states that she had reservations about the move towards oralism (ibid.), Sr Nicholas was very vocal in her push for an oral policy in education, but this did not come into effect until 1972, with the government publication of *The Education of Children who are Handicapped by Impaired Hearing* (Department of Education 1972).

In the interim, an influencing factor behind St Joseph's shift to an oral policy in 1957 seems to have been the establishment of Beechpark School in 1956: it would be responsible for the boys' continuing education (Crean 1997). Indeed, Crean notes that St Joseph's shifted to oralism following from an '*express request*' (original emphasis) from Archbishop McQuaid in 1952. From Sr Griffey's writings, it is clear that she was influential and had the ear of the Archbishop for many years. Thus, oral policy in the schools seems to have been introduced in a de facto manner as a result of the influence that Sr Nicholas Griffey had on Archbishop McQuaid, who in turn influenced the Christian Brothers. Earlier, Christian Brothers' representatives had in 1948 visited nineteen oral schools in the UK, but decided to remain with the manual approach to education (ibid.). It is also possible that the fact that the Claremont School had established oral training, and that Catholic parents were also sending their children to Britain for oral training around this time, also increased pressure on St Mary's to offer oral training locally.

The outcomes of the shift to a strict oralist regime have been well documented (Conama and Grehan 2002; Conroy 2006; Crean 1997; Griffey 1994; Leeson 2007). However, it is important to note that oral instruction itself – that is, the inclusion of some speech training rather than a rigidly enforced oralist approach with no place for sign language – was not seen as a problem by the Deaf community in Ireland in the 1940s. This remains true today (Leeson 2007). The major problem was that the implementation of a strictly enforced oralist policy went hand in hand with the rigid suppression of sign language use, which in turn made it virtually impossible for many students to access the curriculum, since they could not understand what their teachers were saying. Students report being forced to sit on their hands, confess signing as a sin, and give up sign language for Lent (Grehan 2008; Leeson and Grehan 2004; McDonnell and Saunders 1993). All of this resulted in ISL being forced underground.

The physical segregation of students who signed from those who spoke led to the establishment of a hierarchy within the schools that suggested that those who spoke were more intelligent than those who signed. This was reinforced by the fact that for many years, only those who were considered 'oral successes' could sit state examinations.

The segregation of girls from boys for educational purposes in Catholic schools remains widespread in Ireland today, but particularly in the period between 1856 (when St Joseph's was established) and the 1950s (when oralism had its heyday in the Irish Catholic schools), led to the development of a gendered-generational lexicon that the anthropologist Barbara LeMaster describes as the most startling differences ever recorded. We discuss this gender differentiation further below.

Each group of students in the 'deaf and dumb', 'partial deaf (oral)' and 'profoundly deaf (oral)' sections formed 'communication islands' (Grehan 2008), and given their relative segregation from each other and the stigma associated with communicating across what we might call the oral–sign divide, cohort-specific variation flourished, but shifted across generations of signers. The process of inventing signs continued and the meanings of these signs are difficult to translate into equivalent single English words. Leeson and Grehan's study (2004) focused on Deaf women who were enrolled in oral education and some were already halfway through their educational careers when signing was banned. They concluded by noting that the women's signs are still used by women ranging in age from mid twenties to their late fifties today. Thus we can claim that gendered signing still exists in ISL, and that the extent and nature of that variation has yet not been fully documented.

This philosophy of strict segregation was, as noted earlier, ratified by the 1972 Advisory Committee on the education of the Deaf and hard of hearing, who saw sign language as something of a last resort for children, most of whom the authors of the report saw as having '*additional handicaps*', and who were '*not capable of making adequate progress when taught by oral methods alone*' (Department of Education 1972: 69–70, original emphasis). Parents – both hearing and deaf – were also advised that they should not sign to their deaf children, and deaf siblings were told they could not sign to each other. This created several generations of Irish Deaf people who could not effectively communicate with their parents, and whose literacy skills were highly problematic (James et al. 1992).

It is important to remember that these issues were not unique to Ireland. However, as we have seen, the Catholic Schools in Ireland introduced oralism much later than schools in other countries, and consequently, Ireland has been much slower to move towards bilingual education than other countries, though a shift towards Total Communication did occur in the 1980s. Total Communication (or Simultaneous Communication, 'SimCom') became widely used across Europe in the 1980s and was hailed as a means of reintroducing a signed component into the classroom without losing the oral element. Total Communication has been severely criticised as the rated of speech and signing are not the same: teachers typically simplify the spoken component of their message or leave out aspects of manual communication (Baker and Knight 1988) and since aspects of the grammar of signed languages are expressed on the face (adverbs, questions, negation, etc.), the co-occurrence of speech with signed elements blocks out these signals, leading to incomplete messages in both modalities. However, recent research (Marschark and Spencer 2009) suggests that this may not always be the case though Total Communication is still widely used in schools for the deaf.

This contrasts with some other countries like Finland, Sweden and Denmark, where Total Communication was introduced in the 1960s. By the 1980s bilingual education was being introduced in Scandinavia (Heiling 1999) and today is a developing force in the UK (Powers et al. 1998).

The dominant approach to education for deaf children in the Western world during the 1960s and 1970s was oralism (see Brelje 1999 for examples), stemming from the twin beliefs that deaf children must be rehabilitated to succeed in a hearing environment, and that signed languages were not real languages and would harm the acquisition of speech (which echoes the views put forward at the 1880 Congress of Milan, described earlier). The view of signed languages as 'real' languages, coupled with the seriously poor academic achievement of students educated orally, has led to the re-evaluation of educational approaches (see Brelje 1999 for examples). In contrast to pre-oral Ireland where literacy was the educational objective, oral communication became the priority and 'the use of any formal sign system has no place' (Watson 1998: 76).

However, this approach failed to account for the fact that deaf children acquiring English do not follow normal development patterns for acquisition, especially if acquisition is delayed (Woll 1998) as is the case for many deaf children in Ireland (Griffey 1994). It also does not take account of the fact that '*Children who have not acquired fluency in a first language by the age of five do not subsequently catch up either in a signed or spoken language*' (Woll 1998: 65, emphasis added; see also Mayberry and Eichen 1991; Loncke et al. 1990). Further, Irish deaf children's cognitive potential, which is the same as that of their hearing peers on the basis of performance IQ (MacSweeney 1998), has not been realised: literacy rates for deaf children graduating from schools with oral policies typically are equivalent to those of 8–9-year-old hearing children (James et al. 1992). Powers et al. (1998) note the almost lack of longitudinal studies on deaf children's attainment and the lack of appropriate assessments for deaf children.

By the early 1990s, the Irish Deaf Society was calling for ISL/English bilingualism, and since then, growing awareness of the linguistic status of signed languages, coupled with a societal shift that engages in dialogue with minority communities and takes on board the recommendations that emerge from such direct experience, has led to greater acceptance of the fact that, regardless of residual hearing level, many deaf and hard of hearing people identify with the Deaf community and thus use Irish Sign Language as their preferred language.

The early twenty-first century has shown that the use of a signed language as the language of instruction, as employed in the early days of deaf education, leads to educational success for deaf people. From most of the deaf and hard of hearing people who forwarded submissions to the government's Advisory Committee from 2001–4 (reported on in Leeson 2007), the overriding message is that Irish Sign Language is the key to accessing information and ISL must be the language of instruction in schools for the deaf in order to facilitate age-appropriate learning. In 2010, the Education Task Force comprising representation from the Catholic Institute for Deaf People, the Irish Deaf Society, DeafHear.ie and the Centre for Deaf Studies, Trinity College Dublin, launched a policy that, among other things, acknowledges the place of ISL in deaf education. This is something that parents of and organisations for the deaf support (Leeson 2007).

Finally, it is worth noting that this Irish call mirrors the international demand for recognition of signed languages in education at the very highest levels, including, most recently, the UN Convention on the Rights of Persons with a Disability (2006), which Ireland signed in March 2007 but has not yet ratified.

3.5 ISL and other signed languages

We have described ISL as a language that developed with influences from British Sign Language and American Sign Language in the nineteenth century. In the twentieth century, ISL became a language that was severely suppressed and isolated. Yet, particularly in the nineteenth century, ISL was also a language that travelled with missionaries, and in some cases deaf migrants, to Australia and South Africa. ISL also made its way to Scotland and other parts of the UK via religious orders engaging in Deaf education and with Deaf emigrants leaving Ireland.

3.5.1 ISL in Australia

The first Catholic school for deaf children in Australia was Rosary School, Waratah, established in 1875 by Irish nuns. They brought Irish signs to Australia and what Robert Adam refers to as Australian Irish Sign Language was used in Australian Catholic schools until the 1950s (Robert Adam, personal communication, 2010). Johnston (1989) reports that in Australia, two fingerspelling systems are in use: (1) the two-handed alphabet that has its basis in BSL, which is most commonly used; and (2) the one-handed ISL alphabet. He notes that Australian Deaf people who were educated in Catholic schools were taught this form, but that through mixing with other deaf people most learn the two-handed variety as well. He also notes that this effectively means that that from the earliest days of signing in Australia, there has been a 'Catholic' variety, based in ISL, and a 'Protestant' variety, based in BSL. What is interesting is that there seems to be a diglossic context in operation with respect to the use of ISL variants: while those who use an ISL-influenced variant can typically also use the BSL-based variant, those who use the BSL variant do not use the ISL variant. Johnston also points out that the one-handed ASL fingerspelled alphabet is growing in popularity because of the global prestige of ASL. Beyond the level of fingerspelling, Johnston notes that partly because of the influence of ISL and partly as a result of Australia's geographic isolation, Auslan grew to become distinct from BSL. While Stokoe (1974) suggested that Auslan was a descendent of ISL, Johnston notes that the evidence does not support this claim; instead, Auslan can be seen as a descendent of BSL (Deuchar 1984) with some influence from ISL.

The ISL influence is a direct result of the establishment of schools for the deaf in the early years of colonisation of Australia, leading Johnston to note that:

> Since a large proportion of Australia's early immigrants were Irish, both free settlers and convicts, the role of the Catholic Church should come as no surprise. Irish Catholics who were dedicated to the welfare of the deaf brought with them Irish signs and the one-handed alphabet. The alphabet was clearly borrowed from the French one-handed alphabet and the signs were presumably a mixture of indigenous Irish signs with French borrowings.[5] France was another Catholic country so we can assume that the connections between them were fairly strong. (1989: 17)

What we do not know is the extent to which ISL has permeated the Auslan lexicon and syntax, and as a result, how much of the Australian ISL variant has become integrated within contemporary Auslan.

3.5.2 ISL in South Africa

A rather different story is that of ISL in South Africa. Aarons and Reynolds (2003) note that in South Africa, the history of signed language is deeply entwined with apartheid schooling policies and complex language policies. They also point out that speech was considered as more prestigious than signing by the authorities, with the result that schools for white deaf children insisted on oral education while those for other races allowed some form of signed language, in most cases a mixture of speech and some signs.

In 1863, the Vicar Apostolic of the Cape of Good Hope, Dr Grimley, invited the Irish Dominican Sisters to work in South Africa. Dr Grimley had previous associations with the education of the deaf in Dublin, which led to this invitation being issued. Sr Dympna Kinsella, the superior of the group of six nuns who travelled from Cabra to the Cape of Good Hope, began to teach some deaf children on her arrival in a purely voluntary capacity, but given the demands on her time, it became clear that a dedicated teacher of the deaf was needed. This led to the immigration of Miss Bridget Lynne. What is particularly interesting here is that Bridget Lynne was a deaf past pupil of St Mary's School for the Deaf in Cabra, and had trained to teach there. She travelled to the Cape of Good Hope in 1873 and ran the school until 1886 or 1887 (Sr Margaret Wall, Archivist, Region House, Cape Town, personal communication, 2010).

The methods employed during the nineteenth century at St Mary's (later known as the Grimley Institute and now known as the Dominican-Grimley School) involved both fingerspelling and conventional signing. Despite the wide range of spoken languages in existence in South Africa, the written language taught was English; and despite the racial politics that existed, the school catered to all race groups (Aarons and Reynolds 2003). In 1920, the school introduced the oral approach – this coincides with the timing of the sisters taking on the running of the school for the deaf from lay principals in 1918 (Sr Margaret Wall, Archivist, Region House, Cape Town, personal communication, 2010). Aarons and Reynolds (2003) note that the shift to oralism at the Grimley Institute followed from a visit to a Dominican School run by some German sisters in Kingwilliamstown, leading to the decision that 'all but the most "backward" children would be taught using the oral method' (198).

In 1937, the Irish Dominicans opened another separate school for 'non-European', 'coloured' and African deaf children at Wittebome in Cape Town. In 1953, with the tightening of the apartheid policy of segregation, the Nationalist government declared that the school was to register only coloured deaf children. In the 1960s, the now white Grimley School for the Deaf moved to Hout Bay and adopted a strict policy of oralism. This oral approach continues to the present day, with the school's motto being: 'Academic Success through the spoken word'.[6]

What is clear is that the presence of Bridget Lynne, an adult Deaf woman in a position of influence, and a sign language user who had been taught through the Dominicans' manual approach, would have been very influential on the cohorts of children she taught. What we do not know is how much signed English was used and what place, if any, ISL had in formal educational instruction. We also have no idea if or to what extent the form of language used in teaching at the Dominican school was influenced by local signed languages. It is also not yet clear what happened after the introduction of oralism in the 1920s: was a South African variant of ISL maintained or did some other variant develop in its place, based on home signing developed by the children? It is suggested that while the principle of oral education was introduced circa 1925, this approach was not strictly implemented until the 1960s (Sr Margaret Wall, personal communication, 2010), allowing for an embedding of signed language in education for a century, with an ISL-influenced substrate at its heart. What we can say is that for graduates of the Wittebome School, even today, some signs used are identifiable as 'different' from other dialects of South African Sign Language (SASL), and there are a number of handshapes that seem to come from ISL. These include the handshapes for *i*, *e*, *h*, *p*, *q*, *s* and *g* (Meryl Glaser, personal communication, 2010). Sr Rennee Rossouw (personal communication, 2010) adds that the South African Deaf Community,[7] who are responsible for the development of teaching materials in SASL, tend to leave out the Wittebome dialect from any descriptions of SASL given that it differs so significantly from how SASL patterns. This includes use of the ISL alphabet in initialised signs, for example. However, for the Deaf Community Centre of Cape Town (DCCT), the Wittebome dialect is considered a core part of SASL (ibid.).

3.5.3 ISL in the UK

We have seen that although the education of Irish deaf children was established while Ireland formed part of the United Kingdom, ISL developed independently of BSL. The usage of BSL or ISL traditionally related to education in a Protestant school such as the Claremont Institute or a Catholic school such as St Mary's or St Joseph's. The link between creed and language was exported, as we have seen above, to Australia and South Africa, with the Irish Dominican Sisters. The language was also brought to the UK, for example with Irish religious orders teaching at St Vincent's School for the Deaf in Glasgow. This was also the case in Northern Ireland, where Catholic children were traditionally educated in the Dublin schools for the deaf, acquiring ISL as their working signed language, while Protestant deaf children were historically taught through BSL.

Even today, British Catholics' signing is heavily influenced by Irish Sign Language because Irish religious orders have delivered Catholic education in the UK and many chaplains to the Catholic Deaf community have been Irish (Sutton-Spence and Woll 1999). Sutton-Spence and Woll go on to note that the form of signing used by Catholics in the UK draws heavily on initialised signs based on the Irish manual alphabet. Beyond the religious connection, ISL also serves as a donor language for some BSL dialects, including London, Glasgow and Liverpool dialects. Sutton-Spence and Woll report that this is because these cities include large Roman Catholic communities who have strong links to Ireland. It is also interesting to note that the founder of the British Deaf and Dumb Association (now the British Deaf Association) was an Irish Deaf man, Francis Maginn.[8]

Of course, language contact does not necessarily operate in one direction: contemporary ISL is also influenced by BSL but it is important to point out that while some BSL signs may be recent borrowings from BSL, others may reflect the original BSL substrate from the 1800s, with some elderly Irish Deaf people knowing, though not necessarily using in their everyday lives, the two-handed manual alphabet, while the sign for GUINNESS (beer) is articulated with two BSL G-handshapes, a sign not found in BSL (Woll and Sutton-Spence 2007). Further, ISL signers have access to BSL through contacts with the Deaf community in Northern Ireland and through access to the British media, which provides a wide range of programming in BSL (Leeson 2005; Sutton-Spence and Woll 1999).

3.6 Who uses Irish Sign Language today?

Having looked at the historical development of ISL, we now turn to the present and the language's current situation, beginning by asking who its users are. The core users are the members of the Irish Deaf community. In addition to ISL usage, the characteristic features of this Deaf community include identifiable cultural and behavioural norms, similar educational experiences, endogamous marriage patterns, close community ties, and a strong sense of communion with other Deaf people both nationally and internationally.[9] These characteristics differentiate members of the Irish Deaf Community from non-sign language users, including those who are hard of hearing or who become deafened after they have acquired a spoken language ('post-lingually' deaf), but who use spoken language as their preferred means of interaction. These people do not typically enter the Deaf community and instead function within the majority culture of their territories (Ladd 2003; Mindess 1999). Furthermore, deafened people often see their deafness as a problem which may be mitigated by medical intervention or therapy, for example cochlear implantation or speech and language therapy. In contrast, many people who are born deaf or who become deaf before they acquire language see being deaf as their natural state of being: that is, they do not experience deafness as a medical problem requiring a solution. Instead, they see recognition of their language as the central issue, and from this flows a demand for the provision of services in their language. The call for recognition of signed languages as the first step in facilitating full citizenship by Deaf people is central to the agenda of the Irish Deaf Society, and is the core mission of the European Union of the Deaf and the World Federation of the Deaf.

If we attempt to identify how many Deaf ISL users there are, we can follow the international rule of thumb and suggest that approximately one person in every thousand is a signed language user (Conama 2008; Johnston 2006), which suggests that there are close to half a million Deaf signed language users in the EU. An estimated 6,500 Irish Deaf people use ISL, with approximately 5,000 Deaf ISL users in the Republic (Matthews 1996b) and 1,500 in Northern Ireland (Janet Beck, personal communication, 2009). These people consider themselves to be 'Deaf' with a capital D, that is members of a linguistic, cultural community as opposed to people with a sensory disability.[10]

The largest populations of Deaf people are found in and around the major cities and towns of Ireland. In great part, this is because there are opportunities for people to come together to socialise and to provide support networks for each other in these locations. While patterns of community organisation have changed over time, often due to the availabilities of new technologies, Deaf communities value 'face to face' communication, and the fact that ISL is a visual language without a written form supports this. But it goes much deeper than the fact that ISL is expressed in a visual modality. Deaf communities value and trust information that is delivered in a face-to-face manner more than information presented in written form (Mindess 1999). For Irish Deaf people, this may in part be because the people who deliver the information to them in ISL are typically known and therefore their trustworthiness has been tested within the community already. We say this because the Irish Deaf community is small, and membership of the Deaf community is predicated on active engagement with other members of the Deaf community. Given this, it is highly unlikely that one Irish Deaf person who is an active, engaged member will come across another Irish Deaf person that he or she does not know who is also actively engaged in the community unless that person is significantly older or younger than him or her. With the widespread education of deaf children in mainstream settings, however, we suggest that this community demographic is likely to change.

Other people who use ISL include a growing number of friends, family members and teachers of the deaf, interpreters, and those who work with Deaf people in a range of capacities, including chaplains, social workers and psychologists. However, given that Deaf people in Ireland, in common with those across most of the Western world, have shared a history of linguistic suppression, 'normalisation' and oppression by (often well-meaning) hearing people, there is a long way to go before ISL usage is as widespread and fluent among hearing people as it might be. A key example is in schools for the deaf.

3.7 The social status of ISL users

In section 3.4 we discussed the role of education in the development of ISL and described how changing attitudes to signing and oralism led to the suppression of ISL within educational environments. Signing was completely banned for children who were considered to be 'oral successes'; teachers were discouraged from signing to students; and children were segregated from each other on the basis of their ability to speak (Grehan 2008). Grehan notes that in St Mary's School in Dublin, the 'deaf and dumb' girls had a different uniform and a different haircut from the 'oral successes', which served to emphasise their difference. In addition, parents were advised to avoid signing to their children since this was considered to encourage 'laziness' with respect to learning speech (Leeson 2007).

These polices had an impact on both the educational prospects of ISL signers and their social status. A student successful in the use of oral language was taught the national curriculum and had access to state exams. Students in signing groups left school without any formal qualifications. In either case, in 1992 the average deaf child left school with the reading age of an 8½–9-year-old child (Conrad 1979; James et al. 1992). Further, the consequences of this on the lives of Deaf adults who survived the system impacts on all areas of life, as illustrated starkly in work undertaken by Pauline Conroy for the Irish Deaf Society and the Combat Poverty Agency in 2006 (Conroy 2006). Conroy reports that of the 354 Deaf people who replied to her survey, 330 had attended a school for the deaf or a unit for deaf children. Despite staying at school until they were 18 years or older, one in four adults left school with no exam qualifications and literacy was identified as a significant issue: 38 per cent said that they were unable to read and write effectively and more than 50 per cent said that they experienced problems in filling out a form or writing a letter.

Conroy reports a significant link between low levels of educational attainment and consequent economic success. Focusing specifically on education, Conroy notes that the educational experience of adults

> reveal a series of grave flaws in Deaf education. The first deficiency is in communication. Deaf children who were able to communicate with each other, reported being unable to communicate clearly with their teachers who did not use Irish Sign Language. (45)

Other flaws with the educational system include:

1. The fact that many deaf children leave school with no formal qualifications (Junior Certificate, Leaving Certificate) or any other formal proof of their educational attainment.
2. The lack of transfer to continuing education at third or vocational level.
3. The high drop-out rate of Deaf students who do continue to third level.
4. The fact that these facts perpetuate the lack of opportunity for the natural evolution of Deaf role models and critical analysis by Deaf people of the educational system.

Conroy notes that the absence of educational qualifications places Deaf people at a serious disadvantage in later life, with Deaf adults often obliged to accept entry-level jobs where they remain for long periods.

For those who do attend third level, many report:

> being isolated from student life and many found no supports or reasonable accommodations or adjustments to enable them to compete on an equal footing with other students. Those who fared best were the Universities. Those who encountered the most obstacles were at Regional Technical Colleges, or Institutes of Technology. In the absence of a 'critical mass' of Deaf students, they were out on their own. (Conroy 2006: 45)

Perhaps the most significant aspect of the Conroy report is the fact that clear links are drawn between educational disadvantage and negative employment outcomes for Deaf people in Ireland. While employment rates for Deaf people are only marginally below those of hearing people – 64 per cent as the national average and 60 per cent for Deaf people – unemployment is much more significant for Deaf people: Conroy notes that, at 12 per cent unemployment, Deaf respondents experienced four times the national average rate of 3 per cent in 2006.

A consequence is that Deaf adults are concentrated in lower-level clerical and manual posts with low levels of pay. Thus Conroy suggests that many Deaf people can be considered to be 'working poor'. Further, Deaf people do not readily move jobs, do not seek or receive promotion, and experience vertical and horizontal blockages to movement in the jobs market. She worryingly notes that work is effectively 'a place of low pay, poor prospects and considerable isolation' (47). She sums up the situation by suggesting that: 'Educational disadvantage and associated low paid, low status jobs should be identified as strong factors explaining poverty in the Deaf community' (46). So, we can say that the stigmatisation of ISL for deaf children has impacted on both educational and employment outcomes for Irish Deaf people.

Today, the tendency to educate deaf children in special schools has been replaced with a trend towards mainstreaming children in their local schools. Indeed, since 1997, there has been a 52 per cent decrease in the number of children attending schools for the deaf. Mathews (2007) notes that while this decrease in numbers coincides with the introduction of the 1998 Education Act, which provided parents with the legal right to mainstream their child, it is possible that this trend had begun before that and was simply accelerated by the passing of this act.

Mainstreaming is not unproblematic: aside from the issue of how a teacher with no specialist training can deliver adequate access to the curriculum for a deaf child in a mainstream setting, other key concerns include social isolation for the deaf child and, particularly, the lack of access to Deaf role models and the lack of development of a positive sense of Deaf identity. Some of this is addressed by an Irish Deaf man who was educated in a mainstream setting:

> I never got a chance to socialize with other people, no opportunity or reason why really. There is a very serious lack of support and appreciation of what the deaf student has to go through. If they can integrate well educationally, everything is considered hunky dory. But in reality that's not the case at all. In my secondary school, there were 1,000 students and I was the only deaf student – very isolated and always on the outskirts of the group. (Gillen 2004: 9)

3.8 Variation within ISL

3.8.1 Gender and age variation in ISL

The impact of educational policy on the development of ISL is clearly reflected in gender variation. Given that the children who attended St Joseph's School for Deaf Boys and St Mary's School for Deaf Girls were on the whole separated from each other, it is not surprising that their language shows marked differences. This is most striking with older signers. LeMaster (1990) studied differences in women's and men's signing, focusing specifically on women who had left school around 1946 and men who had left school around 1957. This period marks the cusp of the introduction of oralism in the Catholic schools for the deaf. All of LeMaster's informants were active members of the Dublin Deaf community, and had had continued access to gender-varied signs that they had used when at school through social interaction with their peers, even though sign language played a diminishing role in education.

LeMaster analysed 106 different male and female signs and found that 63 per cent of the signs were related to each other in some way, with the remainder unrelated. For example, related signs may have the same hand shape but they a different movement or location. She argues that given that such a high percentage of the vocabulary she analysed was in fact related, one would expect some degree of mutual intelligibility between male and female signers using these related signs. This, however, was not the case with both men and women reporting that they had actively to learn the vocabulary used by the opposite sex.[11]

LeMaster (2002) evaluated semantic lists for gender variation and demonstrated the occurrence of variation across all lexical categories analysed (for example, GIRL (noun), WORK (verb) and YELLOW (adjective)). However, LeMaster's informants also reported that female signs were no longer in use as women adopted the male variety as the standard form for daily interaction, suggesting that male signs were more accessible to both male and female signers than were female signs (ibid.).

What we should note is that the women and men about whom Barbara LeMaster wrote are now very elderly, and given changes in educational policy (that is, the impact of oralism as well as greater interaction between pupils in both schools) and societally, greater interaction between the sexes, there is no longer as clear cut a set of lexical variation in existence in ISL as with LeMaster's generation of signers. However, that does not mean that younger generations of ISL signers do not demonstrate variation in their language.

For example, Leeson and Grehan (2004) report that while the widespread lexical differences described by LeMaster have a corollary in generation, and thus are not generally used by younger signers, contemporary signers have another lexicon of gendered signs which originated in the segregated schools for the deaf in Cabra. That is, gendered signing continues to be found in the Irish Deaf community but more reduced than in previous generations. Despite being 'school signs', many continue to be used today by Deaf women ranging in age from their mid twenties to their late fifties. Cormac Leonard (2005) found that young signers of ISL (aged 18–30 in 2004) have also created and use gendered lexical items, and while some of these gendered variants are the same as those used by older cohorts, new gendered vocabulary items have also been established, and crucially, these tend not to be used in formal settings.

3.8.2 Geographical variation

Educational policy has always impacted on language outcomes in ISL: gendered signing emerged due to segregated schools for boys and girls (LeMaster 1990; LeMaster 1999–2000; LeMaster and O'Dwyer 1991) and continues to impact on today's cohort of signers (Leeson and Grehan 2004; Leonard 2005). Further, the segregation of students according to cohort and oral success or 'failure' led to cohort-specific variants (Leeson et al. 2006). As signed language users are increasingly dispersed nationally and educated in the mainstream, the potential for regional variation increases (ibid.). Indeed, we are seeing some of this already, with respondents in the Mid-West region reporting that the dominant variant of ISL (that is, the variant used in Dublin) is not understood by some deaf people in the Mid-West, particularly those who have been educated locally (Conama 2008). That is, with the establishment of the Mid-West School for Hearing Impaired Children in 1979, for the first time, in the 1980s a significant cohort of deaf people from across the Mid-West region were educated locally and did not come into contact with the variants used in the Dublin schools. This seems to have given rise, over the past thirty years, to a growing local variant that deserves further attention. We can add that with the advent of moves toward mainstreaming for a majority of deaf and hard of hearing children, with small clusters of children attending 'partially hearing units' across the country, the potential for destabilisation of ISL is significant, leading to additional, educational policy-led fragmentation of ISL and increased variation, not just in terms of region but in terms of a cohort by cohort shift. This will present significant challenges for the Deaf community moving forward, and also will present significant challenges in the provision of language-driven services, most notably signed language interpreting services.

Finally, it is worth noting that in Northern Ireland, Irish Sign Language may vary quite significantly from usage in the Republic. As yet, no empirical studies have been conducted to compare and contrast the use of ISL north and south of the border, but this is something that deserves research attention.

3.9 Children's acquisition of ISL

Only 5–10 per cent of deaf children are born to Deaf parents, and these children generally acquire ISL as their first language. That is, deaf children with Deaf parents, acquire signed language in a natural way, following the same general milestones that hold for hearing children acquiring a spoken language. For the other 90–95 per cent of deaf children in Ireland, the acquisition of a signed language does not follow a normative path. For the majority of deaf children then, the acquisition of a signed language is bootstrapped on 'home sign' use – a highly idiosyncratic and systematised use of gesture developed in individual hearing families to bridge the language gap – with fully grammatical signed language use developing only when a deaf child comes in contact with other deaf children and adults, as described in Goldin-Meadow (2003). Either way, there are milestones that hold for the acquisition of sign language for deaf children, and while very little has been examined in terms of ISL acquisition paths to date (see the unpublished work of Deirdre Byrne-Dunne (2005) as an exception to this), it is clear that this is a gap that needs to be closed if we are to better understand how ISL develops for children from Deaf families and for the majority who come from hearing families.

From international studies, we know that deaf children from Deaf families who acquire a signed language as their first language do so in a similar pattern to hearing children acquiring their spoken-language mother tongue. This includes the development of both vocal and manual babbling, with vocal babbling decreasing after the first few months in deaf babies (in contrast with hearing infants, where babbling increases over time) (Woll 1998). Woll goes on to note that this difference may lead to changes in interaction patterns between a deaf baby and its hearing parents, which may have long-term implications for social and cognitive development in addition to language development. Woll notes that gesture plays a significant role in early social interaction between children (deaf and hearing) and adults, and she points out that a well-defined pattern of gesture development has also been identified. She suggests that 'Gestures develop from early expressions of deixis (pointing or otherwise indicating objects or people) to referential gestures (labelling or naming of objects and actions)' (59). While hearing and deaf children make use of two gesture combinations, only children exposed to signed languages seem to develop combinations of referential gestures like DOLLY BIG (Volterra 1983).

The 'critical period' hypothesis suggests that late acquisition of language has ramifications for cognitive and social development. Similar research on a number of signed languages suggests that where deaf children are not exposed to a language by 5 years old, they do not simply 'catch up' when they are later exposed to either a signed or spoken language (Mayberry and Eichen 1991). Given this, those deaf children born into Deaf families have a linguistic and cultural advantage insofar as they have access to a natural language acquisition pathway which parallels the pathway to language acquisition for hearing children born into hearing families. Indeed, Gascon-Ramos (2008) suggests that Deaf parents have a closer and more accurate view of what being deaf means in terms of understanding of capacity for learning and language use, and also in terms of having to cope with what are frequently negative representations of Deaf people in hearing society. For deaf children born into hearing families, the situation is more complex: for most hearing families, their deaf child is the first deaf person they have ever encountered, and societal views around deafness and language tend to support a pathologised view of deafness, with medical interventions, and a focus on speech development typically prioritised. This can contribute to negative psychological outcomes for deaf children: for example, research suggests that while Deaf people grow up to accept and appreciate themselves, they acknowledge painful and negative experiences at school and at home which have contributed to negative feelings about themselves (Corker 1996; Gascon-Ramos 2008). Gascon-Ramos (2008) suggests that:

> The lack of knowledge about the nature of deaf children makes it difficult for hearing parents to look beyond their own life experiences to

> understand the deaf child's needs. The acknowledgement of a world where language and life is visually experienced is not part of their lives. Deaf children, in the early stages of their development, have no need to produce oral expression, as it is not a part of their living experience. They are in need of a language to model and scaffold their experience (Garton 1994) and to grasp their reality in visual terms, so that communication (i.e. language) becomes part of a social visual experience. (69)

She continues to suggest that the well-being of deaf children is in great part determined by the provision of adequate cultural and social nurturing that is aligned with the deaf child's nature and life experience. She suggests that this requires hearing parents' participation in the Deaf community in order to facilitate their understanding of their deaf child's experience from a Deaf perspective.

Many deaf children born to hearing families, for many reasons, do not have access to a signed language during stages when language is normally acquired. Such deaf children often cannot access the spoken language of their environment and have no recourse to natural signed language models. In the absence of accessible language, deaf children build on the natural use of gesture (which is a feature of all human communication) and do something rather special with it: they generate structures that are more language-like than those generated by the hearing people in their environment. Adam Kendon, a key researcher in the area of gesture and language (spoken and signed), notes that this is a normal response; when communication is blocked from the oral modality, the manual modality assumes the functional burdens of speech (Kendon 1980). Goldin-Meadow and Morford (1994) report on the resilience of communication for deaf children who typically cannot process the oral language surrounding them and have not yet been exposed to a conventional signed language (like American Sign Language, or in our case, Irish Sign Language). Despite their language situation, such children 'have been observed to spontaneously exploit the manual modality for communication and to invent their own gestural systems' (249). Citing a range of international empirical literature, Goldin-Meadow and Morford note that these gestural systems are organised in language-like ways and are typically more complex structurally than gestures produced by the children's hearing parents. Research also suggests that such created gestural communications systems are structured similarly to the communication systems of children acquiring language in traditional linguistic environments. These systems, as used by deaf children, have been found to have structure at the level of the sentence (that is, there are patterns identifiable across gestures in a string), and there is some evidence that gestures also have internal structure (Goldin-Meadow and Mylander 1994). Clearly, there is a need for closer examination of the pathway to language for Irish deaf children and the role that gesture plays in bootstrapping communicative development.

For Irish hearing families who do 'discover' ISL, and seek to provide access to the language for their deaf children, there are some pathways in place. The Department of Education and Science established the ISL Home Tuition Scheme in the mid 1990s, which offers a very valuable resource to deaf and hearing children and their families. Given that some 90 per cent of deaf children are born to hearing parents, it is recognised that the need to facilitate communication and language development is vitally important for these children. The Department funds this programme to facilitate learning of ISL in a family setting for children who use ISL and their families. A knowledge of ISL subsequently allows for a greater degree of communication between family and children, and as we have seen earlier, communication is fundamental to children's social, emotional and language development.

In Ireland, an average of 100 hours of tuition a year per family is approved and funded by the Department of Education and Science. In 2004, some sixty families are recorded of having availed of this service (Mathews 2007) rising by 2007 to an estimated one hundred families, but many parents report not knowing that this service exists (Leeson 2007). An Advisory Committee on Deaf Education set up at the turn of the twenty-first century heard examples of the problems met by parents of deaf children due to lack of information and financial supports (ibid.). Parents also highlighted the problematic nature of attempting to support ISL acquisition in a context where not all visiting teachers or teachers of the deaf can sign, since there is no requirement for signed language competency for positions as teachers of the deaf. A later report commissioned by the National Council for Special Education recommended an aggressive programme of providing deaf children and their families with instruction in Irish Sign Language (Marschark and Spencer 2009), though this has yet to be implemented.

Traditionally, access to ISL occurred on arrival at a school for the deaf and as a result, the schools are seen as the 'cradle' of ISL and Deaf culture by many. However, in the current context, educational policy has moved away from the provision of special education per se towards a policy of mainstreaming or 'full inclusion services' (Mathews 2007). This has led to a decline in student numbers that is close to 50 per cent at the schools for the deaf, as parents choose to educate their children at regional units for the deaf and in local mainstream educational settings. Educational policy is important here, as one of the unintended outcomes of this is a destabilisation of a central context for language transmission. Given that teachers of the deaf and those non-specialist teachers working with deaf children are not required to have any fluency in Irish Sign Language, there are no guarantees that a deaf child in a mainstream setting will naturally acquire competence in ISL. Given the ever decreasing number of deaf children attending special schools for the deaf, and the fact that so few deaf children are born to Deaf parents, the core of ISL-fluent members of the Deaf community looks likely to decrease over the coming decades. This may well leave many deaf people without fluency in any language, and thus limited access to Deaf culture and the Deaf community. It also potentially positions ISL as an endangered or threatened language (Johnston 2006).

3.10 The official status of ISL

ISL is not currently an official language in the Republic, although it is recognised formally in Northern Ireland, along with British Sign Language. This lack of recognition together with the fact that Deaf people are generally seen as disabled rather than as members of a linguistic community means that Deaf people are a disadvantaged minority (Krausneker 2001; Timmermans 2005). However, the international community clearly recognises signed languages as 'real' natural languages worthy of protection: the European Parliament has passed two resolutions on signed languages (European Parliament 1988, 1998),[12] while in 2003 the Council of Europe's parliamentary assembly passed a resolution calling for the protection of signed languages (Leeson 2004; Timmermans 2005). UN documents also recognise the value of signed languages: both UNESCO's Salamanca Statement (UNESCO 1994) and the UN Convention on the Rights of Persons with a Disability (United Nations 2006) call for the use of signed languages in education. The most recent addition to the range of international documents recognising (or calling for the recognition of) signed languages is the Brussels Declaration. In November 2010, the European Union of the Deaf (EUD) launched the Brussels Declaration on Sign Languages in the European Union on behalf of the national associations of Deaf people across the EU, and signed by the Presidents of the World Federation of the Deaf (WFD), the European Forum of Sign Language Interpreters (EFSLI), the World Association of Sign Language Interpreters (WASLI) and Hungarian (Deaf) MEP, Dr Ádám Kósa. In parallel, EUD published a volume documenting the current legal status (or lack thereof) of signed languages in all European Union countries (Wheatley and Pabsch 2010).

Despite this gloomy history, many teachers today are more open to ISL learning and use, and in recent years there has been an increase in the number of Deaf teachers working in the schools for the deaf. The Department of Education and Science also provides support to parents who wish to avail of home sign tuition (Leeson 2007). However, without a fundamental shift in (1) state policy regarding requirements for teachers of the deaf, (2) entry requirements for teacher education at primary level and (3) inclusion of ISL on the curriculum and not just in special schools, the situation is unlikely to improve.

Outside of education, over the past twenty years, ISL has come to be used in the media, for example the television programmes *News for the Deaf*,

Hands On and its precursor, *Sign of the Times*, at conferences and in tertiary education. These developments were made possible by the availability of professional interpreters, with the first cohort graduating in 1994. In criminal legal contexts, the requirement for sign language interpretation has long been established as a right but in medical contexts the critical barrier to informed consent arising from use of another language still does not seem to be adequately recognised.[13]

3.11 Summary

In this chapter we have considered the historical development of ISL and its current social context. We have seen how important a role has been played by the schools for the deaf. We have seen that BSL was present in the Protestant schools for the deaf until the twentieth century, and that modern ISL displays a complex pattern of sign language contacts: combining an LSF substrate with input from the pre-existing 'Old ISL', which included a BSL substrate. We also saw that educational policy impacted significantly on the form that ISL took, for example with regard to the use of ISL-based variants in the Catholic schools and BSL-based variants in the Protestant Claremont Institute, and with gender-segregated schools leading to gendered variants of ISL. We have seen too that the implementation of oral education at different times has influenced variants. More recently, the establishment of schools in other parts of the country is leading to the evolution of regional variants, for example the Mid-West School for Hearing Impaired Children being associated with an evolving Mid-Western dialect of ISL.

We considered the impact of ISL on Auslan and South African Sign Language. ISL has also had a strong presence in parts of the UK, including Scotland, parts of England and in Northern Ireland. We also noted that while the influence of BSL on modern ISL is often discussed, the historical influence of BSL on ISL is frequently overlooked.

We have tried to show something of the contemporary Irish Deaf community and outlined the range of social issues that impact on language use. Primary amongst these is educational policy, which affects how the majority of deaf children come into contact with ISL, how they acquire the language, and the extent to which ISL is used in academic domains. We outlined the impact that the suppression of ISL in previous generations has had on ISL usage today, including the development of gendered variants and the delayed development of an academic register of ISL. We have also talked about the likely impact of mainstreaming on ISL in the coming decades. In considering the path to language acquisition for deaf children, we discussed 'home sign', and we outlined how home sign can support access to ISL. We compared and contrasted the developmental pathways for deaf children from Deaf families with that of deaf children from hearing families. We then turned to look at issues of language recognition and we saw that while the British government has recognised ISL in Northern Ireland, the Irish government has not yet formally recognised ISL within the framework of any language-related legislation.

Notes

1. Matthews (1996b) lists fourteen educational services, but this includes the various locations that Orpen operated at: Smithfield Penitentiary in 1816, Brunswick Street in 1817 and then Claremont in Glasnevin in 1819. He also lists St Joseph's School, Prospect Avenue, Glasnevin, separately from St Joseph's School for Deaf Boys, Cabra, as well as St Mary's School for Deaf Girls, Cabra, while McDonnell (1979) combines these under the heading of the Catholic Institution for the Deaf.
2. See Pollard (2006) for a detailed account of the work of Dr Charles Orpen and the history of the Claremont Institute.
3. See for example McDonnell and Saunders (1993), Griffey (1994), for discussion of the Irish situation and Knoors (1999) for the Netherlands.
4. It is not clear from Griffey's writings exactly when strict segregation was implemented in St Mary's School for Deaf Girls, but we know from Knoors that Van Uden implemented a strict segregation policy in the 1960s, so Sr Nicholas Griffey seems to have been a forerunner in implementing this approach.
5. As we have seen, the link to LSF did originally come about as a result of the establishment of the first Catholic school in Ireland.
6. The school currently has a website at <http://www.dominicangrimley.org> (accessed 25 November 2011), which states its continuing commitment to oralism.
7. See SLED (Sign Language Education and Development) website, <http://www.sled.org.za> (accessed 25 November 2011).
8. Maginn was born in Mallow, Co. Cork, in 1861 to a Protestant family. He became deafened post-lingually at age 5 years. He was educated in London, and later attended Gallaudet College (now University) where he was inspired to improve the situation of Deaf people in the UK. In his later years, Maginn focused his efforts in Northern Ireland, where he died in 1918. It is worth noting that Maginn was multi-lingual. He was a fluent writer of English (as evidenced by his school and College reputation); while in the USA, he would have used ASL to engage with the Gallaudet environment, and we know that he communicated in BSL with his contemporaries in the UK. While he did not graduate from Gallaudet College, Maginn was highly regarded, and was later conferred with an honorary degree by the College (see <http://www.bris.ac.uk/Depts/DeafStudiesTeaching/dhcwww/chapter3.htm#5> (accessed 25 November 2011)).

9. See Matthews (1996) and Leeson and Sheikh (2010) for further discussion regarding the Irish Deaf Community; Lane et al. (1996) for discussion of the American Deaf Community; and Ladd (2003) for discussion of Deafhood and the British Deaf Community.
10. In the field of Deaf Studies, the term 'deaf' (with a lower case 'd') is used to refer to those with a hearing impairment and those who are deafened, while 'Deaf' (upper case 'D') refers to those who see themselves as members of a cultural community. Of course, there are 'fuzzy categories', which we will return to later, where it can be difficult to assign membership to one of these categories, for example deaf children with hearing parents, who have not yet encountered Deaf culture; and hearing children of Deaf parents who acquire a signed language as a first language.
11. Interestingly Stan Foran (1979), writing as a leading member of the Deaf community at the time, suggests that a process of standardising ISL occurred in order to make it easier for hearing learners of ISL, that is, they would only have to learn one sign variant.
12. Indeed this resolution was raised by an Irish MEP, Eileen LeMass.
13. See RTÉ *Hands On* reports from 2008. The archived data is only available to Irish viewers but content is available at <http://www.rte.ie/tv/handson/archive.html>. Particularly, see the programme about access to health care aired on 24 February 2008, available at <http://www.rte.ie/tv/handson/thisweek24022008.html>. A more recent addition is a *Hands On* segment on access to maternity care on 27 November 2011 at <http://www.rte.ie/tv/handson/thisweek27112011.html> (all accessed 30 December 2011).

4 The Phonetics and Phonology of ISL

4.1 Introduction

This chapter introduces readers to the first aspect of linguistic analysis proper: the phonetics and phonology of ISL. We begin by defining phonetics and phonology, outlining the importance of being able to identify what data are considered significant in linguistic terms. We show how the notion of minimal pairs helps us to identify the phonological units of ISL that make up signs. We discuss manual, non-manual and multi-channel signs and introduce Stokoe's (1960) original parameters for analysis of manual signs: handshape, movement and location. We look at the handshapes that are used in ISL and discuss the issue of allophonic variation. We then identify other parameters of the signs: movement and orientation of the hands and non-manual features.

4.2 Phonetics

Phonetics is typically taken to be the study of speech sounds. Phoneticians are concerned with what people do when they speak, and aim to describe the sounds that occur in human spoken languages. They ask questions about how the articulatory parameters of speech are affected by speech; for example, how does the vocal tract produce the sounds of spoken languages? Phoneticians are also concerned with creating a phonetic inventory for each language, which contains the list of sounds that occur in a given language. In turn, each sound is associated with a symbol that represents the sound, and these symbols together make up the International Phonetic Alphabet (IPA). The symbols listed in the IPA are based on the Roman alphabet and allow for phoneticians to write down the sounds of any spoken language that occurs using the IPA. Phonetics, then, is concerned with the transcription of the sounds of a spoken language while phonology is the description of the systems and patterns of sounds that occur in a language. As Ladefoged (1993: 25) notes, phonetics 'involves studying a language to determine its distinctive sounds and to establish a set of rules that describe the set of changes that take place in these sounds when they occur in differing relationships with other sounds'. Ladefoged describes a phonological unit, a phoneme, as occurring when two sounds can be used to differentiate between two different semantic units, for example in the English words '*wh*ite' versus '*r*ight' or '*c*at' versus '*b*at' (ibid.).

It is important to note that as a phonological unit a phoneme is not a single sound, but a group of sounds. Phonemes are abstract units that function in the grammatical system of a language and may form the basis for writing down languages systematically and unambiguously (ibid.). Because English pronunciation has changed so much over time, but spelling has remained the same, we see differences arising between phonemic transcriptions of English and the established writing system. In contrast, for Swahili, the transcription system and the orthography are very similar (ibid.). If we take the English examples 'pat' and 'sat', we can see that these words appear to differ only in terms of their initial consonants. What we can say is that this difference, known as contrastiveness or opposition, is sufficient to distinguish these words from each other. Because of this, we can say that the [p] and [s] sounds represent different phonemes in English. Pairs of words that are identical except for such a sound are known as a minimal pair, and minimal pairs are the most frequent demonstration that two sounds are separate phonemes. If no minimal pair can be found to demonstrate that two sounds are distinct, it may be that they are variants of the same phoneme.

Such variant sounds, though distinguishable by phonetic analysis, may be perceived by speakers of the language as essentially the same sound and are known as allophones. These allophonic variations are especially likely to happen if the sounds occur in different environments. An example of allophonic variation in English exists with the /l/ phoneme. In most accents the 'dark' l sound [ɫ] that comes at the end of the word *wool* is quite different from the 'light l' sound [l] at the beginning of the word *leaf*.

4.3 The phonetics of ISL

With this description of traditional phonetics and phonology in mind, we turn to the application of these principles to signed languages generally, and to Irish Sign Language in particular. We have seen that phonetics is the study of the sounds that occur in a given language and how they are articulated while phonology describes both how those sounds form linguistically significant units and how these units combine to create words in a given language. Since the word phonology derives from the Classical Greek word *φωνή*, *phōnē*, 'sound, voice', it might be no surprise to learn that William Stokoe, one of the founders of modern sign linguistics, proposed using the term cherology, from Greek *χείρ*, *cheir*, 'hand', to discuss the hand patterns that arise in signed languages (Stokoe 1960). However, this term did not enter into widespread use and instead the same terms, phonetics and phonology, are used in identifying the building blocks of signed languages and the patterns that they follow (Johnston and Schembri 2007). So just as phonetics is concerned with the segmentation of the sound stream produced by speakers, in signed languages it is concerned with the segmentation of the fluid movement of the signer's hands, body and facial movements. Forms such as handshapes are abstracted from the gestural stream by phonetic analysis, as their linguistic function is identified. Thus far, there is no agreement on the phonetic alphabet inventory for ISL: Ó Baoill and Matthews (2000) identified sixty-six handshapes while Matthews (2005) identified those listed in Figure 4.1. As we shall see, other linguistic forms include bodily orientation, mouthing and eyegaze.

The description of the phonology of a signed language involves exploring the way that phonological units are formed by the combination of handshapes and other phonetic features, and trying to discover the rules that govern how these units are combined to form higher-level elements like words.

An important issue to consider is the fact that while ISL makes use of the one-handed alphabet, as discussed in Chapter 2, signs can be either one-handed or two-handed. For example, the signs for DEAF and HEARING are both one-handed signs, as are the signs for KNOW, LIKE and WALK. However, signs for MOTHER, FATHER, OLD, YOUNG, LOVE, JUMP and FISH are two-handed. We should also note that in certain conditions, two-handed signs can become one-handed and one-handed signs can become two-handed. For example, in informal situations, if a signer is nursing a pint of Guinness or holding a cup of tea or a baby, the non-dominant hand is omitted (though in some conditions, another point of contact may be substituted, for example the non-dominant arm or the leg of a signer). Another possibility is that over time, what was a two-handed sign has become a one-handed sign. SISTER is an example. It is articulated with the dominant hand making contact with the ipsilateral shoulder. For older signers (or for emphasis, as we shall see later), this sign may be articulated as a two-handed sign.

When we talk about two-handed signs, sign linguists use terms like 'dominant/non-dominant' or 'strong/weak' or 'active/passive' to describe the relationship between the hands, with the dominant/strong/active hand being the hand that the signer uses to fingerspell. However, as Nilsson (2010) points out, the non-dominant hand is anything but passive. It has a range of functions, which we discuss later, that have particular importance for the structure of discourse in ISL.

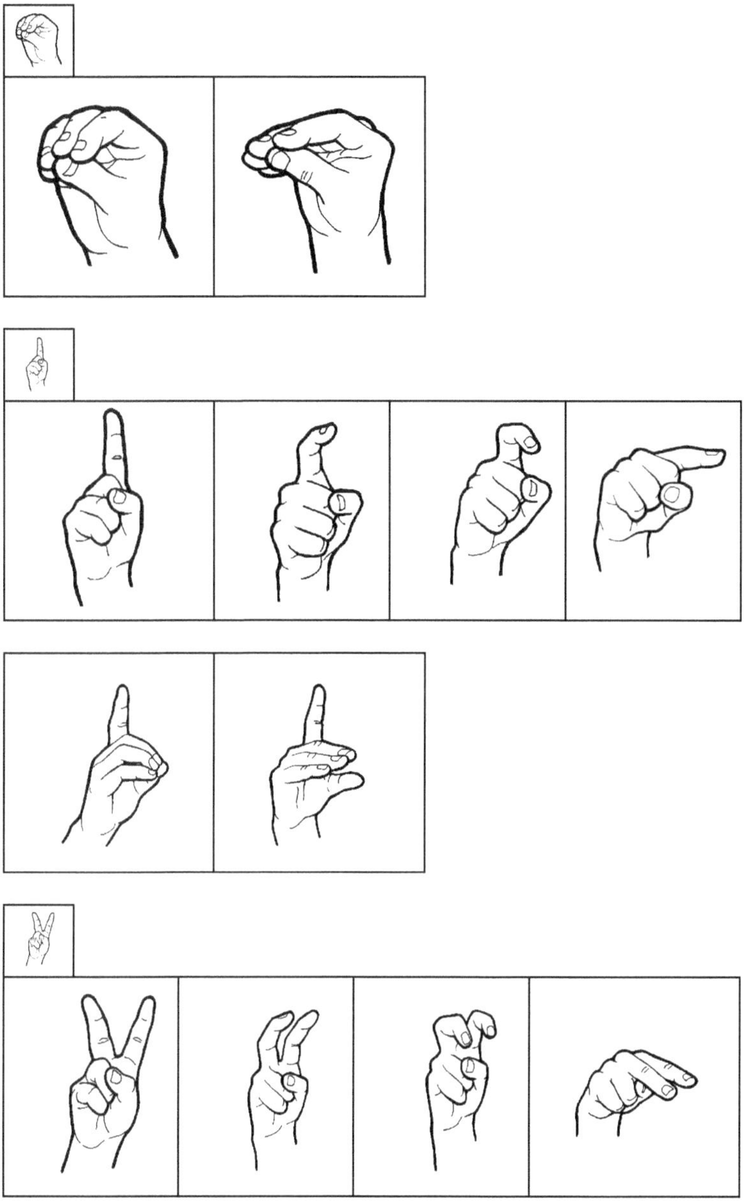

Figure 4.1 ISL handshapes

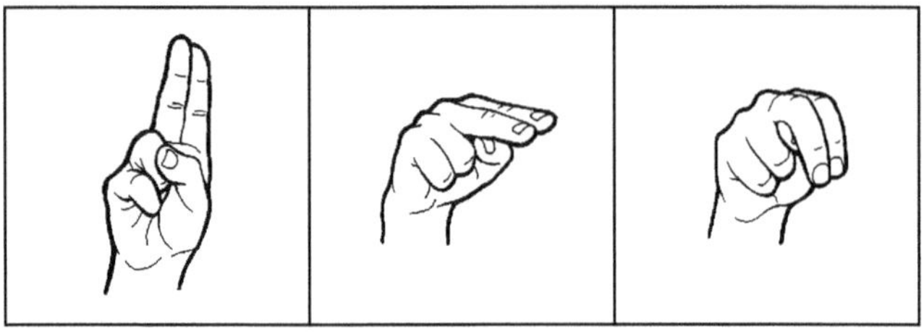

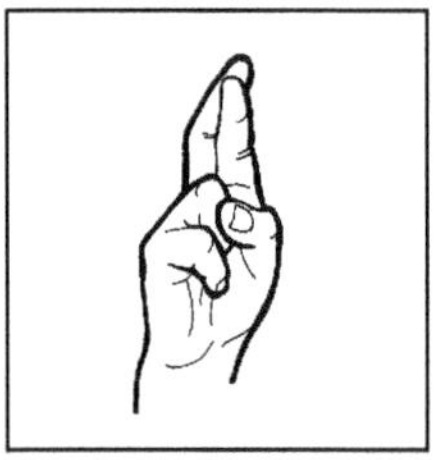

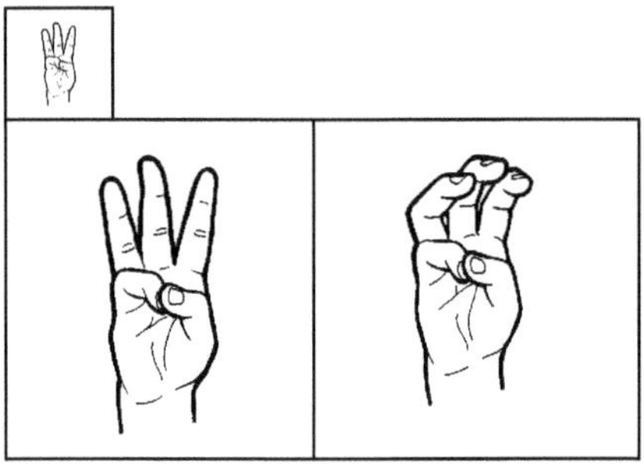

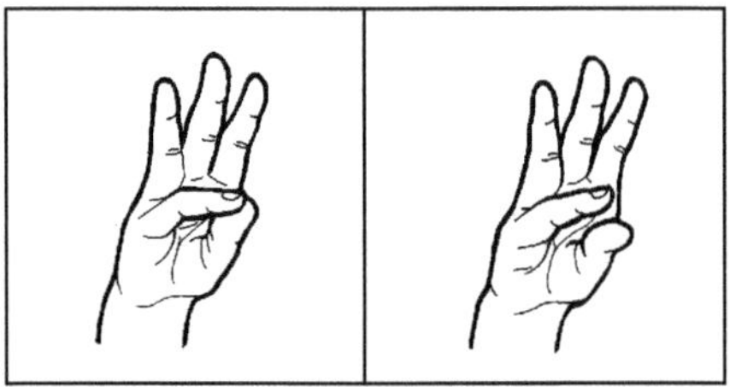

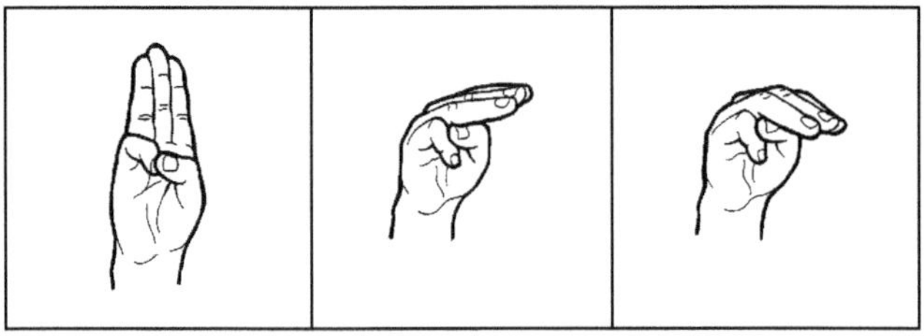

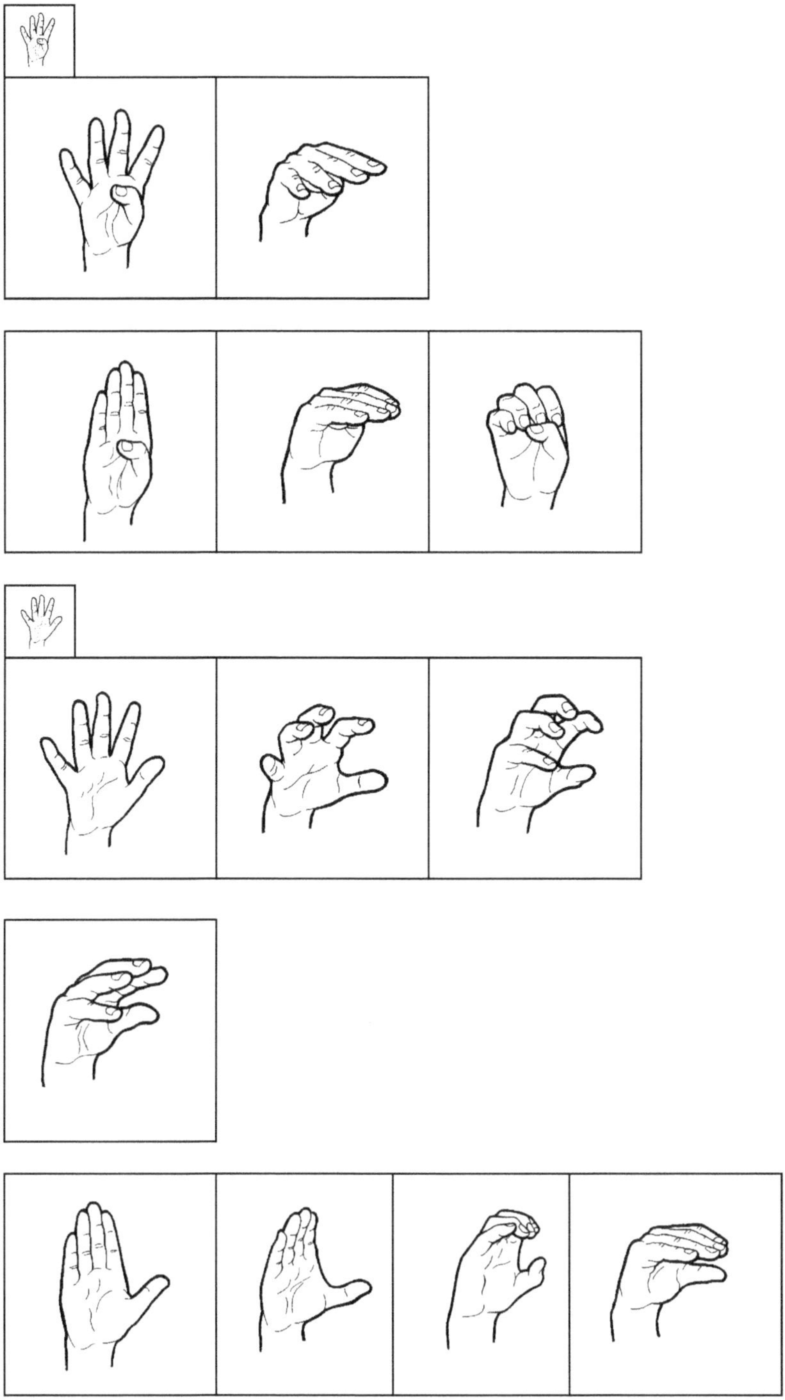

Figure 4.1 (*cont.*)

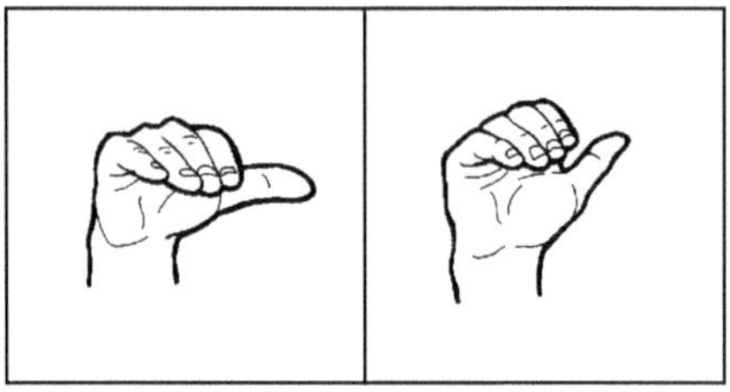

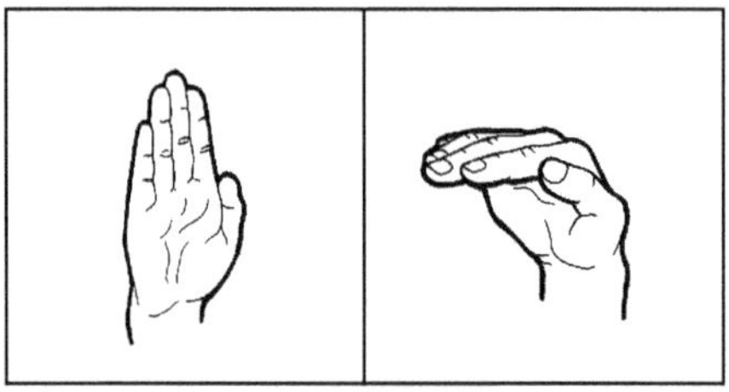

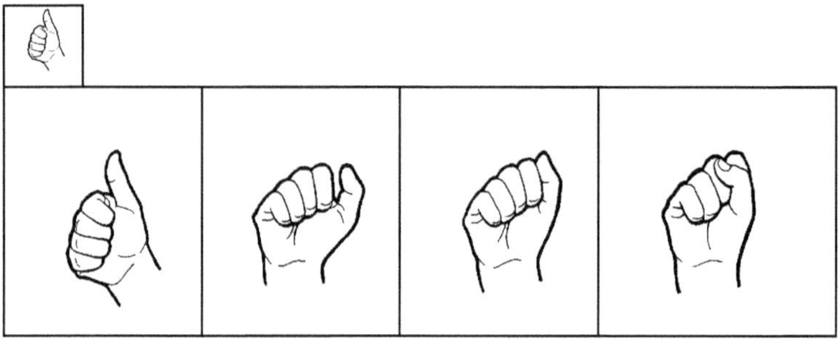

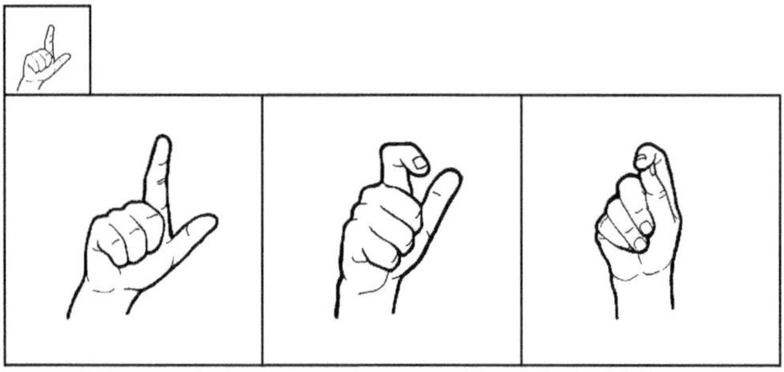

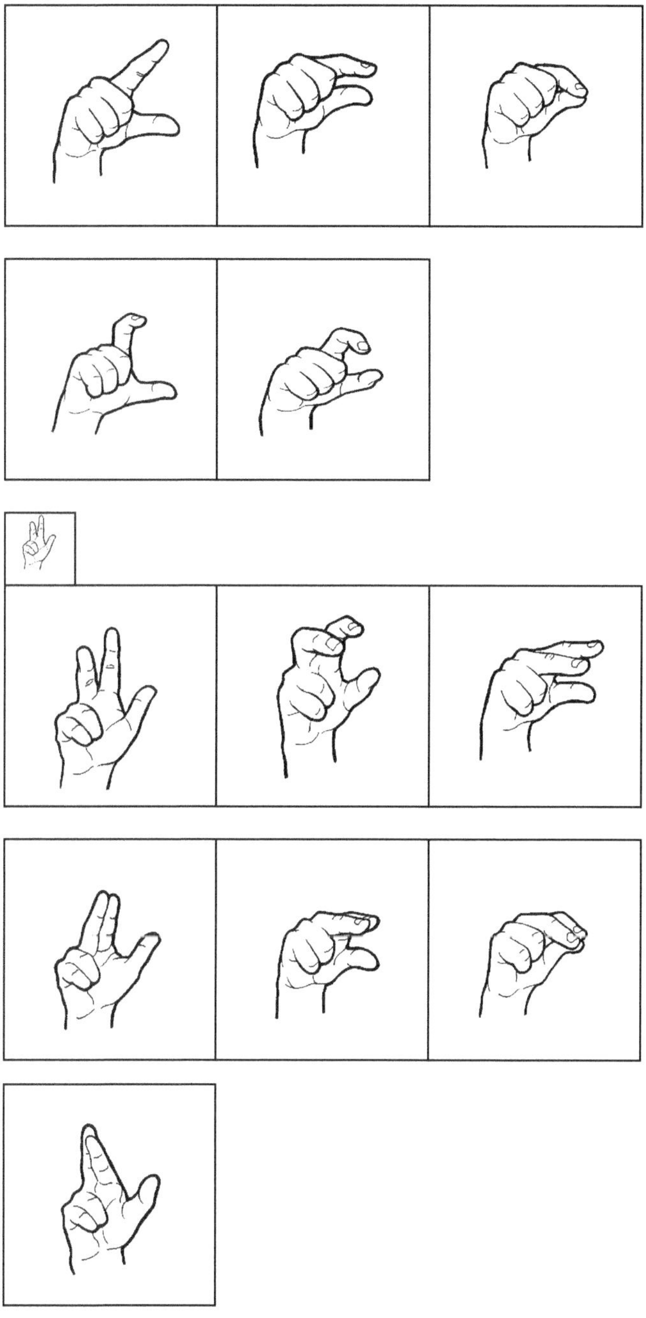

Figure 4.1 (*cont.*)

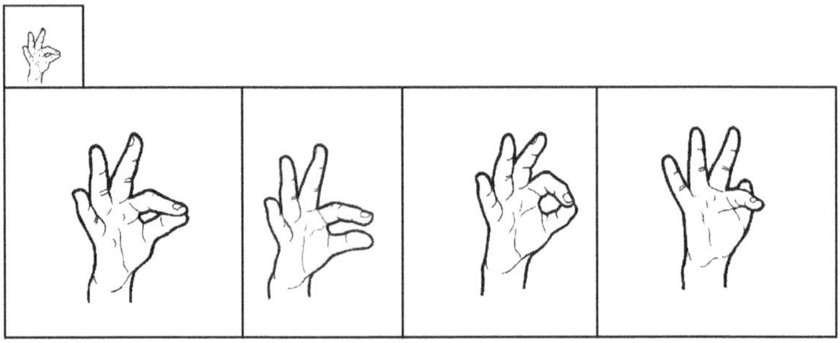

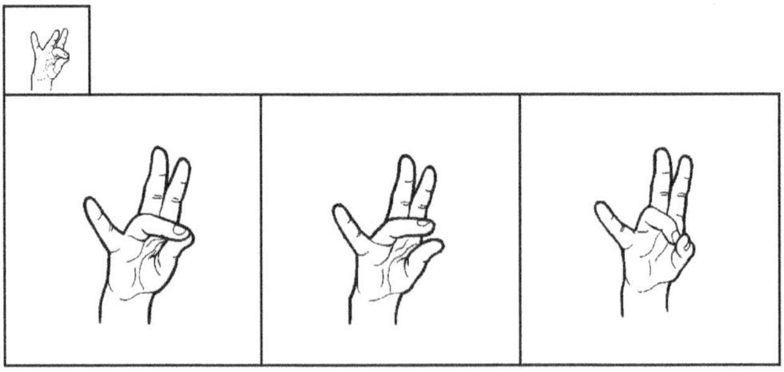

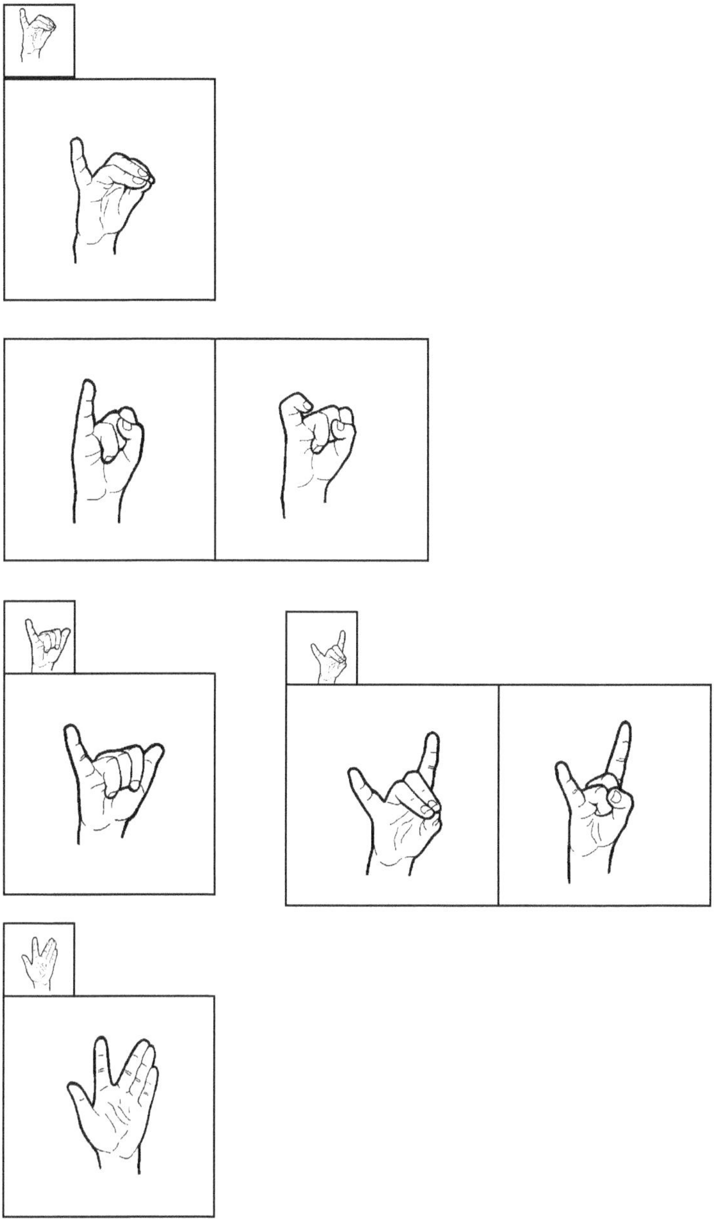

Figure 4.1 (*cont.*)

4.4 The phonology of ISL

As we have noted, phonology describes formal units that allow contrasts in meaning. While two handshapes may show detectable differences, these may not be significant for meaning in a given sign. In ISL, for example, some spreading of fingers can occur in handshapes in certain signs, but this phonetic difference may not cause signers to perceive the sign as meaning something different. The ISL sign for MOTHER, for example, is articulated with two P-handshapes, which entails the fingers being closed. In Example 4.1, the first signer articulates MOTHER in this prototypical way. In contrast, the second signer articulates MOTHER with the fingers spread, using what would otherwise be described as a W-handshape. However, contextually, these variant handshapes are not perceived as different signs. These two variants do not form a minimal pair; they are just phonetic variants of the sign MOTHER, or an instance of allophonic variation.

Example 4.1

Allophonic variation in the articulation of MOTHER
Fergus M. (07) Personal Stories (Dublin)
Lianne (14) Personal Stories (Dublin)

4.5 Manual signs

Handshape is a necessary, but not sufficient parameter in the creation of a sign: several other parameters are required to co-occur simultaneously. Stokoe (1960) identified three parameters as essential to the formation of a manual sign:

1. handshape or 'designator' (DEZ)
2. location or 'tabulation' (TAB)
3. movement or 'signation' (SIG).

To these Battison (1978) suggested adding a parameter of orientation (ORI): the spatial relationship of the palm and fingers to the signer's body. The parameters that are basic to the make-up of any sign in any given natural sign language can be said to be the phonological properties of a sign language (Sutton-Spence and Woll 1999).

As we have seen, handshape refers to the configuration of the hand(s) in the articulation of a sign. Handshape can be said to represent one of the phonetic possibilities of a signed language and use of particular handshapes is linguistically determined. For example, while the middle finger extended is a handshape that occurs in some dialects of BSL, for signs like for IDLE, UNEMPLOYED, HOLIDAY and MOCK (Brien 1992: 381), this handshape does not occur in ISL.

In the following sections we look at handshape and the other manual parameters, movement, location and orientation, in ISL. More recent research suggests that we need to consider non-manual features (NMFs), particularly mouthing and mouth gestures, as important parts of the phonological structure of signs. As we shall see, NMFs have an important role to play at morphological and syntactic levels. However, for simplicity we begin with the four manual phonological parameters that are the basis for the formation of a sign in ISL.

The identification of 'minimal pairs' allows us to identify phonemes in a language. A minimal pair can be said to arise when only one parameter is altered, but this alteration leads to a change in meaning. For example, in ISL, where orientation, movement and location remain the same, and only the handshape parameter varies, we can identify handshapes that are phonemes.[1] Examples include the ISL signs KNOW and UNDERSTAND, where location, movement and orientation of the palm are the same for both signs, and only the handshape parameter differs. KNOW takes an ISL-L-handshape while UNDERSTAND takes a U-handshape, at the side of the head. In many cases in ISL, minimal pairs differing only on the basis of handshape tend to share the same semantic class, as can be seen in Examples 4.2–4.6.

Example 4.2

AUNT UNCLE COUSIN

Example 4.3

MOTHER FATHER

Example 4.4

SON DAUGHTER

Example 4.5

KNOW UNDERSTAND THINK

Example 4.6

HOLY BLESS BLESS (as done by the Pope)

Examples 4.2–4.6 clearly show that higher-level semantic categories are shared by individual signs. In Examples 4.2–4.4 all the lexical items are kinship terms; in Example 4.5 they are related to cognitive processes; and in Example 4.6 they are related to a central notion of blessedness. These more abstract semantic classes share elements of the phonological form. In Chapter 6 we will discuss these semantic relations between words in more detail.

In the next sections we discuss the manual parameters of (1) handshape, (2) location, (3) movement and (4) orientation. Handshape, as we have seen, refers to the configuration of the hand or hands (for two-handed signs). Location relates to the position of the hands relative to the signer's body or in signing space. Movement relates to the movement path that the hands and arms follow in signing space. Movement can also include reference to the internal movement of the fingers and/or thumbs. The orientation of the palm is an important phonological factor that can lead to minimal pairs. An ISL example of this would be MOTHER versus POOR (Example 4.7).

Example 4.7

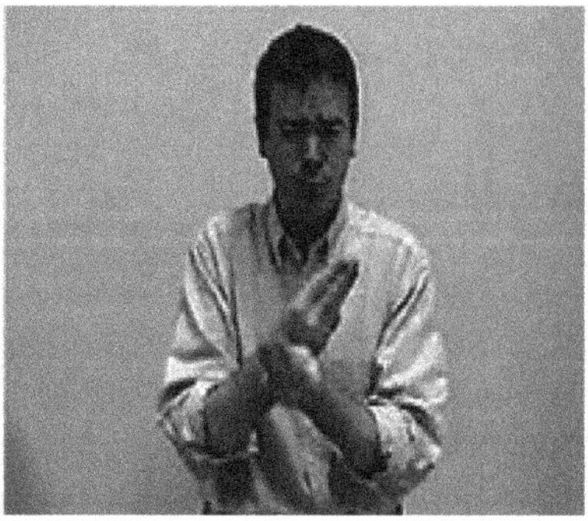

Minimal pairs arising from a difference in orientation: MOTHER and POOR

Kevin (17) Personal Stories (Dublin) Senan (01) Personal Stories (Dublin)

4.5.1 Handshape

Earlier, we presented a characteristic inventory of handshapes in ISL (see Figure 4.1). Internationally, many phonologists are adopting the HamNoSys inventory in their work. We include elements of the inventory here too, as it offers an articulatory phonetics approach to the description of manual signs, and, with input arising from the analysis of an ever increasing number of signed languages, it has the potential to form the basis of an International Phonetics Alphabet for signed languages (Figure 4.2).

As Thorvaldsdottir (2010) notes, when we attempt to transcribe or code phonetic features in a signed language with the aim of using the information

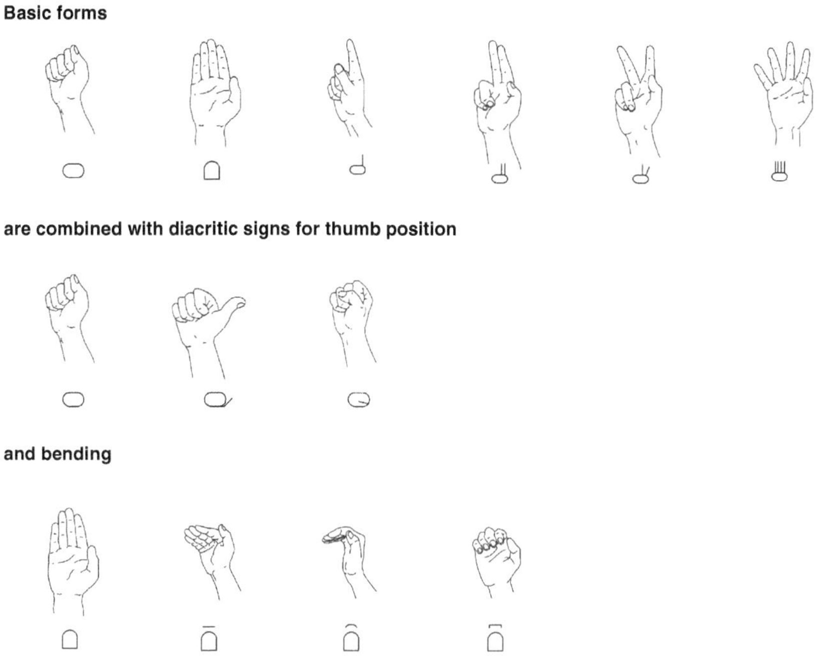
Basic forms
are combined with diacritic signs for thumb position
and bending

(a)

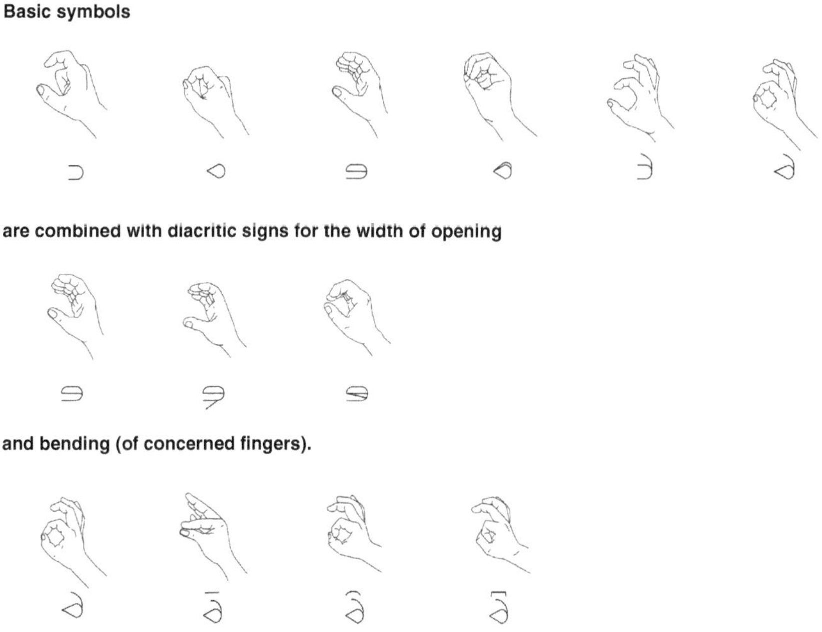
Basic symbols
are combined with diacritic signs for the width of opening
and bending (of concerned fingers).

(b)

Finger specifications replace default finger(s)

or specify derivations **or specify concerned fingers with connections.**

(c)

Crossing fingers are notated with fingers digits (lower first) and the finger part where the upper finger meets the lower one:

Hidden thumbs are notated as follows:

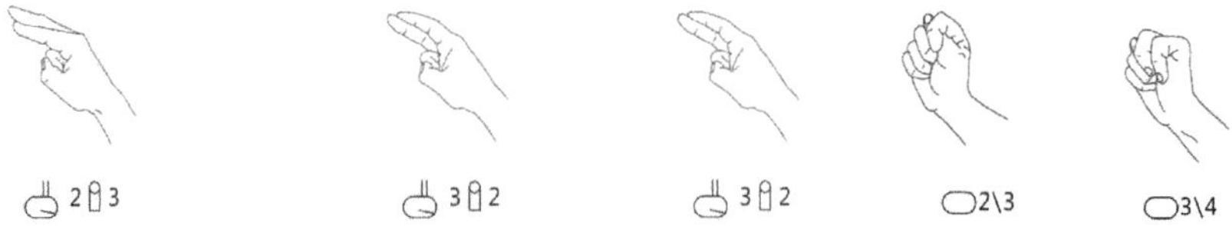

(d)

identical finger base direction:

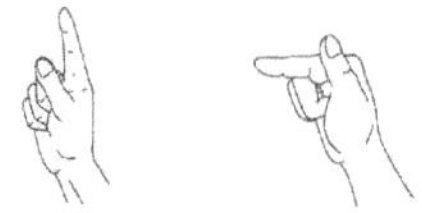

Inventory:

(e)

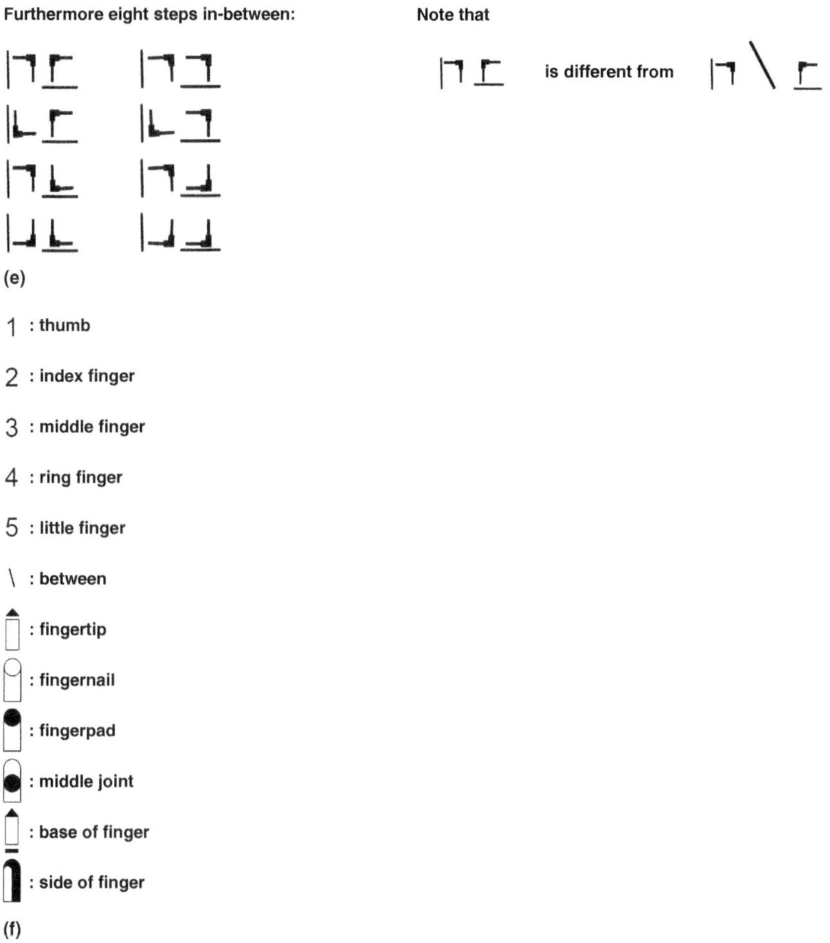

Figure 4.2 The HamNoSys inventory: (a) handshapes, (b) thumb combinations, (c) finger specifications, (d) finger parts, (e) finger base orientation, (f) finger parts, denotations

for phonological analysis, we face the challenge of making the coding functional for later phonological work. Ideally, we would know the phonology of the language before we begin to code the phonetics of a given signed language, but this rarely happens in practice. Crasborn (2001) and Van der Kooij (2002) call this the database paradox. To overcome this problem, it becomes necessary to rely on research from other signed languages alongside our preliminary observations for ISL. Thorvaldsdottir (2010) notes that one issue that arises is that international databases of handshape do not necessarily capture the range of ISL-specific handshapes that arise. She gives the examples in Figure 4.3.

(a) ISL handshape not found in HamNoSys

(b) Handshape not noted before in ISL (but used in signs like BOY)

Figure 4.3 ISL-specific handshapes? (a) ISL handshape not found in HamNoSys, (b) handshape not noted before in ISL (but used in signs like BOY)

Another issue is that there are phonetic variants that arise in ISL, as illustrated in Example 4.8, which are further instances of allophonic variation as described earlier.

Example 4.8

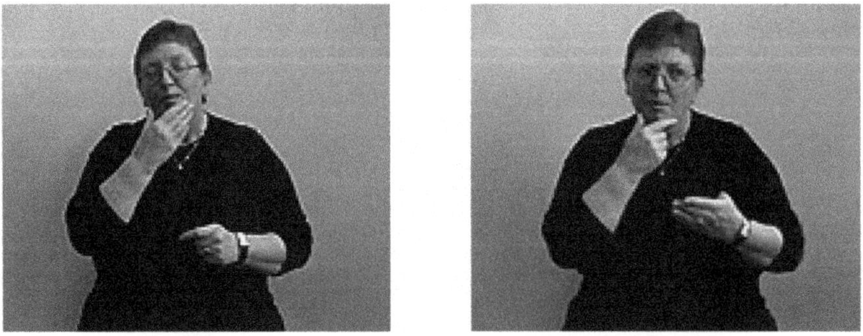

(a) Citation form for BOY:
articulated with four selected fingers
Noeleen (03) Personal Stories (Dublin)

(b) Variation of the sign BOY:
articulated with one selected finger

4.5.2 Location

Describing British Sign Language, Brennan et al. (1984) identify five distinct spatial locations: the head (including the neck), the trunk, the arms, the hands and the area in front of the signer's body. They subdivide each location into specific tabs. For example, the head area is reported to have ten tabs, each allocated due to the fact that certain signs differ only in terms of their position on or near the head (35). So in BSL, the eye, ear, nose, mouth and forehead are considered to be separate tabs.

The same pattern is discernible in Irish Sign Language since many minimal pairs can be identified on the basis of tab differences. An example of an ISL verb which has the side of the forehead as a tab is THINK, while the ISL verb TELL begins at the mouth and has this as its tab. The verb GIVE uses the space in front of the signer, neutral space, (c.) as its tab, although as we will see, direction of movement is another influencing factor. Currently work is underway to identify the tab operations for ISL. In the absence of a comprehensive list, we can still identify minimal pairs in ISL on the basis of tab difference. For example, Matthews (1996a) gives the ISL examples of MY and STUPID as minimal pairs, where the feature that changes, creating meaning change, is location. MY has the signer's chest as a tab, while STUPID has the forehead as a tab.

We can also note that constraints exist with respect to the use of signing locations in ISL. For example, no sign is normally articulated outside signing space, or on the signer's back, though poetic licence may allow for this rule to be broken occasionally. When this happens, we can say that the prototypical phonological constraints have been breached. An example of this in British Sign Language occurs in the poem 'Morning' by Dorothy Miles. In one section, the poet signs 'TWIN TREES', a novel creation that shows the reflection of a tree in a pool. The poet breaches typical BSL phonological rules because it is not usual for two-handed signs to touch at the elbows (Sutton-Spence et al. 2005; Sutton-Spence and Woll 1999). Signers of ISL also recognise when location constraints have been breached; signers can, for example, breach location constraints for metaphoric effect. One example of this is where the ISL sign BOIL is articulated on the signer's body at lower-torso level instead of in neutral signing space. The change of location indicates a shift in meaning from the literal verbal meaning of 'to boil' to a metaphoric rendition, meaning that 'I was boiling with anger', as discussed later in Chapter 9.

4.5.3 Movement

Analysis of the movement parameter is considered the most difficult to describe adequately (Brennan et al. 1984; Kyle and Woll 1985; Maguire 1991; Stokoe 1978). Just as the number of handshapes permitted within a sign language is subject to constraints, the range of movements allowed is also governed from within the language. Brennan et al. (1984) consider the argument that 'the type of movement may in part be conditioned by what is performing the action' (40). Indeed, more recent work suggests that there is an analogue between movement in the real world and some kinds of movement that arise in signed languages. For example, Slobin and Hoiting (1994) note that signed languages use space to represent space, and motion to represent motion. For now, we can consider the feature analysis of movement offered by Friedman (1977) which includes four fundamental features:

- **Interaction:** whether one or both hands move and if they perform the same movement or interact with each other.
- **Contact:** whether the hands make contact with the body, and if so, what kind of contact do they make? (For example, continuous or punctual, etc.)
- **Direction:** of movement in space described in terms of three axes: horizontal-width, horizontal-depth and vertical.
- **Manner:** relates to the type of movement, be that of the entire arm ('macro') or of the joints of the hands and wrist ('micro').

If we take the following Irish Sign Language utterance, we could describe the ISL verb 'GIVE (a thick book)' in terms of the movement parameter as in Example 4.9.

Example 4.9
c.(2h)1GIVE2 (h/s 13⇒⇐)f.
'I am giving you a (thick) book'

We can describe the movement as:

- **Interaction:** two hands move, performing the same movement, using the same handshape.
- **Contact:** no body contact occurs. Movement takes place in neutral space (c.).
- **Direction:** moves forward along the 'horizontal-width' axis. (c.→f.).
- **Manner:** macro. Both arms are involved in the movement.

The movement parameter also allows us to differentiate direction of movement in relation to person agreement, for example 1GIVE2 and 2GIVE1 differ only in relation to the direction of movement.[2]

4.5.4 Orientation

The final manual parameter to consider is that of orientation (Ori). Orientation, as we saw earlier, can be considered the relationship of the hands to the signer's body and to each other (Brennan et al. 1984; Kyle and Woll 1985). The inclusion of orientation as a fundamental parameter for description was originally hotly debated. Friedman (1977) argued for the inclusion of this parameter, though she proposed that orientation must be defined for each individual handshape to allow us to determine the hand direction in relation to the body, while Stokoe (1978) argued that it was unnecessary.[3] Brennan et al. (1984) include the orientation parameter in their analysis on the basis of two main influencing factors: the fact that orientation can be a sole distinguishing feature between two lexical signs, and the fact that hitherto transcription systems that excluded the parameter of orientation have proven inadequate.

In Irish Sign Language, orientation can also be said to be a defining factor in differentiating between sets of minimal pairs (Matthews 1996a). One example of this is the minimal pair LESSON and BLOOD, as seen in Example 4.10.

Example 4.10

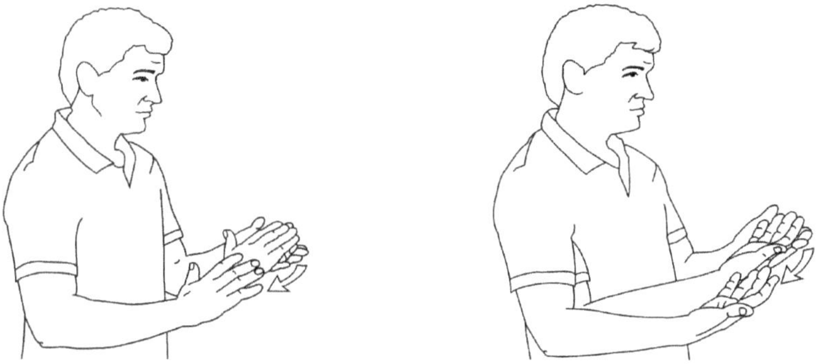

(a) LESSON (b) BLOOD

Brennan (1992) notes that there are other features that need to be taken into consideration in addition to those outlined above. She lists hand arrangement and point and place of contact as important when discussing sign production. Our discussion has concentrated on manual parameters; in section 4.7 we discuss an important non-manual parameter in ISL: mouthing. Before that, we turn to the phonological constraints that we can identify as operating on the production of signs.

4.6 Non-manual features

4.6.1 Beyond the hands

Sutton-Spence (2007) points out that while we often think of signed languages as being manual in nature, important linguistic information is also produced through non-manual channels, including the mouth. Research on sign languages has revealed the contribution to meaning of non-manual markers such as facial expressions, head movements, bodily posture and mouthing. Examples of the types of non-manual features used by ISL signers are given in Table 4.1. We will see examples of the grammatical and discourse roles played by some of these features later in this book, for example with

Table 4.1 Articulatory descriptors for non-manual features in Irish Sign Language (following Nonhebel, Crasborn and van der Kooij's description of ECHO Project conventions (2004))

Feature	**Annotation**
Headnod	headnod
Headshake	headshake
Headtilt	TILT+[direction of tilt]
Head turn	TURN+[direction of turn]
Chin to shoulder	cs
Brows raised	raised
Brows furrowed	furrowed
Eyes wide	WD
Eyes squinted	SQ
Eyeblink	//
Eyes closed	CLOSED
Eyes averted	+[locus of gaze]
Cheeks: sucked in puffed out	 in puffed
Lips: closed open round forward stretched	 closed open round forward stretched
Air: in/out	 in/out
Mouth corners: up/down	 corners up corners down
Tongue position: in/out	10% out of the mouth 30% out of the mouth 60% out of the mouth 100% out of the mouth
Tongue shape: pointed/relaxed	pointed relaxed
Teeth: labiodental up/labiodental low	labiodental up labiodental low

respect to how topic-comment structures are marked, the ways in which the clustering of certain non-manual features can mark the difference between statements and questions, the marking of WH-questions versus yes–no (or polar) questions, the role played by NMFs in differentiating between volition and non-volition on the part of the signer, and in the marking of adverbials. Identifying this lexical use represents a claim that the non-manual feature is an obligatory part of the sign rather than an optional modifier, belonging more properly to the sentence level. However, in many cases such features combine with manual features to form what have been called 'multi-channel' signs (Lawson 1983), to emphasise the interdependence of manual and non-manual features in these signs. An example of this is the minimal pair APPLE/PROSTITUTE. APPLE is articulated with an A-handshape, with contact at the ipsilateral cheek, and the sign has a circular movement. The mouthing that co-occurs with this sign is 'apple'. PROSTITUTE is made up of the same manual components, but for some typically older signers there is no mouthing and instead, the signer's tongue is extended into the hollow of the ipsilateral cheek and is visible to the interlocutor. Younger signers tend to mouth 'prostitute'. We discuss the role of mouthings and mouth gestures in the next section.

4.6.2 Mouthings and mouth gestures

In this section we discuss meaningful linguistic information conveyed by signers' mouth movements. Rainò (2001) suggests that there are two major categories of mouthed elements in signed languages. The first main category is referred to as 'mouthings'. Mouthings are derived from a spoken language, and are evidence of the contact between English and Irish Sign Language, as in the APPLE/PROSTITUTE example discussed above. We will also see that mouthings were introduced into ISL as a consequence of the introduction of oral educational practices. The second category of mouthed elements is that of 'mouth gestures'. Sutton-Spence (2007) points out that these are idiomatic gestures of the mouth and cannot be traced back to a spoken language. We will see that even signers who do not make use of mouthing, mostly elderly male signers, do make use of mouth gestures. We will also see that there are some mouth gestures that were originally gender specific but, in some cases, have become more widely used across the Irish Deaf ISL-using population (Leeson 2005; Leeson and Grehan 2004).

Boyes Braem (2001) has shown that mouthings may be used lexically, grammatically, prosodically and for discourse and stylistic reasons in Swiss German Sign Language. Sutton-Spence (2007) finds the same range of functionality for mouthings in British Sign Language, while work in progress on the form and function of mouthings in ISL suggests the same range of function holds true (Fitzgerald forthcoming). For BSL, Sutton-Spence (2007) reports that in all cases, the simultaneity of the mouthing with the hands is an essential feature, with just 1 per cent of the mouthings in her corpus having no accompanying manual component. The majority of these mouthings were for interjections such as 'yes', 'no', 'well', 'of course' and 'oh'. However, as we shall see below, in ISL, while mouthings co-occur with manually produced lexical items, there are instances where no mouthed accompaniment arises, and we shall see that this feature is sociolinguistically motivated.

Militzer (2009) has conducted a preliminary analysis of the gendered use of mouthing in ISL and substantiated what was claimed for ISL, namely that considerable differences arose in terms of how men and women use mouthing, and that age plays a significant role in the occurrence of mouthing. Her work substantiates earlier claims of differences associated with the introduction of oral education in Ireland and how this impacts on use of mouthing and mouth gestures by ISL users. Militzer suggests that for ISL, the signer's educational background (primary and secondary school education influenced by oralism or not) is decisive for their use of mouthing. This is evidenced in the personal stories from the Signs of Ireland corpus, which demonstrates that generational differences have a major impact on the mouthing behaviour of the signers. Militzer subdivided the Signs of Ireland corpus into three age categories for her study: (1) 18–35 years, (2) 40–55 years and (3) 55+ years.

She found that Irish Deaf women aged 55 years and above use mouthing much less frequently than younger female signers. She also suggests that there is a correlation between use of mouthing and mouth gestures: usage of mouth gestures is inversely related to use of mouthings. Given this, younger female signers make much less use of mouth gestures than their older female counterparts. Militzer suggests that this is a result of the educational experience of the Irish Deaf community: she suggests that the younger signers were educated in the heyday of oralism and were subjected to spoken English more than the older generation, which explains the differences in mouth actions. We would suggest an additional set of considerations: while oralism was introduced and implemented with determination in St Mary's School for Deaf Girls from the 1940s, the availability of hearing aids and other systems to support auditory input was quite limited. Today, due to the increased availability of more powerful technologies (for some, including the cochlear implant, for example), there is scope for increased potential contact between the spoken use of English and that of ISL. This would go some way towards accounting for the fact that younger Deaf women make greater use of mouthings than older Deaf women, but it still does not account for the fact that male signers of all ages make less use of mouthing than Deaf women.

For the male signers, we must also remember that oral education was introduced some ten years later in St Joseph's School for Deaf Boys, in 1958 (Matthews 1996b), and as we have seen, significant lexical differences between male and female variants of ISL have been documented (LeMaster 1990). Militzer found that for the older male signers (aged 55 years and above), many of whom were educated before the introduction of oralism,

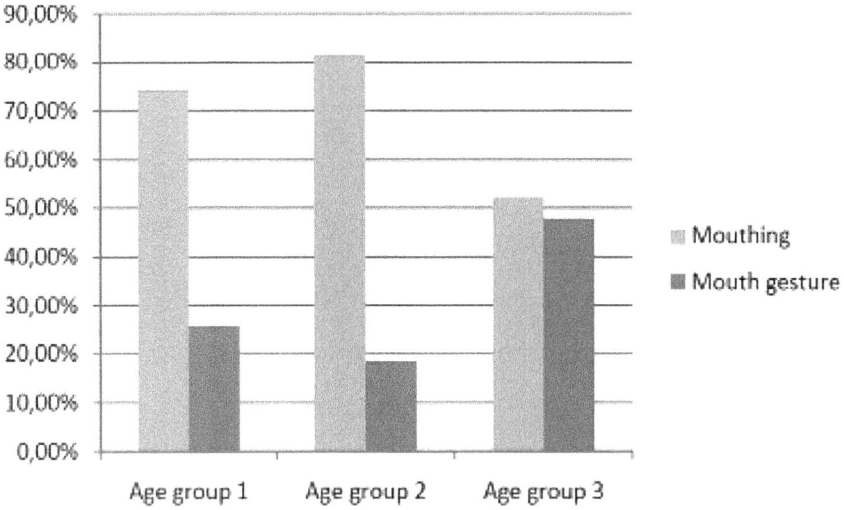

Figure 4.4 Mouthings and mouth gestures as used by Deaf women in the SOI corpus

some 53 per cent of lexical signs articulated are accompanied by no mouth action at all. This contrasts with the female signers of the same age where 89 per cent of all lexical signs co-occur with a mouthing or a mouth action.

She found that 75 per cent of the lexical items articulated by women in the 18–35 year age group were accompanied by mouthings while only 52 per cent of lexical items articulated by men in this age group co-occurred with mouthings.

In the 40–55-year age group, 60 per cent of lexical items articulated by women co-occurred with mouthings while only 39 per cent of lexical items produced by men co-occurred with a mouthing.

For those aged 55 years and above, 45 per cent of lexical items produced by women co-occurred with mouthings and only 12 per cent of those produced by men used mouthings. (See Figures 4.4 and 4.5.)

Militzer's preliminary findings can be generalised by saying that Irish Deaf women use language contact-induced mouthing much more consistently than men, regardless of age, with younger women using mouthing most. She also found that the use of mouth gestures and mouthing seems to be interrelated. For example, women aged 55 years and above used mouth gestures in 31 per cent of all mouthed instances. Where the use of mouthing increases, the rate of mouth gestures decreases. For men, the use of mouth gestures is much more stable, with younger Deaf men using mouth gestures in 34 per cent of all mouthed situations.

If we now turn to examine what mouthings and mouth gestures look like,

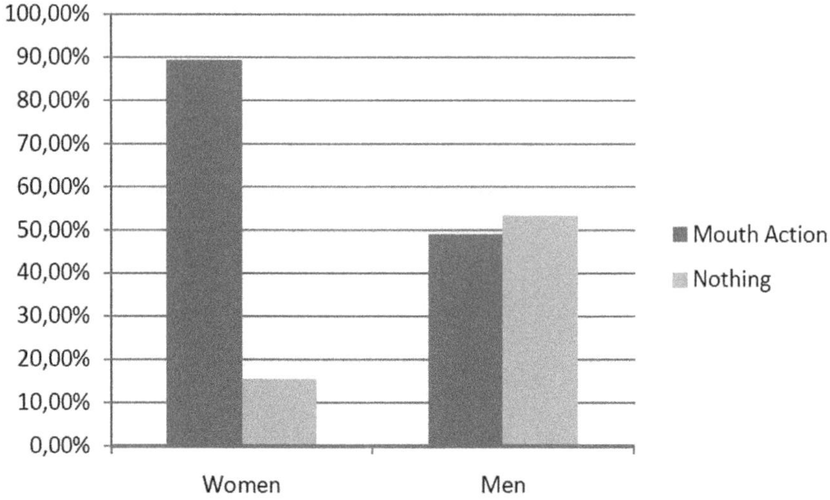

Figure 4.5 Mouth actions (combined) used by ISL signers aged 55 years and above

and whether they have a phonological basis (in addition to the morphological, lexical and syntactic bases noted earlier), then we need to consider whether mouthings can serve as the basis for minimal pair formation in ISL. That is, are there signs which have the same handshape, location, movement and orientation, where meaning difference arises solely on the basis of the mouthing or mouth gesture?

In Example 4.11(a) the signer signs FEEL and mouths 'feel'. Compare this with 4.11(b) where she signs LIVE and mouths 'live'.[4]

Example 4.11

(a) FEEL

(b) LIVE

Michelle (05) Personal Stories (Dublin)

The salient point for consideration here is the fact that the manual articulatory parameters for the signs LIVE and FEEL are identical. They both are one-handed signs, articulated with the middle finger bent, making contact with the signer's torso at the centre of the chest and travelling upwards along the sternum. The only phonological feature which distinguishes them from each other is the mouthing accompanying the manual sign. Another example is the pair HARD and STRICT, which are both two-handed signs, where the dominant hand adopts a baby-C-handshape and makes contact with the non-dominant hand, which takes an ISL-L-handshape, palm facing downward. The only distinguishing feature is the mouthing of either 'strict' or 'hard'. What we should also note, given Militzer's preliminary findings, is that this kind of minimal pair is more likely to occur in the signing of women, and more so in that of younger women. In contrast, older men are much less likely to use a mouthed element and would either expect the lexical items to be differentiated from each other on the basis of context or, if there is the potential for confusion or a desire to clarify, they may fingerspell the item in lieu of or in addition to using the manual sign.

Mouth gestures can also serve to create minimal pairs. Mouth gestures are mouth patterns not derived from spoken languages.[5] The category of mouth gestures in ISL includes the adverbials created on the mouth including those which we gloss as 'mm', 'th', 'ee' and 'cs'. We will discuss the form and function of these non-manual features in Chapter 5, but here, we wish to point out that these mouth gestures can serve a phonological purpose: they can serve to create minimal pairs where only the mouthed element is different in a sign that is otherwise manually articulated in the same way. For now, we can simply note that mouthed elements – both mouthings and mouth gestures – serve a phonological role for most signers in ISL. The exception to this rule may be older male signers, and the SOI corpus data suggest that the increased role of mouthing in ISL is pervasive, suggesting a shift arising from language contact.

4.7 Constraints and phonological processes

Not all combinations of features that play a role in the phonetic and phonological production of signs are possible in Irish Sign Language. As in other sign languages, ISL draws on a portion of the possible permutations for the combination of features, imposing constraints on yet other combinations of features. We need to remember that physical constraints apply to the articulation of all sign languages. In addition, there are language-specific constraints imposed by the rules of a specific language. These relate to the manner in which we perceive and produce spatial and visual data. McDonnell (1996) lists two forms of constraint that are brought to bear on sign formation: production constraints and perceptual constraints. In the next section, we outline some of his findings for ISL.

4.7.1 Perceptual constraints on ISL

We can begin by noting that signs are characteristically produced in 'signing space', that is the articulation space confined to the area at or near the signer's body, which is readily visible to interlocutors. This was illustrated in Chapter 2 (Figure 2.1).

It has been noted that signs produced at the periphery of signing space tend to exhibit larger handshape distinctions, larger movements and consequently, increased temporal duration (McDonnell 1996). In contrast, the central focal area in signing space is an area of 'optimal and visual acuity' where it is easier for interlocutors to detect relatively smaller handshape and location distinctions (34). McDonnell lists PARTY, TREE and SUN as ISL signs that illustrate larger handshape distinctions occurring at the periphery of signing space, while ORANGE, YESTERDAY and APPLE illustrate some of the smaller distinctions that occur at the central focal area in ISL (ibid.).

4.7.2 Production constraints on ISL

Certain physical constraints apply to the production of signed utterances. Typically, signed utterances must be produced in a way that makes them visible to their interlocutor, with signers typically facing their interlocutors, having gained eye contact before commencing their 'turn'. Other constraints are imposed by linguistic criteria. For example, Battison (1978) proposed two constraints on sign formation in American Sign Language: a symmetry constraint and a dominance constraint. These can be considered to be a single feature, which applies to the formational constraints on two-handed signs. These constraints seem to hold across other documented signed languages, as proposed for example by Sutton-Spence and Woll (1999) for British Sign Language, with variation for feature inventories across languages.

The symmetry constraint applies to signs that are articulated using two active hands. This constraint demands that both hands use the same handshape in the same relative location and perform similar motor acts. The symmetry constraint is very pervasive in ISL and some examples from the SOI corpus are shown in example 4.12, where in the articulation of the signs for NEED, MOTHER, JOB and GO-OFF-TO, both hands take the same handshape.[6]

The dominance constraint proposed by Battison also applies to two-handed signs, specifically those signs in which the dominant hand acts upon the non-dominant hand. The dominance constraint specifies that the dominant hand may assume any handshape that is compatible with 'contact signs', that is the handshape held by the non-dominant hand. The non-dominant hand is restricted with respect to the handshapes it can utilise: it must use the same

Example 4.12

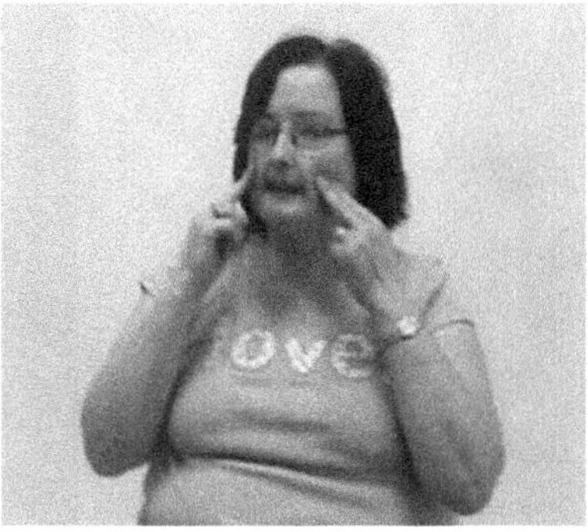

(a) NEED
Valerie (12) Personal Stories (Dublin)

(b) MOTHER
Fergus M. (07) Personal Stories (Dublin)

(c) JOB
Fiona (36) Personal Stories (Waterford)

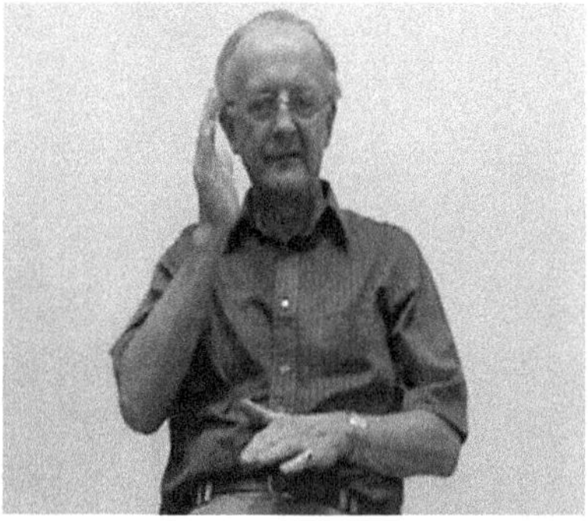

(d) GO-OFF-TO
Peter (18) Personal Stories (Dublin)

handshape as the dominant hand or one of a restricted set of other handshapes. The signs in Example 4.13 illustrate the dominance constraint in ISL: HUSBAND, PLAN, MONEY and TIME.

In the signs in Example 4.13, the non-dominant hand takes what are considered to be unmarked handshapes, in each case a flat ISL-L-handshape, while the dominant hand takes more complex handshapes. Here, we use the convention of referring to ISL-specific handshapes that align with the manual alphabet, and where these handshapes are also common to American Sign Language, we simply list the handshape (for example, V, K, L, etc.) as is common in signed linguistic descriptions of this kind.

The signer in Example 4.13(a) is using an open-ISL-G-handshape, whose citation form is also known as the F-handshape in other signed linguistic research. In 4.13(b) we see the V-handshape. In 4.13(c) and (d) the signers use the ISL-T-handshape, though the point of contact between the dominant hand and non-dominant hand differs between the two signers.

Example 4.13

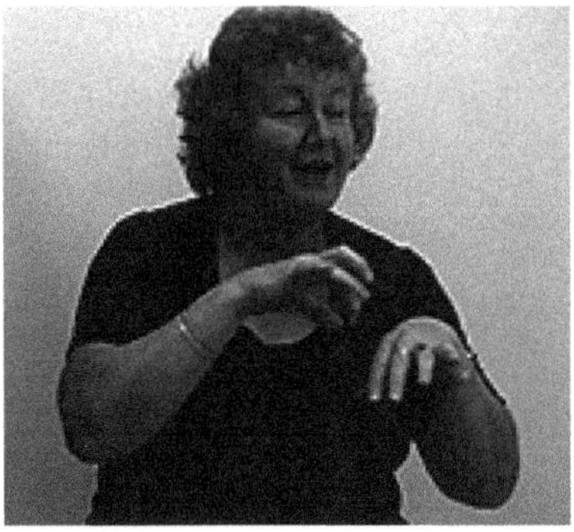

(a) HUSBAND
Eilish (10) Personal Stories (Dublin)

(b) PLAN
Bernadette (02) Personal Stories (Dublin)

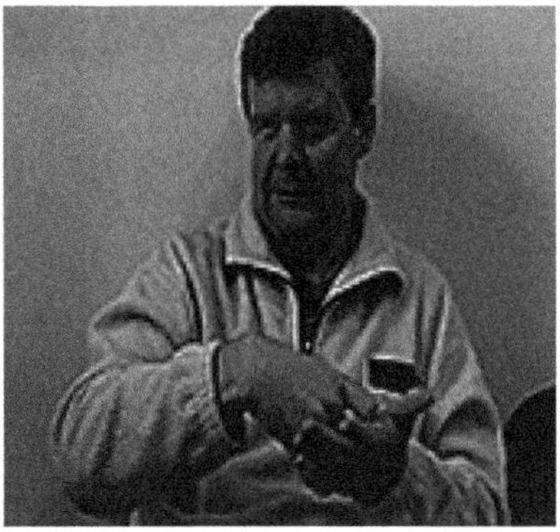

(c) MONEY
Michael (34) Personal Stories (Galway)

(d) TIME
Eric (32) Personal Stories (Cork)

In addition to signs composed using a dominant and non-dominant hand, we can also consider signs that require sequential contact with the body. Wilbur (1987: 29) outlines some constraints on production for such American Sign Language signs. She reports that in ASL, first contact may occur at the head and second contact at the chest area. However, a move from contact at the head to the edge of the hand may breach ASL-specific linguistic constraints. McDonnell (1996) reports that similar sequential contact constraints appear to exist in ISL and other sign languages, but as yet, it is not clear if this is a universal feature. When we come to discuss compound formation in ISL, we will make reference again to this movement constraint.

4.8 Summary

In this chapter we have introduced the idea of a phonetics of ISL, and outlined the range of handshapes that arise in ISL (following the work of Matthews

(1996a, 2005); and Ó Baoill and Matthews (2000)). We noted that when we consider the phonology of signed languages, we are concerned not only with the form of the handshape that arises but also, fundamentally, with whether the handshape difference is perceived as leading to a meaning difference. That is, whether a variation has phonemic or allophonic status. We noted that one way of testing for the phonological status of handshapes is to explore the existence of minimal pairs. We also found that we can test for the phonological status of other parameters such as location, movement and orientation. This discussion reveals that ISL displays the duality of structure found in all human languages: there are structural units (phonemes) that while themselves meaningless contribute to the formation of meaningful elements.

We also looked at the non-manual features of signs and discussed in particular the role of mouthings and mouth gestures in ISL. We saw that the use of mouthing and mouth gesture is interrelated and has gendered-generational associations. We found that women make greater use of mouthings than men, and that amongst men, older men make very little use of mouthings, in great part because they were educated before the introduction of oralism in St Joseph's School for Deaf Boys or just on the cusp of the introduction of oralism. From a phonological perspective, we noted that for most signers, other than older male signers, mouthing and mouth gesture can serve as the basis for minimal pairs in ISL, demonstrating that mouthings have a phonological function in ISL in addition to lexical, morphological and syntactic functions, which we will address in later chapters. In the next chapter, we consider another level of structure: the morphology of ISL.

Notes

1. As with spoken languages it is possible to analyse phonemes further as combinations of more abstract elements, often called features. Thus Sandler and Lillo-Martin (2006) analyse handshapes in terms of individual fingers and finger positions.
2. These are directional verb forms that inflect in the signing space for first person and second person. We discuss directional verbs later in Chapter 5.
3. It should be mentioned that despite Stokoe's resistance towards inclusion of a separate orientation parameter, his notational system does in fact specify orientation via subscript or handshape.
4. Here the non-dominant hand maintains a fragment of the preceding sign, WHERE, in what Liddell (2003) calls a fragment buoy, which we discuss further in Chapter 8.
5. See Sutton-Spence and Boyes Braem (2001) for discussion.
6. For an extended piece of discourse that demonstrates the pervasiveness of the symmetry constraint, see Lawrence, personal story no. 19, at <http://www.lat-mpi.eu/tools/elan/download> (accessed 25 November 2011).

5 Inflectional and Derivational Morphology

5.1 Introduction

This chapter deals with the identification of morphemes in ISL, an essential precursor to our discussion on how words are formed in ISL. We will discuss the forms of modification of signs that can be considered morphological in nature; and we will examine the role of inflectional morphology, in particular in verbs, and discuss its relationship to verb classes. We will consider a range of topics including the marking of agreement and of number on verbs; the marking of aspect; classifier predicates; and compound formation. First, we begin by considering the status of words and morphemes in ISL.

5.2 Words and morphemes

We begin by asking whether it is appropriate to consider individual signs as words. Brennan (1994) concludes that while there are difficulties with terms that originate in the examination of spoken languages, the unit that is known as the 'sign' in signed languages

> clearly functions as the linguistic unit that we know as the word. We do not usually exploit a separate term for this unit in relation to written as opposed to spoken language, even though notions of written word and spoken word are not totally congruous. (13)

We will follow Brenan in using the term 'word' in a general sense to incorporate spoken, signed and written language. We will use the term 'sign' when referring only to signed languages, taking as given that 'signs' are equivalent to 'words' in terms of grammatical role.

We note in passing that though there is evidence that words in spoken languages have cognitive salience for speakers (McQueen and Cutler 1998; Sapir 1921), and it is notoriously difficult to provide a universal definition. Critical criteria in one language, for example phonological criteria, do not necessarily apply in another. We encounter similar issues in signed languages where the notion of a sign may be clear in ideal or isolation cases, thus satisfying McQueen and Cutler (1998) and Bloomfield's (1926) criterion for a word that it be a 'minimal free form', but there may be difficulties in segmenting and extracting these units from the flow of signing.

A morpheme is the smallest meaningful unit in a language (Bloomfield 1933). The word 'meaningful' is important here. Some meaningful units can stand alone and function as words, like English *bike* or *shoe*: these morphemes cannot be pared back any further and still be said to be meaningful. Indeed, if we try to analyse further, we find ourselves working at the level of phonology. Morphemes like *bike* and *shoe* are considered to be 'free morphemes'. In contrast, morphemes like *–s* (in *shoes*), *-er* (in *biker*) and *-ing* (in *going*) cannot stand alone as words, but they also carry meaning. Units like these are called 'bound morphemes'. Signed languages also exhibit free and bound morphemes. For example, there are ISL morphemes that function as words in their own right like HOUSE, GIRL, SISTER and HAVE. Other signs are made up of both free and bound morphemes, such as verbs inflected for agreement, as we shall see.

In Chapter 4, we talked about the phonological parameters that facilitate word formation in signed languages. Here, we have to consider whether some or all of the phonological features we described (handshape, movement, location, orientation and non-manual features) might also function as morphemes. For example, most sign linguists argue that the movement parameter can be morphological. For example, it has been shown that zero movement of an item is associated with existence (EXIST). A stamping movement is associated with the establishment of a locus (BE-LOCATED). The physical movement of an entity through signing space is associated with physical (and often also metaphorical) movement (MOVE), while a movement that traces the extent of an item's size or shape is also considered morphemic in nature (EXTENT). These movements are said to combine with specific handshapes, often called 'classifier handshapes' in the literature, to produce classifier predicates, which we discuss below in some detail. Before that, we can look at the articulation of the ISL verb GIVE-TO in Example 5.1. Here, the signer marks the onset of the verb at the forward side right (+sr) of his signing frame, which we will call the +sr locus. The offset of the verb is at the signer's torso, which is designated the 'canonical' locus or 'c' (Engberg-Pedersen 1993).

We can say that to articulate sr+GIVE-TO+c the location +sr is needed to complete the sign, so this location is a phoneme in this sign. But the locus +sr also carries meaning: at the location that +sr refers to, a person other than the signer gives something to the signer (or indeed, the person who is co-referential with the +c locus). Because of this, we can say that +sr is a morpheme in this analysis, as argued for ASL by Padden (1988). We can also note that if the onset and offset points for the verb were reversed (that is, the signer signs

Example 5.1

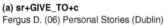

(a) sr+GIVE_TO+c
Fergus D. (06) Personal Stories (Dublin)

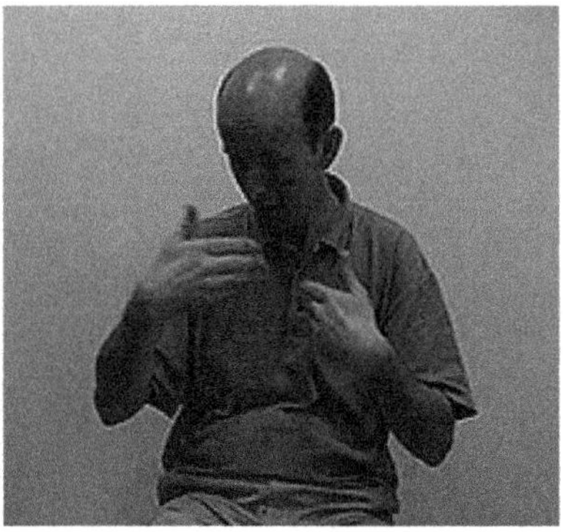

(b)

c+GIVE-TO+sr), then the meaning of the sign would change to 'I gave (it) to (someone)(the named/un-named person co-referential with locus +sr)'.

5.2.1 Loci

At this juncture it is necessary to say something about the concept of loci in signed languages, drawing on Scott Liddell's work (Liddell 1990). Firstly, we can say that a location in space where an entity has been established is referred to as locus (ibid.). The signer can establish an entity by articulating a lexical sign, or as we will describe later a classifier, at a certain location in space, or by producing the sign and then pointing or directing eyegaze to a location in space. Once an entity has been assigned a locus, it can be referred to later in the discourse, in ways that we shall talk about later. A locus does not necessarily have to be a location in the signing space: a location on the signer's body is also referred to as a locus. When a sign has to be articulated at a certain location on the signer's body, this locus is phonologically important. When locus has such a phonological purpose, Liddell refers to it as having an articulatory function.

A locus can also have a three-dimensional function, in which case it stands for a spatial location (ibid.). When this function arises, the signing space may be thought of as a stage on which entities are located. Signers use classifier predicates to represent entities in the real world and the entities will be located in relation to each other as they are in the real world. This kind of space is referred to as topographical space in some of the literature (Sutton-Spence and Woll 1999).

When a locus is established using a classifier predicate, the signer will first typically articulate the lexical sign for this entity and then produce the classifier predicate at a certain location. For example, a signer might produce a name sign (see Chapter 6) for a person and then locate the person in space using a classifier handshape. The person is now considered to be at this location in signing space. Producing a sign and then pointing at a location to establish a locus is very common when using topographical space. A signer can, for example, produce the name sign for a particular place and then point at a certain location in space to establish the locus for this place. If more than one place is to be assigned a locus, the second locus will be established in relation to the first one, like referring back to a map. A good illustration of this is seen in Example 5.2 where the signer is talking about the war in Iraq. He assigns IRAQ a locus in canonical space (a), and then positions Kuwait to the south of the locus for IRAQ (b). Later, Turkey is introduced and assigned a locus to the north of the position for IRAQ (d). With these three loci established, the signer then can talk about how American and allied forces discussed a possible invasion of Iraq (c) via Turkey in the north and Kuwait in the south without having to re-establish these points of reference. That is, the signer builds on the established loci positions and then embeds semantic relations by creating associations between the geographical locations and the logistics of war-time planning on the part of the Americans and allied forces.

Example 5.2

(a) IRAQ
Senan (01) Personal Stories (Dublin)

(b) KUWAIT (relative to IRAQ)

(c) INVADE-IRAQ

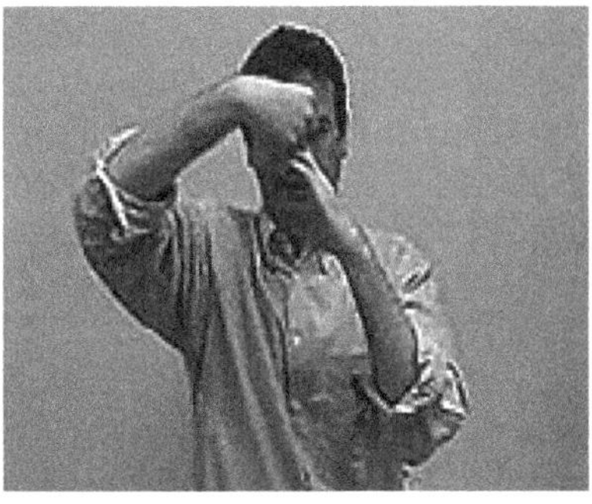

(d) (TURKEY) BORDERS IRAQ

A locus can also be established by articulating a lexical sign, often at a point in space that differs from where the citation form is normally articulated, and then directing eyegaze towards a certain location in space. This way of establishing a locus seems to occur less frequently than the way described above. For example, in the narrative on the war in Iraq, the signer does not assign Turkey a locus by using a classifier to refer to its position in signing space, as he does in setting up Iraq (with a CL-B-handshape) or Kuwait (an INDEX to the locus's relative relationship with the previously established IRAQ). Instead, he gives the sign for TURKEY, then fingerspells Turkey, and then implies its location via the use of the CL-5-spread-handshape used to illustrate the possible path of invasion from the north, that is through Turkey, on the dominant hand. Later in this piece, the signer talks about how the allied forces sought to secure Turkish government approval for this plan of action. In doing this, he notes that Turkey is located at the northern border of Iraq (5.2(d)), where he is building on the previously established descriptions of the position of Iraq and the intended simultaneous invasion via northern and southern borders.

As we shall see in the next section, agreement verbs are verbs that make use of space to link with a subject or object, or both. The verb is directed at a point in the signing space and in this way the form of the verb shows what kind of agreement is involved. In sentences that include agreement verbs, the signer first typically establishes an index, that is he or she locates an entity at a particular place in the signing space and then directs the agreement verb towards this place. In ASL it is also possible to produce the agreement verb first and then mention the referent (Liddell 1990). When entities are assigned to a locus in space, it is referred to as the frame of reference (Engberg-Pedersen 1993). According to Engberg-Pedersen, the frame of reference in Danish Sign Language can be either deictic or anaphoric. It is deictic when the signer points at the entity he or she is referring to and the point of reference can change if the signer changes position in space or if the entities referred to change locations. Thus, the deictic frame of reference 'is determined by the actual locations of the entities or places to which the signer refers' (71).

The anaphoric use of space follows some conventions with regard to how relations between established entities can be structured in the signing space (ibid.). When two entities are compared or contrasted, the signer uses the convention of comparison and locates one entity in the space on the left and another entity in the space on the right (ibid.).

Sometimes, as we saw in the last example, entities that are semantically related will have the same locus in the signing space, unless a separate locus is necessary in the narrative, thus exhibiting a relationship based on semantic affinity. These relationships include, for example, those that hold between a person and a place, such as a workplace or a club. It is also possible to think of these relationships as being layered or nested at a locus, creating and then building on associated relationships that hold between entities established at that locus.

The conventions for loci in Danish Sign Language take place in two dimensions: (1) a side-to-side dimension and (2) a diagonal dimension which goes from the signer's right side and forward-left, or from the signer's left side and forward-right. If the entities being referred to are equivalent in the discourse, the signer can use the side-to-side dimension. Engberg-Pedersen (1993) reports that in DSL, if the signer, or the person represented by that locus, has semantic affinity to one of the entities being referred to, he or she will place that entity on his or her left or right side and place the other more forward in the signing space.

Even though the same referent can be situated at different loci, between texts or in the same text in DSL, Engberg-Pedersen argues that the choice of locus is not arbitrary: 'The conventions for choosing loci show that, even though loci have a deictic basis, they also reflect discourse-dependent semantic-pragmatic features of the referents' (40). This is a point that we return to in Chapter 8 when we come to look at discourse in ISL. Another issue we consider in more depth in Chapter 8 is the functionality of 'list-buoys' (Liddell 2003). For now, we can say that entities can also be assigned a locus on the fingertips, with each fingertip then being activated as a locus that is co-referential with that entity.

A number of constraints operate on the formation of loci. For DSL, the signer does not exploit the locus behind his or her back if using agreement verbs, polymorphemic verbs or reported speech. In these cases, a locus behind a signer's back will be moved to his or her side (Engberg-Pedersen 1993). This seems to be a characteristic generally shared by ISL, as discussed in Chapter 4.

Shifting locus or 'reference shifting' is a common way to show different perspectives in signed languages (Engberg-Pedersen 1993; Janzen 2005; Padden 1990). In Chapter 8, we discuss this phenomenon in greater detail, but for now, we can say that in shifted reference, a signer can take on the role of another person by shifting into the locus that has been established for that person (Engberg-Pedersen 1993) or remain static and change his or her facial expressions, eyegaze and/or head orientation, to reflect the character and emotions of the target referent (Janzen 2005). When a signer is quoting another person, he or she can shift reference and articulate pronouns from this person's point of view so that the signer is speaking as the other person, rather than using reported speech as might be the case in English (Engberg-Pedersen 1993). Shifted reference can then occur to report the speech of other participants, and signers can also use shifted reference to report action, states and thoughts (Poulin and Miller 1995). We will discuss these strategies in more detail in Chapter 8.

5.3 Grammatical morphemes

Signs are inflected for grammatical information in ways that sometimes parallel spoken languages. Thus while plural in English nouns is often marked by suffixation of a bound morpheme, for example *–s* in singular/plural pairs like *girl/girls*, *tree/trees* and *noun/nouns*, in other spoken languages plurals are marked by full or partial reduplication, for example in the Philippines language Pangasinan, where *manók*, 'chicken', has the plural form *manómanók*, 'chickens' (Rubino 2001). Similarly in ISL, plurals are often formed through a process of full reduplication. In Example 5.3, the sign HOUSE+++ (each + stands for a repetition of the sign) communicates the meaning 'houses' and not 'three houses'.

Example 5.3

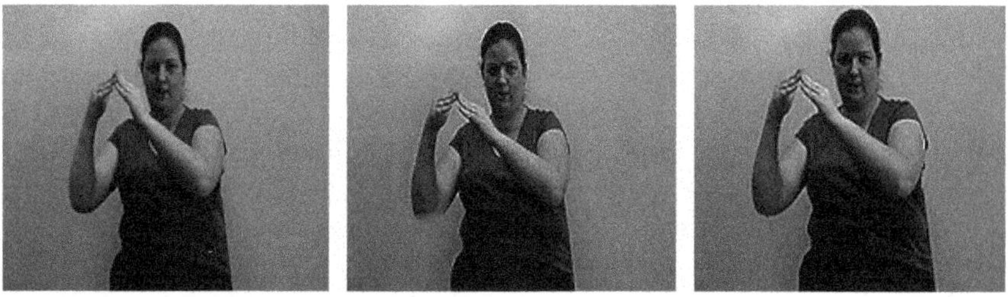

Reduplication to mark plurals: HOUSE+++ ('houses')
Geraldine (20) Personal Stories (Dublin)

Klima and Bellugi (1979) describe the growing realisation that American Sign Language displays morphological patterning. They report that American Deaf informants would comment, when asked about the kind of event that allowed specific forms of inflected signs, that a form would be used, depending on the mood of the signer. Initially, Klima and Bellugi interpreted this to mean that such inflections were not governed by grammatical rules but were optional or stylistic additions. Subsequently, however, the obligatory nature of morphological rules became clear:

> Such judgments suggested that the occurrence of modulations [. . .] like morphological inflections in spoken languages – was motivated by and restricted to certain linguistic contexts. (246)

In the next section we look at the morphological marking of verbs in ISL.

5.4 Morphological verb classes in ISL

Following McDonnell (1996) we can begin with a basic distinction in ISL between plain verbs, following Padden (1988), which are uninflected and therefore do not take agreement affixes, and agreement verbs whose affixes show agreement with person or location. Somewhat separate from these two basic groups are classifier verbs, which comprise a hand configuration and a movement, with the hand configuration giving information about predication and semantic classification. We deal with classifier verbs in section 5.5. Agreement verbs can be further divided into those that show person agreement with subject/actor, object/undergoer, etc. and those whose affixes are controlled by locations.[1] We begin by discussing person agreement verbs.

An example of a person agreement verb is GIVE as in Example 5.4, where the onset of the verb agrees with the actor argument and the offset corresponds to the undergoer argument, here a recipient. The theme, the thing given, must be represented independently, here by an independent nominal.

Example 5.4

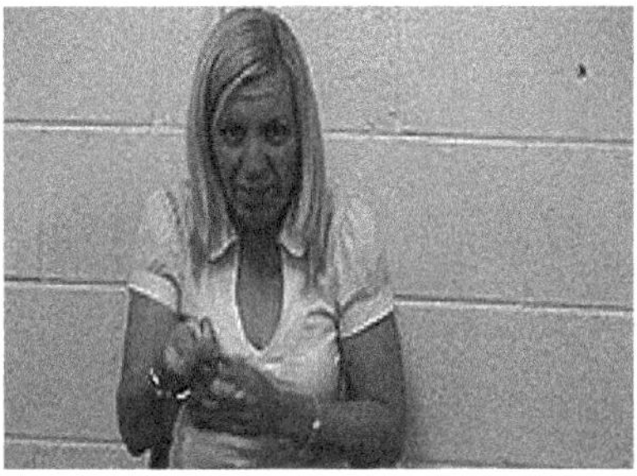

c+GIVE+f (protoypical form) '(I) gave (the dog) (food)'
Rebecca (38) Personal Stories (Waterford)

There are a number of variations on this basic type of person agreement. One is reciprocal agreement verbs, for instance CONSULT (also frequently glossed as DISCUSS) in Example 5.5. In this type of verb the morphological markers of both actor and undergoer occur on both hands, indicating the dual or reciprocal nature of the action.

Example 5.5

c+DISCUSS+f
f+DISCUSS+c
'We discussed the issue'
Annie (26) Personal Stories (Wexford)

A further type is the reverse or backward agreement verbs, where the relevant participants are inflectionally marked but the position of the affixes is reversed and the verb begins at the location of the undergoer and moves towards the location of the actor, for instance CHOOSE in Example 5.6.

Example 5.6

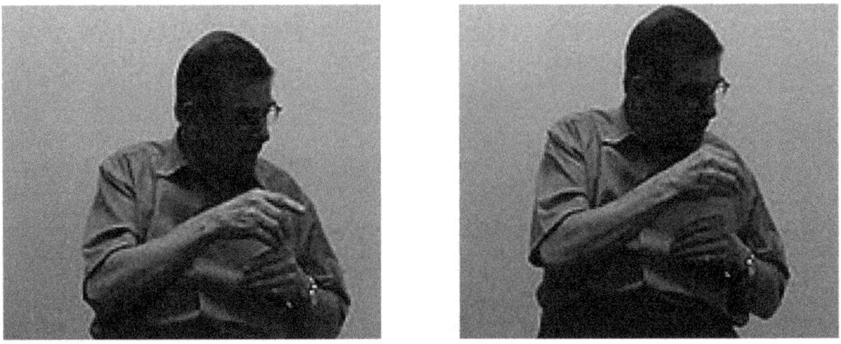

c+CHOOSE+sl
'I chose/picked (someone/something)'
Kevin (17) Frog Story (Dublin)

A final type is single agreement verbs, such as SAY-TO and SEE, where agreement is shown with only one argument. The onset is uninflected and therefore there is no agreement with a subject/actor, while the offset agrees with an object/undergoer argument, as can be seen in terms of dominant hand activity in Example 5.7.

Example 5.7

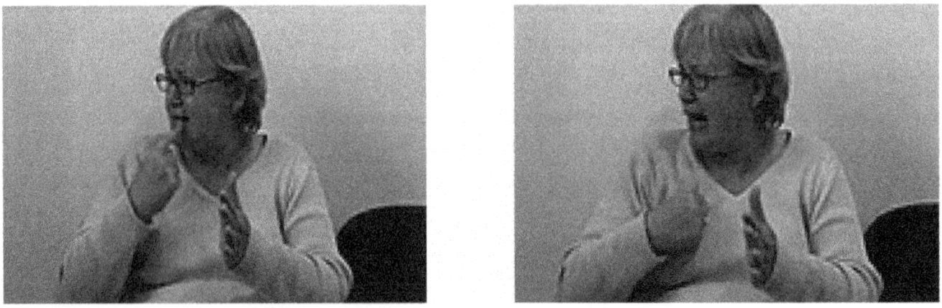

TELL-ME
'(The tour guide) told me'
Mary (33) Personal Stories (Galway)

Locative agreement verbs are morphologically linked to locations rather than participants. In semantic terms they agree with source, goal or location rather than actor or undergoer and give the location of an entity or the path of its movement. The verb may agree with a single location as in Example 5.8(a) or two as in 5.8(b).

Example 5.8

(a) DRIVE+f (onset)
'(I) drove home'

(a) DRIVE+f (offset)
'(I) drove home'

(a) HOME
'(I) drove home'

Fergus D. (06) Personal Stories (Dublin)

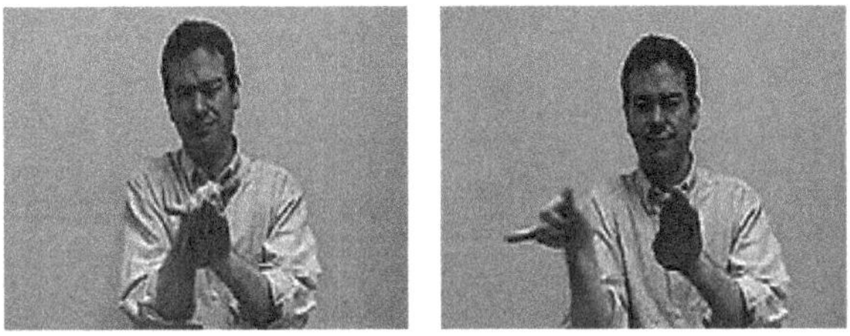

(b) c+FLY-TO+sr (onset)
'The plane flies from (x) to (y)'

(b) c+FLY-TO+sr (offset)
'The plane flies from (x) to (y)'

Senan (01) Personal Stories (Dublin)

Patrick McDonnell (1996) identifies a subclass of locative agreement verbs, which instead of marking agreement with locations in space incorporate specific locations on the body, such as SLAP and CATCH-Y-HAND, or, as in Example 5.9, LICK-MY-FACE, where the signer is telling how a bear at the zoo licks a boy's face. Here, his non-dominant hand is representing the bear's tongue while the rest of his body (including his facial expression) represents the boy's experience of the event (see Chapter 8 for discussion of 'body partitioning').

Example 5.9

f+LICK-BOY'S-FACE+c
'(The bear) licked (the boy's) face'

If we accept this last subdivision of verb patterning, we can summarise the morphologically defined classes of verbs as in Figure 5.1.

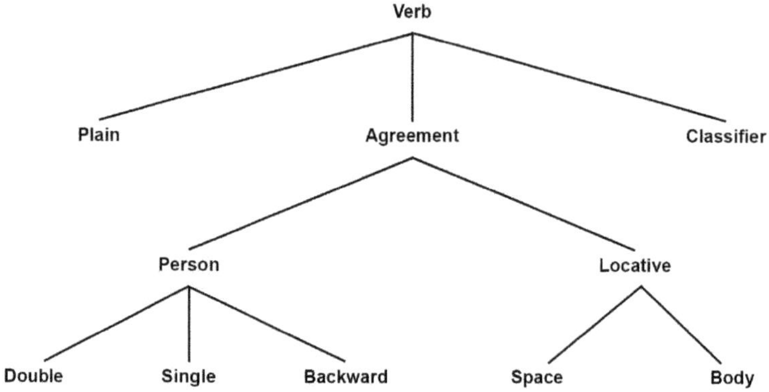

Figure 5.1 Morphological verb classes

5.5 Number

An important means of marking plural on nouns is reduplication, as described earlier, although, as we shall see later, classifier handshapes are important in counting, or quantifying entities. Verbs too have a role: person agreement verbs, for example, show a distinction between singular and plural arguments. The singular form, which is used as the basic or reference form, involves agreement with a single locus. Variations from this can give information about plural arguments. There is a general or non-specific plural, which is formed by a smooth horizontal concave arc placed before the offset of the verb, as in Example 5.10.

Example 5.10

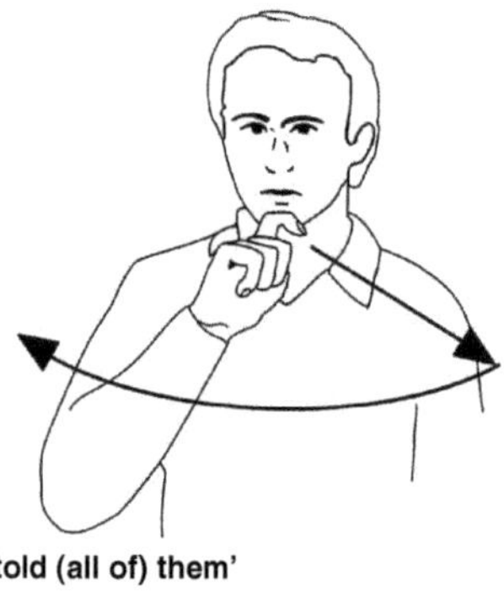

'I told (all of) them'

A dual form can consist of two separate offset points, located close together and connected by a small convex arc, as in Example 5.11.

Example 5.11

TELL-ALL
Fergus M. (07) Personal Stories (Dublin)

Alternatively, it may be formed by a two-handed sign in which each hand replicates the same form, as in Example 5.12.

Example 5.12

'I told both of them'

It is also possible to form an exhaustive plural where the action is allocated to each of the group, by a series of short convex arcs, as in Example 5.13.

Example 5.13

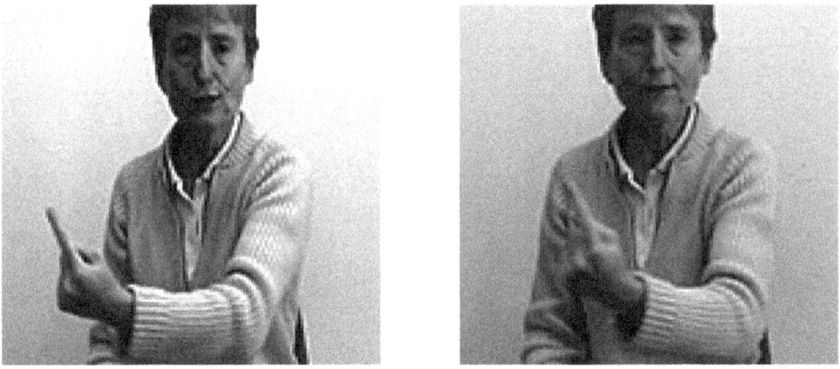

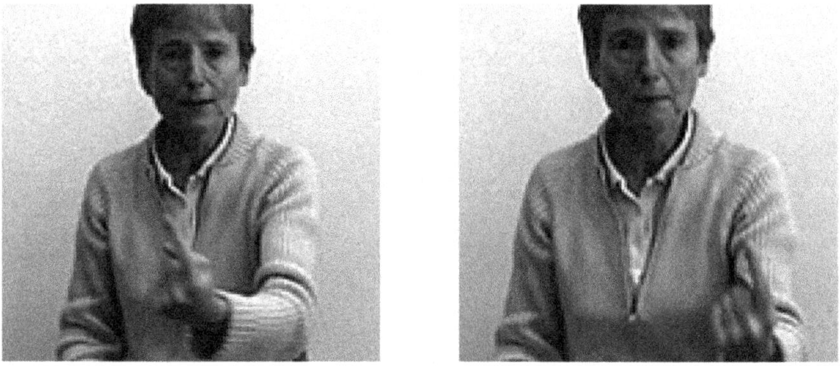

c+CL: INDEX 'ONE'+sr+c+f+sl
'I gave one to each of them'
Frankie (11) Personal Stories (Dublin)

The repetitions can be viewed as a modification of the verb, especially where the focus is not on the individuation of a plural argument, in which case the term 'attributive aspect' has been used. This form occurs with a distributive sense, as in Example 5.14.

Example 5.14

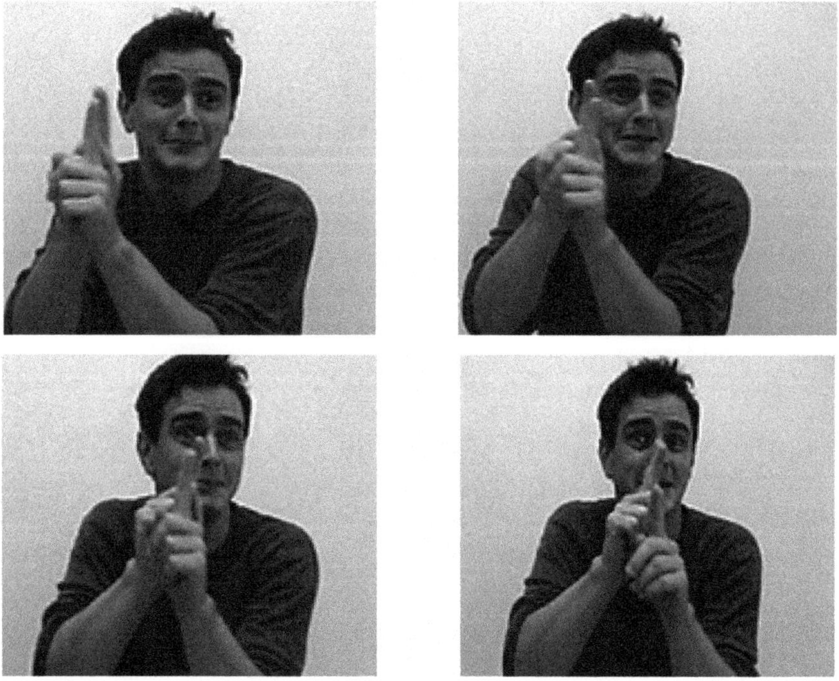

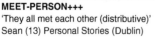

MEET-PERSON+++
'They all met each other (distributive)'
Sean (13) Personal Stories (Dublin)

While Example 5.14 is an example of a person agreement verb, locative agreement verbs also behave in the same way.

5.6 Aspect

Although tense is not marked morphologically on verbs in ISL, aspect is an important inflectional category. Aspect systems allow speakers to relate situations and time, but instead of fixing situations in time relative to the act of speaking like tense does, aspect allows speakers to view an event in various ways: as complete, or incomplete, as so short as to involve almost no time, as something stretched over a perceptible period, or as something repeated over a period. As Charles Hockett (1958: 237) described it, '*Aspects* have to do, not with the location of an event in time, but with its temporal distribution or contour.'

Describing aspectual morphology in ASL, Klima and Bellugi (1979: 245) noted that the distinctions were primarily marked by dynamic qualities of movement superimposed on signs employing differences in speed, tension and length. We shall see that in ISL too aspectual marking is associated with modifications to the movement parameters, but that reduplication, seen earlier in nominal plurals, is particularly significant. The meaning conveyed by reduplication depends on the inherent situation type of the verb. Thus verbs may inherently describe situations that are static, unchanging for a period, or dynamic, involving change. Among the latter, different verb types correspond to different dynamic situations. Some, which may be termed durational, describe processes continuing through time, while others, punctual verbs, describe point events that are perceived to involve very little time. These verb types interact with aspectual morphology to produce different interpretations. Aspectual distinctions give information about clauses and we will see that they may be marked in ISL on verbs and other elements, such as time phrases. We will look at three types of imperfective aspect, beginning with repetition or iterative aspect.

In Example 5.15, the signer produces an aspectually modified variant of the punctual verb KNOCK. In citation form, KNOCK typically has two repetitions. Here, signifying iterative aspect, there are four. The movement parameter in citation form involves a straight line from close to the signer to the locus associated with the object (typically a door) that is knocked on. Here, the signer reports knocking repeatedly, and with urgency, on her neighbour's door when she discovered her son was missing from his bedroom.

We see the straight-line movement motif repeated in other punctual verbs such as HEART-BEATING+++++ (with multiple reiterations of the sign) in Example 5.16 from the same narration and REMOVE-PARTS-OF-ENGINE+++++ in a story about a mechanic taking parts of the car's engine out, one after the other in Example 5.17.

Example 5.15

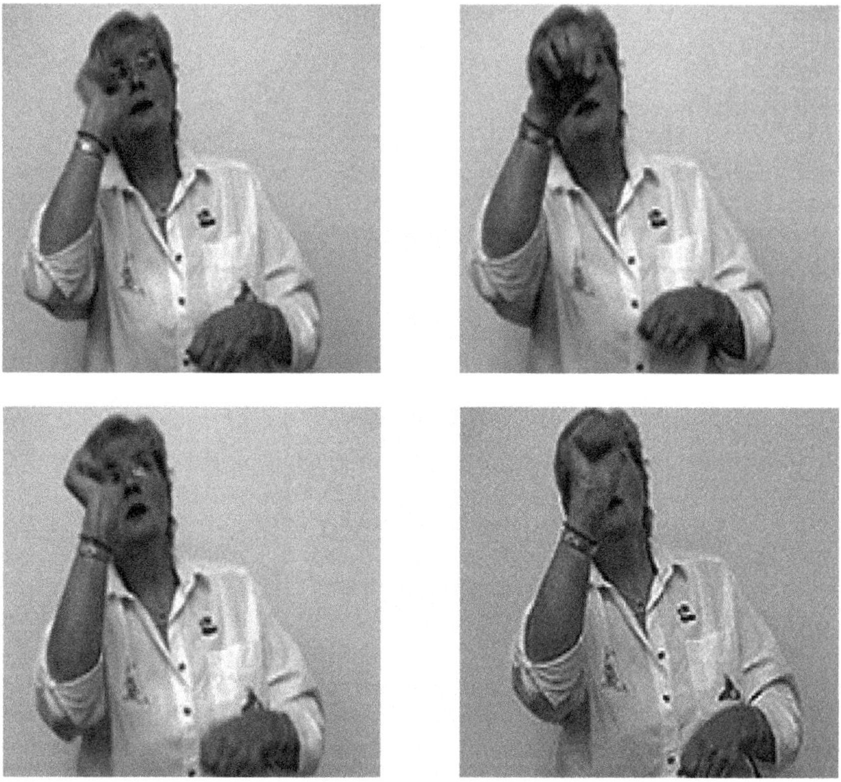

KNOCK++++
'I was banging down (the neighbour's) door'
Catherine (31) Personal Stories (Cork)

Example 5.16

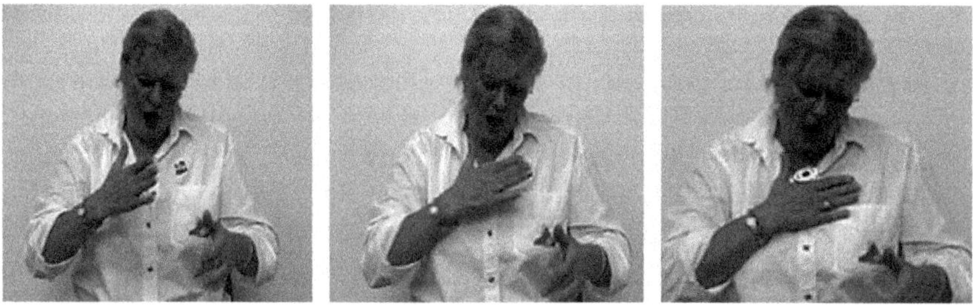

HEART-BEATING+++++
'My heart was pounding'
Catherine (31) Personal Stories (Cork)

In Example 5.18 the reduplicated form of the durational verb SIGN produces a durative aspectual reading that could be translated as 'kept on signing'.

Example 5.17

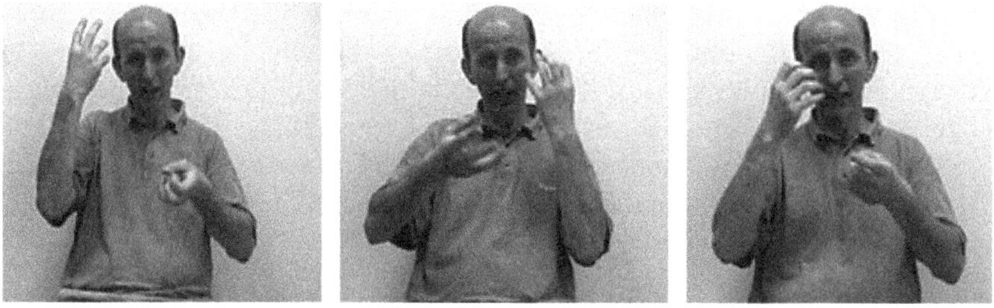

REMOVE-PARTS-OF-ENGINE+++++
'(He) removed all of the parts (of the engine)'
Fergus D. (06) Personal Stories (Dublin)

This is premodified by a gesture which is glossed as 'calm face' and adds the meaning 'I put on a brave face'. The 'mm' morpheme adverbial indicates that the action occurred 'in the normal way' or 'normally' (Baker-Shenk and Cokely 1980; Liddell 1978; Liddell 1980; Ó Baoill and Matthews 2000).

Example 5.18
Presenter: HELLO [sign name] // YOUNG PRESENT-ER JOIN SIGN OF TIMES BEFORE-BEFORE // HOW YOU (c INDEX f) FEEL FIRST PRESENT
'Hello (name). You joined us as a young presenter some time ago. How did you feel about presenting?'

mm

Interviewee: ME NERVOUS ['repeated regularly'] // 'calm face' SIGN SIGN SIGN // BUT GOOD
'At first my heart was thumping but I put on a brave face [and kept on signing normally] and it was OK'
Sign of the Times (RTÉ, June 1996)

Aspect operates at the level of the clause and similar morphological marking can be applied to time expressions, as in Example 5.19 from a story about football training. Here the time phrase THURSDAY-THURSDAY is reduplicated and articulated with a repeated, small, straight-line action, similar to that described for ASL by Baker-Shenk and Cokely (1980), which indicates that Thursday evening meetings were occurring regularly. Similarly, THERE-THERE-THERE is articulated in the same manner, reinforcing the message that these sessions occurred without fail.

Example 5.19
THERE TRAINING **THURSDAY-THURSDAY** THERE-THERE-THERE // STAY SAME 'permanency' (on sequence line)
'(Those picked) were training every Thursday without fail'
(Leeson 1996: 83)

A further aspectual distinction is created where the inflection is formed with a repeated circular movement as shown in Example 5.20 where the reduplicated form of the durative verb CRY shows this circular movement. The meaning communicated is of the extended duration of the event, the crying. This parallels aspectual forms as described for ASL by Baker-Shenk and Cokely (1980) and Klima and Bellugi (1979). The aspectual information is augmented by the non-manual features that communicate that the subject cried over a long time and with distress.

Example 5.20

CRY++
'(The participants) bawled their eyes out'
Sean (13) Personal Stories (Dublin)

A second example, Example 5.21, is taken from *Sign of the Times* (August 1995) where a young man talks about going to the cinema:

Example 5.21
GO CINEMA ENJOY WATCH WATCH A LOT LAUGH LAUGH **ENJOY ENJOY** GREAT TIME
'I go to the cinema and enjoy watching the actors. Comedies can be very funny and really enjoyable; a great time'
(Leeson 1996: 85)

In this example, ENJOY ENJOY is presented with a circular motion similar to that described for 'CRY-CRY-CRY' above, giving a durative interpretation; although with fewer repetitions of the verb than in the previous example. This may be influenced by two factors. First, this sentence also includes other aspectually inflected verbs (WATCH WATCH / LAUGH LAUGH) and includes the lexical item 'A LOT' which may constrain the need for further reduplication of 'ENJOY'. Second, the sign 'ENJOY', when presented in citation form contains inherent movement. Bergman (1983) discusses the constraints which operate on modulation of signs which have such inherent movement in Swedish Sign Language (SSL). In some cases, only one repetition of the citation form occurs.

A further illustration is in Example 5.22 from an interview of a middle-aged deaf man, talking about his schooldays.

Example 5.22

WHEN ME WAS ABOUT NINE / ONE TIME ME GO TO at f.r. LEARN ORAL // TEACHER (his sign name) fingerspells name // r.s. **TEACH-TEACH** // r / s ME

'One time when I was about 9 years old I had to go to a speech class. The teacher, a Christian Brother, taught me for (what seemed) a long time'

(David Breslin, interviewed in the TG4/Irish Deaf Society documentary, *Angry Silence*)

The aspectual distinctions described thus far have been imperfective in nature, in that they focus on the internal structure of the event or process rather than expressing the external, perfective viewpoint that focuses on the event as a whole, in particular its end points. This basic distinction between perfective and imperfective types of aspectual distinction is well documented in the languages of the world: Dahl (1985) and Bybee et al. (1994) identify it as the most commonly found and in many senses the most basic distinction. ISL marks a perfective aspect, the completive, by the use of the verb FINISH as a supporting or auxiliary verb, as in Example 5.23(a).

Example 5.23

(a) FINISH (perfective)
Peter (18) Personal Stories (Dublin)

(b) COMPLETION (perfective)
(onset)
Nicholas (22) Personal Stories (Wexford)

(c) COMPLETION (perfective)
(offset)
Nicholas (22) Personal Stories (Wexford)

Example 5.24

(a) *PLAN FOR MY DAUGHTER CL-INDEX+sl WELCOME HOME CL-INDEX+fl PLAN READY 2xGOOD FLY TOGETHER PARTY FINISH

'We planned to welcome my daughter home. We had already planned (what we would do). We would go to the airport together. We had planned the party. It was all organised'

(Peter (18) Personal Stories (Dublin))

(b) . . . PLAY-VIOLIN SWEATING / COMPLETION HAVE SLEEP / RELIEF / WALK-OFF / 'F' / SECOND / NO HOPE / PLAY-VIOLIN / NO HOPE /

PLAY-VIOLIN+++ / COMPLETION SLEEP / RELIEF . . .

'. . . and he played the violin, sweating buckets as he played. Eventually, one lion slept. Relieved, he was walking away when he realised that the second lion was still awake. There was nothing for it but to keep playing. And so he played the violin. He played and played and played. Eventually, the second lion slept . . .'
(Derek (28) Personal Stories (Cork))

Examples 5.23(b) and (c) illustrate another perfective marker that is widely used: COMPLETION (Leeson 1996). Example 5.24(b) situates the use of COMPLETION in the context of a joke about a violinist who finds himself in a lion's enclosure with three lions. In this example we see that he successfully lulls the first two lions to sleep with his music (with COMPLETION used to signify the successful end result).[2] COMPLETION thus functions as a marker of resultatives, marking the successful outcome of a process. This is in line with Matthews's description:

> It may signal the completion of an action which happened over time as in **building a house**. It may signal success as in having **made a new date** or **got a new girlfriend**. It may mark a change of state as in the repair of a broken television. (1996a: 158, original emphasis)

COMPLETION can precede the verb as in Example 5.25(a) and (b), or come before a noun as in (c) and (d).

Example 5.25

(a) HOUSE COMPLETION BUILD
'The house has been built'

(b) t.v. BROKE COMPLETION REPAIR
'The broken TV has been repaired'

(c) COMPLETION DATE
'I got a date'

(d) COMPLETION GIRLFRIEND
'I got a girlfriend'

(Leeson 1996: 73–5; Matthews 1996a: 158)

5.7 Classifier predicates

The term 'classifier' is often used in relation to a set of handshapes (sometimes with movement components) that provide information about motion, location, handling and the visual-geometric description of entities in a signed language. This kind of verbal construction has been identified in more than thirty signed languages (Schembri 2000, 2003). These predicates can be categorised according to morphosyntactic criteria and we outline the range of so-called 'classifiers' that have been identified for ISL below. Schembri (2000) notes that the handshape parameter, which is considered to be the carrier of meaning in these constructions, has typically been described as a 'classifier' morpheme. This is due to the fact that the handshape that is used in these constructions varies depending on the salient characteristics of the referent: for example, the size and shape of the referent can influence the choice of handshape that is used. Example 5.26 provides a sample of some of the kinds of classifier handshapes that can arise in ISL.

Example 5.26

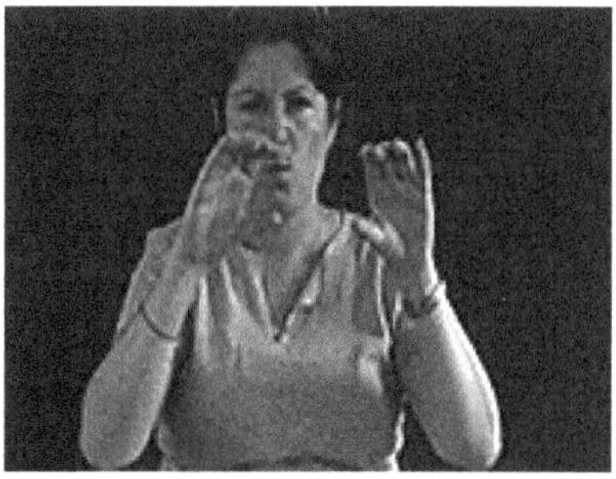

(a) extent, size and shape specified (brick)
Annie (26) Personal Stories (Wexford)

(b) flat-surface, extent and shape specified (cooker hood)

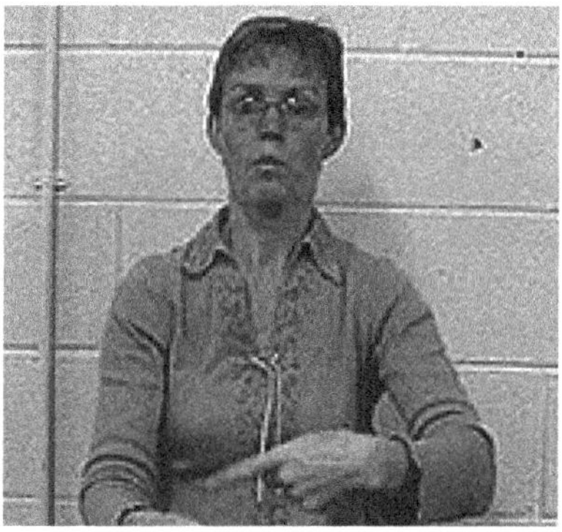

(c) long-thin-entity (hosepipe, pipe extended)
Fiona (36) Personal Stories (Wexford)

(d) handle-entity (motorbike)
Helen (27) Personal Stories (Wexford)

The use of the term 'classifier' was first introduced by American Sign Language researchers, including Frishberg (1975), Kegl and Wilbur (1976) and Supalla (1978). Following Allan (1977), they drew comparisons between the constructions they found in ASL and the classificatory morphemes in verb systems in Athabaskan languages like Navajo. While Allan established a typology of classifiers that grouped these morphemes into four categories –

(1) numeral classifiers, (2) concordial classifiers, (3) predicate classifiers and (4) intra-locative classifiers – it is the third group, predicate classifiers, that have been related to constructions in signed languages. Predicate classifiers are morphemes associated with verbs that allow speakers to classify the subjects or objects according to certain semantic features, typically the shape, number or distribution of the entities concerned (Aikhenvald 2000).

Applying this notion to ISL, McDonnell (1996) draws on the work of Mary Brennan (1992) who identifies six categories of classifier handshapes: (1) semantic, (2) size and shape, (3) tracing size and shape, (4) instrumental, (5) handling and (6) touch. However, McDonnell incorporates these into four broader categories of classifier predicates as follows:

1. **Whole entity-CL stems:** includes discussion of hand configurations that refer to semantic, size and shape, and instrumental categories.
2. **Extension-CL stems:** includes reference to tracing size and shape configurations.
3. **Handle entity-CL stems:** includes reference to handling and touch categories.
4. **Body-CL stems:** where the signer's body functions in a way that is similar to the way that handshape functions in certain two-handed configurations.

5.7.1 Whole entity-CL stems

In these classifier stems, the hand configuration typically represents a whole entity. McDonnell argues that in ISL, many whole entity CL-stems occur in constructions where the whole entity-CL combines the semantic roles of actor and theme. Several subcategories of whole entity-CLs have been identified: a semantic-CL stem refers to an entity in terms of its semantic features (for example, + animate). A size and shape-CL stem refers to an entity in terms of its shape (for example, rectangular) or in terms of an entity's dimensions (for example, 'two-dimensional object'). McDonnell proposes that these stems can combine with the same types of movements in ISL, namely MOVE, BE-LOCATED and EXIST.

Example 5.27 illustrates a semantic-CL stem in an ISL narrative: the handshape referred to by McDonnell as the 'multiple entity-CL handshape'. This is identifiable as the '5-hand/s', which in formational terms means that the signer's fingers are open and spread. Typically, the multiple entity-CL-handshape represents entities as members of large groups, for example a large number of participants in an event or a shoal of fish. In this example, the multiple entity-CL listed here as 'CL-5+open' represents a large number of Deaf people travelling from the UK to Ireland to attend a Deaf youth camp. This is an important use of a classifier to quantify, as mentioned earlier.

Example 5.27

CL:5+sr+hi+trace-path+c
'. . . They all came over (from the UK to Ireland)'
Sean (13) Personal Stories (Dublin)

5.7.2 Extension-CL stems

McDonnell's extension-CL stems are like those described by Brennan (1992) for BSL as 'tracing size and shape classifiers'. McDonnell proposes treating this set of hand configurations as a separate category because the hand configurations found in these stems in ISL trace rather than represent the entities that they refer to. Extension-CL stems combine only with EXTENT movements. Example 5.28 below offers an example of an extension-CL stem in ISL, which we have glossed as 'trace-arc'. Here, the signer traces the extent of the shop sign, then tells us what is written on the sign.

Example 5.28
. . . SHOP TITLE g. 2/h CL.C. (trace-arc) (thumb and forefingers) g.l.f.t.s.CL.C. (trace-arc)
'. . . was a shop which had a big arched doorway with the word "gifts" emblazoned on it'
(Informant H: narrative)
(Leeson 2001: 73)

Another example, this time from the SOI corpus, involves the signer describing the extent of the storage box to the rear of her motorbike. She traces the outline of the box, illustrated in Example 5.29.

Example 5.29

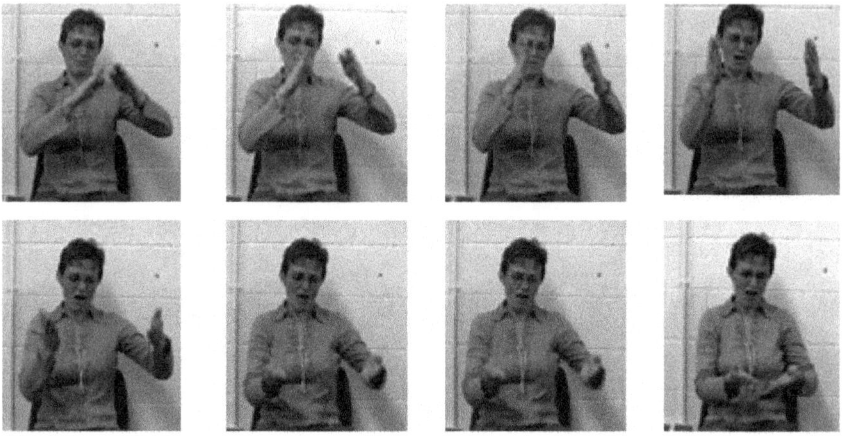

CL:ISL-L trace-outline 'box'
Fiona (36) Personal Stories (Waterford)

5.7.3 Handle entity-CL stems

Handle entity-CL stems have handshapes that typically denote the configuration of the hand as it moves, touches or uses an object or part of an object rather than denoting the object itself as a whole. These stems typically imply an animate agent, that is the signer him- or herself or another agent who is indicated through a reference shift. McDonnell notes that such stems typically occur in transitive constructions where the hand configuration represents the direct object argument. Handle entity-CL stems combine with MOVE, BE-LOCATED and EXIST movements. Example 5.30 offers an example of a handle entity-CL in ISL.

Example 5.30
'blah-blah'
. . . c.+CL.C.+move-to-mouth . . .
'. . . I can use the radio . . .'
(Informant T: interview, *Hands On* footage)
(Leeson 2001: 48)

In this example, the signer is describing the safety options available to Deaf sailors. One option that he describes includes using a radio to transmit a pre-recorded message calling for help. The segment above includes use of a CL-C-handshape to represent the position of the hand in handling a typical hand-held radio. As discussed above, use of handle entity-CL stems indicate an animate actor. In this case the animate actor is the signer.

Another illustration, this time from the SOI corpus is in Example 5.31.

Example 5.31

CL:ISL-T (tap-stick-on-blackboard) (handle-think-long-object)
'The teacher tapped her stick on the black-board, then hestitated;
Marion (08) Personal Stories (Dublin)

In Example 5.31 we see the signer recounting a story about a time when she brought a kitten into her classroom, and hid it in her desk. As the teacher was teaching, the kitten started to meow. At this point in the story, the signer has taken on the role of the teacher in her classroom, stick in hand, pointing to the blackboard. At this juncture, she hears something and pauses. Of interest to us here is the fact that the signer is using an ISL-T-handshape to represent a whole entity, the stick. The signer's handshape choice implies both an animate agent who handles the entity that we conceive of as being a stick as well as the stick itself, and this interpretation is something we return to in later chapters.

Interestingly a number of stems take the same surface forms across the whole-entity-CL and the handle entity-CL distinction. McDonnell (1996) gives an example of the whole entity-CL stem, 'three-dimensional entity-CL', which is used in a sentence meaning *There was a bun on the table*, while a handle entity-CL stem, 'handle three-dimensional entity-CL', is used in a sentence meaning *I put a bun on the table*. McDonnell states that these stems both share the same hand configuration and movement types. Other stems such as 'cylindrical entity-CL' and 'handle cylindrical entity-CL' also exhibit this shared pattern.

5.7.4 Body-CL stems

ISL has a category of stems where the signer's body functions in a way that is similar to the way that handshape functions in certain two-handed configurations. Here body-CL stems play a significant role in backgrounded constructions. While body-CL stems might perhaps be considered to fit into the category of whole entity-CL stems, the contexts where they are used suggest that a separate category of body-CL stems should be considered for ISL. Typically, the body classifier involves the body of the signer and is used as an independent articulator to refer to a single animate entity, which is typically an individual. This type of classifier is typically used in ISL to refer to the actual body of the animate entity as opposed to the semantic category of the shape of the entity itself. Several constraints on operation have been identified:

- A body classifier can only be used when the referent is animate (or where an inanimate object has assumed animacy as a result of anthropomorphism, for example where a tree has human-like feelings and can walk or (as in the LSF example outlined in Sallandre (2007),[3] an apple experiences fear as the chef's knife moves towards its 'head').
- Where a body classifier is part of the verb complex, it can only refer to one object referent at a time.
- Body-CLs can combine with morphemes that denote manner of locomotion, but they cannot combine with morphemes that denote the path of motion.
- Body-CLs do not take locative agreement markers.

In ISL, classifier predicates that involve a dominant and subordinate articulator (that is, non-dominant hand) occur frequently. Typically, such constructions see the non-dominant hand functioning as a backgrounded element with respect to the action of the dominant hand, as seen in Example 5.32.

Example 5.32

PROBLEM Solid-round-entity-CL+MOVE-imit: sunrise
Flat-surface-entity-CL+EXIST----------------
SOON MORNING
'There's a snag. The sun is beginning to rise and soon it will be morning'
(McDonnell 1996: 224, Example 6.111)

In Example 5.33 we see that the signer's body can also function as a subordinate articulator in relation to the action of the dominant articulator.

Example 5.33

Index-CL+fr+MOVE+contact-c
Body-CL+EXIST+chest-------
'(Someone) bumped into me'
(McDonnell 1996: 225, Example 6.113)

Finally, several body-CL stems, such as PERSON-BUMP-INTO-ME, as with many other classifier predicate forms, have become lexicalised. As a result, the separate elements that make up the sign no longer have separate significance in relation to the features of the nominal that they refer to.

We have continued the traditional use of the term 'classifier' here for the most part because the term has entered into mainstream discourse about the description of this type of complex predicate, and because it has been widely used to refer to this particular category of verbs (Frishberg 1975; Kegl and Wilbur 1976; McDonnell 1996; Schembri 2003; Supalla 1978). However, it is important to note that other researchers have argued against this position, for example arguing that these signed language forms are not classifiers in the sense put forward by Allan (Engberg-Pedersen (1993)), while others have queried the appropriateness of using the term 'classifier' itself to denote these constructions (Brennan 1986; Deuchar 1987; Schembri 2003; Sutton-Spence and Woll 1999). For example, Schick (1990) notes that some of the constructions typically analysed as being verbal classifiers could perhaps be more appropriately analysed as adjectival in nature. Another argument is that this term implies that the handshape performs a classification function in these structures, while in fact it functions in a selectional rather than classifying way, with handshape selecting certain characteristics of entities, for example size and shape, or how the entity is handled, while imposing selectional restrictions on other characteristics. Schembri (2003) often refers to this category simply as complex predicates (CPs) to overcome these problems, rejecting the alternative term 'polymorphemic' because of problems in justifying the morphemic status of the signs' elements.

5.8 Compounds

Compounds are words that are made up of two or more free morphemes which can themselves function as separate words within the language. The meaning of the resulting form may not be directly predictable from the component parts. Generally speaking, we can identify several kinds of compound signs in ISL, including sequential compounds and loan translations. We will also briefly consider what have been called 'simultaneous compounds'.

5.8.1 Features of ISL compounds

Sequential compounding combines signs in what we can term 'linear space': signs are articulated one after the other, but in such a way as to be identifiable as different signs from the component parts. What is important is that compound formation involves free morphemes: bound morphemes are not fundamental building blocks for compounds. In many cases the meaning of the compound is distinct from the meaning of a phrase with the same words. For example, in ISL, signers know that the sign OLD-MOTHER means grandmother, not a mother who is old, just as speakers of English know that a greenhouse is not a house that is green in colour.

A number of principles have been identified for compound formation across a range of signed languages, including, for example, that the sign to be articulated highest in signing space will be signed first; that there will be a reduction or omission of movement in the first part of the compound sign; and that articulatory emphasis is usually on the second part of the sign (Brennan et al. 1984). We also find that when the second part of the sign uses a non-dominant hand as a base, this hand finds its position during the period of production of the first part of the compound sign. These are general principles, though there are exceptions. Before we consider those, we can look at how these principles apply to the formation of sequential compounds in ISL. As compound signs are made up of two free morphemes, and as each of these is typically articulated at a different point in signing space, we can say that compound signs usually involve a location change and sometimes a change of handshape (for example, ISL THINK-EXTRA 'exaggerate'). The transition process between the elements in the compound is smoother than the usual transition between two separate signs; the morphemes that make up a compound transition into each other. The duration of the compound sign also differs from the production of the component morphemes individually: compound signs tend to have similar productive duration time to a simple sign rather than the duration period of two separate signs, for example in Example 5.34 we see POLICE-HOUSE 'police-station' rather than the sequence POLICE, HOUSE 'police', 'house'.

Example 5.34

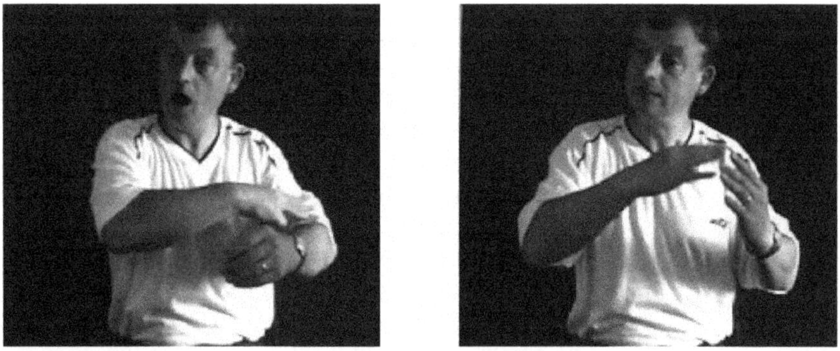

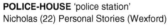

POLICE-HOUSE 'police station'
Nicholas (22) Personal Stories (Wexford)

Note that in this example the first element of the compound has a place of articulation on the arm, and is a one-handed sign, while the second component is a two-handed sign, articulated in neutral signing space. However, the citation forms of compounds are subject in context to local phonetic processes like assimilation. For example, if we consider Helen's story, we can identify several ways in which the articulation of the compound SICK-

HOUSE ('hospital') differs from citation form. Helen discusses how she injured herself in a childhood accident and had to go to hospital. She signs GO-OFF SICK-HOUSE, and the fact that SICK-HOUSE is articulated with a higher onset than in citation form is a result of the fact that the offset of the previous sign, GO-OFF, has a fairly high offset point, that is a process of assimilation occurs.

Example 5.35

SICK-HOUSE 'hospital'
Helen (27) Personal Stories (Wexford)

In Example 5.35, we see an atypical articulation of SICK: normally SICK is articulated with the non-dominant hand taking a flat-5-handshape, palm facing down, as in Example 5.36.

Example 5.36

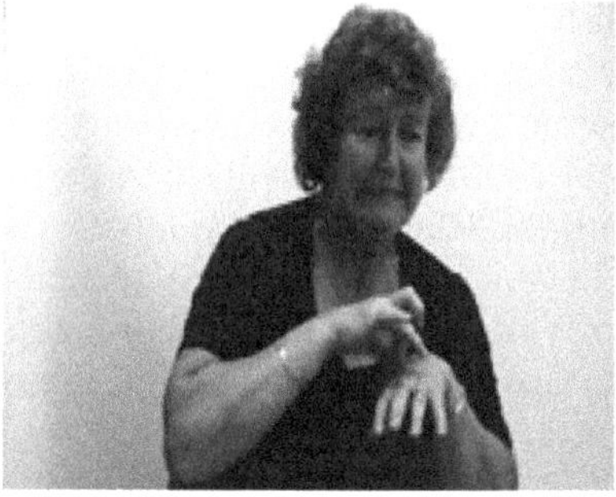

Citation form of SICK
Eilish (10) Personal Stories (Dublin)

However in Example 5.35 Helen is anticipating the handshape and location that the non-dominant hand will take for the articulation of HOUSE, though what is interesting is that here, the non-dominant hand never quite opens to the expected flat-5-handshape, to mirror that of the dominant hand, as was the case in Example 5.33. Given this, the expected conformity with the symmetry constraint does not occur.

Movement may also be reduced in compounds: when the component signs are produced independently, movement is generally away from the signer, but where they are the initial component of a compound, this movement is usually greatly reduced or completely omitted. In the example of ISL POLICE-HOUSE, the usual repeated movement in POLICE is lost, as the dominant hand moves instead towards the non-dominant hand. The movement of HOUSE is also reduced: while the citation form is articulated with a repetition of the sign, in the compound, the repeated movement is lost, though in many sequential compounds, the second element is given additional emphasis. This often involves an increase in muscle tension or a longer final hold than is normal. Indeed, Klima and Bellugi (1979) found that in ASL compounds, repetition in the final component of a compound sign is often omitted where in regular production repetition would be usual. This is reported as sometimes occurring in BSL signs too, but more often, repetition is retained but the sign is held for longer in space. In ISL, the evidence seems to suggest that repetition at the end of compounds is omitted, as in POLICE-HOUSE and SICK-HOUSE above, and while the final component may be held for longer in space, this may be dependent on where the compound occurs in a clause. Another example of this process is BLESS-HOUSE 'church' where the BLESS component has been drastically reduced.

5.8.2 Constraints on compound formation

A range of articulatory constraints have been found to apply to sequential compounds in signed languages. Wallin (1983) reports that in genuine compounds in Swedish Sign Language, the first sign always has a single articulator (that is, is a one-handed sign). The only exception he found was PROMISE-GIVE 'permit', which has a double articulator. Bergman (1977) describes an articulator as 'the hand involved in performing the movement' and a double articulator as 'when two hands having the same handshape are used in the movement', which Battison (1978) refers to as the symmetry constraint. In contrast to Wallin's findings, ISL has compounds that have both one- and two-handed signs as the first morpheme. Some ISL compounds that have one-handed signs as the first morpheme are given in Example 5.37(a), while some that have two-handed morphemes as the first component are given in Example 5.37(b).

Example 5.37

(a) BOY-DAY 'day-boy, day-pupil', SEE-EXAMINE 'check', GREEN-AREA 'field', CANDLE-LIGHT 'light'

(b) MOTHER-FATHER 'parents', SICK-HOUSE 'hospital', SICK-SPREAD 'epidemic', MARK-MIND 'affected'

It is also been claimed that the component sign that is articulated at the highest point in signing space is articulated first (Brennan et al. 1984). In ISL, if the first element in a compound is one-handed, it will typically be articulated at a higher plane than the second morpheme. We see this in BOY-DAY 'day-boy, day-pupil', SEE-EXAMINE 'check' and GREEN-AREA 'field' but not in CANDLE-LIGHT 'light', where the iconicity associated with the second component demands an overhead location for articulation, while CANDLE is articled at lip level. If the ISL compound is made up of two two-handed morphemes, there is a strong likelihood that both will be articulated in neutral space, as all of the examples we mention below. Where two two-handed morphemes combine to create a compound in ISL, it is more typical for both morphemes to conform to the symmetry constraint. This is evident in compounds like MOTHER-FATHER 'parents', TRAIN-HOUSE 'train station', SIT-ROOM 'sitting room' and HOME-WORK 'homework'. Where a compound comprises two two-handed morphemes and one upholds the dominance constraint and the other the symmetry constraint, the typical formation is that the first element will uphold the dominance constraint and the compound final element will be symmetrical. Examples that illustrate this include SICK-HOUSE 'hospital', SICK-SPREAD 'epidemic', WEEK-END 'week-end' and BLACK-BOARD 'blackboard'. We also find that deletion of a repeated movement in the final component of a compound may occur, but this does not seem obligatory. It may even be the case that in citation form, signers may tend towards a morpheme final hold, though this may differ in extended discourse.

We could also add that in some instances, ISL compounds are accompanied by mouthings which reflect the donor morphemes, for example 'mark-mind' and 'boy-day', but in many instances, the English word associated with the meaning of the compound is mouthed, perhaps a reflection of the bilingual reality of Deaf people's lives. For some signers, probably older signers (but not those from the pre-oral education era), genuine compounds are accompanied by mouthings of the donor morphemes or one element thereof. For example, some signers would mouth 'mother-father' while others mouth 'parents'. It is also important to note that there is diachronic and other variation in the way some compounds are articulated and mouthed, for example it seems that older signers use TRAIN-HOUSE, while other (perhaps younger) signers sign TRAIN-STATION, and while some signers sign FOOD-EVENING 'supper', others sign FOOD-NIGHT and mouth 'supper' or just 'eat'.[4] This may be indicative of a changing functionality for mouthing in ISL (Militzer 2010) as well as being directly related to educational policies and their impact on ISL usage, as outlined earlier in this volume.

As signs with two or more elements are more complex than signs with one element, it is generally reported that compounds have an upper limit of two component parts. This is known as the 'duality constraint' (Kyle and Woll 1985: 118). The effect of the duality constraint includes the movement reductions we talked about earlier. However, there are exceptions to this

Compound	Translation	1st element higher in signing space than 2nd?	Movement reduced in 1st element?	Repetition of final element deleted?	If two-handed sign occurs, is it the final element?	Does two-handed sign uphold symmetry or dominance constraint?
WHITE-RAIN	'snow'	✓	✓	✓	✓	Symmetry
GREEN-AREA	'field'	✓	✓	× An extended hold is typical at offset	n/a – both one handed morphemes	n/a
SICK-HOUSE	'hospital'	× Both components articulated in neutral space	✓	✓	✓	Dominance-Symmetry
TRAIN-HOUSE	'train station' (perhaps generational)	× Both components articulated in neutral space	×	✓	n/a – both two-handed morphemes	(Both morphemes) Symmetry
PLANE-HOUSE	'airport' (perhaps generational)	× Both components articulated in neutral space	✓	✓	✓	Symmetry
BLESS-HOUSE	'church'	× Both components articulated in neutral space	✓ Movement of BLESS is so reduced that most signers would be unaware of this morpheme having independent meaning in its compound form.	✓	✓	Symmetry
THINK-BRIGHT	'intelligent'	× BRIGHT moves upwards from the head, so here, the 2nd component moves upwards, away from the head of the signer.	× Although THINK can be modulated aspectually, the SOI corpus data suggests that in discourse, there is no repeated movement of THINK, so there is no way of reducing the movement of this morpheme when it forms part of a compound.	× An extended hold is typical at offset	n/a – both one-handed morphemes	n/a
MOTHER-FATHER	'parents'	× Both components articulated in neutral space	✓	✓	n/a – both two-handed morphemes	(Both morphemes) Symmetry
THINK-EXTRA	'exaggerate'	✓	×	× An extended hold is typical at offset	✓	Dominance
MONEY-PAIN	'expensive'	× Both components articulated in neutral space	✓ While both signs are articulated in neutral space, the plane of articulation of the first morpheme is higher than the second.	×	× Here, the first component is a two-handed sign.	Dominance
SICK-SPREAD	'epidemic'	✓	✓	× An extended hold is typical at offset	n/a – both two-handed morphemes	Dominance-Symmetry
CANDLE-(overhead) LIGHT	'light' (generational sign)	× The onset of movement of the sign LIGHT is at a high locus in signing space	Maybe – depends on context of appearance.	× An extended hold is typical at offset	n/a – both one-handed morphemes	n/a
BOY-DAY	'day-pupil'	✓	✓	An extended hold is typical at offset	✓	Dominance
MORNING-FOOD	'breakfast' (generational)	× It may be that the upward movement inherent to the sign MORNING takes precedence here (i.e. redundancy of movement principles operate)	×	×	×	Symmetry
FOOD-EVENING	'supper' (perhaps generational)	✓	✓	×	✓	Symmetry
SEE-EXAMINE	'check'	✓	✓	×	✓	Symmetry
MIND-MARK	'affected (mentally) by something'	✓	✓	× An extended hold is typical at offset	✓	Symmetry
MIND-DISAPPEAR	'to lose one's train of thought'	✓	✓	×	✓ (though younger signers may sign the final element with one hand only)	Symmetry

Figure 5.2 Features of ISL compounds

rule in ISL and we can find examples with up to three component parts, for example BLUE-MARK-BE-LOCATED-ON-ARM 'bruise (on arm)' or FALSE-INFORMATION-SPREAD 'propaganda' (Ó Baoill and Matthews 2000: 243–4).

Compound	Translation	1st element higher in signing space than 2nd?	Movement reduced in 1st element?	Repetition of final element deleted?	If two-handed sign occurs, is it the final element?	Does two-handed sign uphold symmetry or dominance constraint?
WEEK-END	'weekend'	✓	✓	✗	n/a – both two-handed morphemes	Dominance-Symmetry
TO-DAY	'today'	✓	✗	✗	✓	Dominance
BED-ROOM	'bedroom'	✓	✓	✗	✓	Symmetry
SIT-ROOM	'sitting room'	✗	✗	✗	n/a – both two-handed morphemes	(Both morphemes) Symmetry
HOME-WORK	'homework'	n/a – both articulated in neutral signing space	✓	✓	n/a – both two-handed morphemes	(Both morphemes) Symmetry
GREEN-HOUSE	'greenhouse'	✓	✓	✓	✓	Symmetry
BLACK-BOARD	'blackboard'	n/a – both two-handed morphemes	✓	✗	n/a – both two-handed morphemes	(Both morphemes) Symmetry
BOY-FRIEND/ GIRL-FRIEND	'boyfriend' or 'girlfriend'	✓	✓	✓	✓	Symmetry

Figure 5.3 Loan translation or 'calque' compounds in ISL

The general principle for ISL signs is that the first component in a compound begins higher up in signing space than the second component, for example BOY-DAY 'day-pupil', where BOY is articulated at the chin and DAY is articulated in neutral signing space. We saw this principle illustrated in Example 5.32. In Figure 5.2, we see a sample of ISL compounds together with some of the features we have discussed.

There are also compound signs in ISL that have been influenced by spoken language compounds. When vocabulary is borrowed into another language like this, the process is referred to as loan-translation. Wallin (1983) reports that in Swedish Sign Language loan-translation compounds are very common. For example, the Swedish *sjukhus* 'sick-house, hospital' is reflected in the Swedish Sign Language sign SJUK-HUS. Thus, we often see that elements of one language are borrowed into another language and adapted phonologically to secure meaning in another language. In Figure 5.3, we some examples where ISL has borrowed from English and which can be considered as loan translations, together with their basic features.

Given the role of simultaneity in signed languages, it is no surprise that a process of simultaneous compounding has been posited (Brennan 1990, 1992). This occurs when two separate free morphemes are combined and produced simultaneously. Each morpheme is articulated on a separate hand at the same time. For example, in ISL we use the compound sign TELEPHONE-TYPE to mean 'minicom'. However, as Brennan (1992) points out, many of the signs that have traditionally been considered as simultaneous compounds are created using classifier handshapes, the bound morphemes discussed earlier in this chapter. Thus it is arguable that they do not fall within the definitional criteria for compounding. In ISL, the range of signs that might be considered candidates for simultaneous compounds include signs that have become lexicalised, like PARACHUTE-JUMP and

JUMP-UP-AND-DOWN. As Brennan notes, the issue in deciding whether these are compounds or blends is the extent to which their components can be identified as free morphemes. We will consider this issue in our discussion of the ISL lexicon in the next chapter.

5.9 Manner

In this section we look briefly at ways in which the articulation of a sign, such as a verb or adjective, may be modulated to convey information about manner, intensity and other qualities, such as size. A motion verb, for example, may be articulated to give information about the path of movement, as in Example 5.38, where the trajectory of the moving figure, to use Talmy's (1985) term, is represented as part of the sign.

Example 5.38

CL:B+f+trace-non-linear-path
Kevin (17) Personal Stories (Dublin)

Similarly, action verbs, such as WALK or RUN, maybe modulated away from the citation form to give information about speed, as in Example 5.39.

Example 5.39

(a) WALK
Bernadette (02) Personal Stories (Dublin)

(b) WANDER-ROUND-BY-FOOT
KEVIN (17) Personal Stories (Dublin)

Non-manual features play an important role in this type of adverbial modification. One particular type of manner inflection conveyed by a non-manual features occurs in Example 5.18 earlier where the morphemes glossed as 'mm' provides the adverbial information that the action occurred 'in the normal way' or 'normally' (Baker-Shenk and Cokely 1980; Ó Baoill and Matthews 2000). A similar non-manual morpheme is reported for ASL (Liddell 1980) and BSL (Sutton-Spence and Woll 1999). This non-manual morpheme co-occurs with the manual signs illustrated in Example 5.39(a) and (b).

In a similar way adjectives may be modulated to give information about the scale of the relevant quality. Thus an adjective like BIG may be articulated to convey 'very big', 'extremely big', as in Example 5.40.

Example 5.40

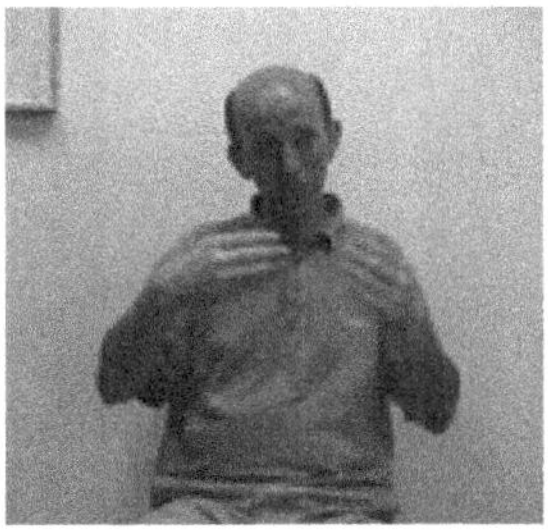

(a) BIG (citation)
Fergus (06) Personal Stories (Dublin)

(b) BIG-BALL
Maria (Dublin) Frog Story

(c) VERY-BIG-WINDOW
Leanne (14) Personal Stories (Dublin)

We note also that temporary states expressed by verbs like HUNGRY, TIRED, ANGRY, etc. can also be modified. Movement of the verb is lengthened, as in the examples discussed above, to mean 'very hungry', 'very tired' and 'very angry'. Clearly these manner modifications are conceptually related to the aspectual distinctions described in the last section, if we view aspect as describing the way in which a process or event unfolds through time.

5.10 Summary

In this chapter we have discussed the morphology of ISL, giving examples of how word shapes are altered by morphological processes to signal the functions of grammatical categories like agreement, aspect and number. We have also seen how ISL users create new signs through compound formation, and something of the rules and principles that govern this. We have also looked at the system of classifiers, where aspects of the form or movement norms of an entity (including aspects of how an entity is handled) are encoded in predicates. This system too is capable of innovation, for example one ISL sign for NOTHING, articulated in neutral space, can be relocated to the forehead to mean KNOW-

NOTHING or located on the palm of each hand to mean KNOW-NO-SIGN. In the next chapter we will look at the lexicon in further detail, discussing what have been called the productive and the established lexicons of ISL.

Notes

1. We discuss the relationship between semantic roles like actor and grammatical roles like subject in Chapter 7.
2. For interested readers, here is the end of the joke: the third lion happens to be deaf, and the violin music doesn't lull him to sleep. So he eats the violinist.
3. For discussion of analysis of such structures in LSF that draw on the work of Christian Cuxac, the reader is referred to Sallandre (2007) and Risler (2007).
4. Carmel Grehan, personal communication, September 2010.

6 The ISL Lexicon

6.1 Introduction

In Chapter 5, we outlined aspects of the morphological system in ISL. We considered what constitutes a word in ISL and considered how plurals are marked and how compounds are formed, amongst other things. This chapter builds on that discussion, focusing on the morphology of the lexicon. We differentiate between the established lexicon, namely those signs that have a fixed citation form and are typically cited in dictionaries of ISL, and the productive lexicon, which makes use of the productive relationship between a narrow set of handshapes that can operate in signing space to create new, dynamic descriptions of entities. In Chapter 5, we discussed these in section 5.5 under the heading of classifier predicates and noted that they have also been referred to as size and shape specifiers (Brennan 1992).

In this chapter we also investigate the role of borrowing from English and other languages. We discuss the relationship of the productive lexicon to aspects of iconicity and gesture before turning to a discussion of the development of dictionaries of signed languages. We will also look at the lexicon in terms of 'cognitive iconicity' (Wilcox 2004a), which adopts a cognitive linguistics framework to analysing, among other things, the lexical level of signed languages, and re-examines the notions of arbitrariness and iconicity, positing that the two are not necessarily wholly independent notions but can co-exist, and that both represent a deeper, underlying cognitive basis for language.

6.2 The ISL lexicon

We have already seen that signs are created with manual and non-manual morphemes. A useful distinction is one that Brennan (1992) suggested for British Sign Language: between the established and the productive lexicon. Some signs in the lexicon are fixed or 'established', that is they have a clearly identifiable citation form, and often they have an established English language equivalent. Typical examples include signs for MOTHER, FATHER,

HOUSE, TREE and JOB. Other signs are constructed using conventional strategies to fit contextual needs. These strategies form the productive lexicon. For example, in the last chapter, in Example 5.28, we saw how a signer used a two-handed CL-C-handshape to trace the outline of the arched entrance to a gift shop at the zoo. He then signed 'gift', locating the fingerspelling for the word along the crest of the arc. Together, this meant that there 'was a shop which had a big arched doorway with the word "gifts" emblazoned on it' (Informant H: narrative, Leeson 2001: 73). The combination includes the creation of a bespoke lexical item, created by the signer 'online', as a 'doorway' for the current context. Though there are iconic elements to this sign, it is produced from conventionalised elements, for example the classifier handshape, in a rule-governed way. In general, while some signs are arbitrary in nature, with no direct relationship to their referent discernible from their form, other signs are more highly iconic – that is, there is a relationship that holds between the form of the sign and its referent in the real world. For example, the sign for DRINK takes a CL-C-handshape, which at the same time tells us something about the size and shape of the referent and about how it is handled. The ISL sign for HOUSE takes two flat-B-handshapes, reflecting the structure of an A-frame roof. Iconicity is not always so easily discernible. Some of the iconic relationships we find underpinning the ISL lexicon are more complex in nature. For example, one ISL sign for SCHOOL sees the non-dominant hand taking a flat-B-handshape, representing a flat entity, interpretable as a page, while the dominant hand takes an S-handshape and moves from the non-dominant hand to forehead. This movement suggests movement of knowledge from the page to the person's head. As we shall see, some of the complexity can be accounted for when we look at the role of metaphor in the formation of the lexicon. We shall see that metaphor and metonymy, along with gesture and initialised handshapes can combine. This can lead to ISL signs being iconic and, at the same time, demonstrating some degree of influence from English as a result of language contact. When we talk about language contact and ISL, we should also bear in mind that other signed languages, historically French Sign Language, British Sign Language and to a lesser extent, American Sign Language, have impacted significantly on the language.

Figure 6.1 provides a schematic overview of the ISL lexicon, with the broken lines suggesting possible relationships at the interface between productive and established elements.

The established lexicon of ISL includes a range of arbitrary and iconic signs, including signs that have been influenced by English, and by British and French Sign Language. More recently there is evidence of influence from American Sign Language. Some of the iconic signs may have gestural roots, many of which appear as metonymic forms, and some of which co-occur with mouth gestures, which have become conventionally associated with particular lexical items, specifically items that are gender-specific in nature. In the productive lexicon, we find that gesture also plays a role as a substrate

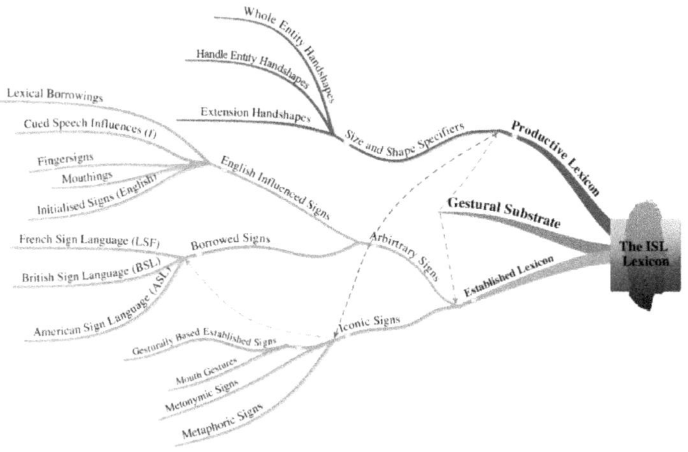

Figure 6.1 Overview of the ISL lexicon

for many productive elements, but that these elements have been conventionalised, giving them linguistic status. The role of size and shape specifiers, also known as classifier handshapes, is significant in this category too.

Given this, it is important to bear in mind that the established and productive components are not wholly separate entities, but, as indicated in Figure 6.1 above, that there are dynamic processes that operate to link them. With this in mind, we begin by taking a closer look at the established lexicon.

6.3 The established lexicon

In Chapter 3 we discussed the origins of contemporary ISL and noted that both British Sign Language and French Sign Language have influenced the lexicon of Irish Sign Language. Much of what has been documented regarding early forms of contemporary ISL relates to English-based descriptions of signs for English words, and this bias has tended to influence what is seen as a word in ISL. As we have shown in Figure 6.1, this is not an accurate reading of the situation, as the lexicon of ISL has had many influences, and as a living language, it continues to change over time, drawing on a range of processes to promote the evolution of the lexicon. Given the stereotyped traditional view of the sign, however, we begin by considering signs that have been influenced by English.

6.3.1 English-influenced signs

English-influenced signs include the following range of items: lexical borrowings, initialised signs, fingersigns, mouthed elements and cued speech influenced items. Lexical borrowings include elements that were created as part of the move to map English to a signed form via the system known locally as manually coded English or signed English. McDonnell (1997) notes that many of the signs used in manually coded English in Ireland were in fact borrowed from ISL, some of which were in turn borrowed from LSF and BSL. Others, though, were invented for words in English which had no pre-existing equivalent in ISL. Typically, the hand configuration for such a sign indicates its relationship to the English manual alphabet (ibid.). McDonnell includes initialised signs such as DEFEND, GUARD, FOSTER and PROTECT as illustrative of this process.

Signs which are initialised typically incorporate the first letter of the English word – as in MOTHER, FATHER, POLICE, TROUBLE, THINK, IDEA, INTERPRETER – and may have been created by educationalists as part of the move towards manually coded English. It is also probable that several such signs had a non-initialised form and that initialisation was imposed on them. Indeed, it seems that several signs are undergoing a process of de-initialisation, perhaps in part influenced by increased awareness among the Irish Deaf community of ISL as a language in its own right, with a concurrent move away from signs seen as having an overt English influence. An example is PROCESS, which, in citation form, takes an ISL-P-handshape, which many Deaf people sign with a B-handshape, thus creating a non-initialised form.

Many initialised signs seem at first glance to be wholly arbitrary in nature, but on closer examination, we find that they are typically grouped so that cognate concepts are aligned to a set of locations, for example the non-dominant hand for 'trouble' (POLICE, PRISON, ARREST, TROUBLE, PUNISH, ANNOY, PROBLEM); the head for literal associations with the head area and for issues of cognition (HEAD, BRAIN, COGNITION, IDEA, THINK, UNDERSTAND, KNOW, INTELLIGENT, IGNORANT, STUPID, etc.); and the heart for issues of emotion and literal associations with that aspect of the body (HEART, LOVE, LIKE, etc.). Thus there is a metaphoric relationship that holds between salient concepts and the conceptual associations aligned to physical locations on the body.

Other initialised signs have a reduced iconic element: for example, the male variety for the signs MONDAY–THURSDAY are initialised for days of the week on a list-buoy, where each finger aligns with the first, second, third and fourth days:

Example 6.1

MONDAY – M-handshape travelling along the index finger of the non-dominant hand

TUESDAY – T-handshape travelling along the middle finger of the non-dominant hand

WEDNESDAY – W-handshape travelling along the ring finger of the non-dominant hand

THURSDAY – T-handshape travelling along the pinky finger of the non-dominant hand

Related to initialised signs are signs that started out as fingerspelled items but which, as a result of phonological deletion and grammaticalisation processes, are now lexicalised. These are typically place names, which may have originally been fingerspelled in full but over time, phonological deletion rules have applied and today a reduced number of letters are articulated, and this, together with an identifiable movement pattern, suggest that the formerly fingerspelled items have lexicalised to a greater or lesser degree. Examples include C-O-R-K ('Cork'), T-I-P-P ('Tipperary'), L-K ('Limerick') and G-W-Y ('Galway'). We know that these are psychologically treated as signs rather than as items that are spelled out as deaf children have been known to ask adults how to spell the proper noun they have just signed. These forms are typically influenced by English orthography. This aligns to findings on perseveration and anticipatory coarticulation affects at the level of phonology:

> Fingerspelling is more than a sequence of canonical handshape–alphabet letter correspondence, since the articulatory movements of segments within the fingerspelled word influence each other. Perseverative and anticipatory coarticulation affects the actual shaping of fingerspelled words, creating a fluid transition between letters that is prosodic and complex. (Wilcox et al. 2003: 140)

A key element in the creation of the range of established signs we have discussed thus far is mouthing, a phenomenon we discussed in some detail in Chapter 4, where we noted that mouthings may be used lexically, grammatically, prosodically, and for discourse and stylistic reasons (following Boyes Braem (2001)). We noted that preliminary analysis of the Signs of Ireland corpus reveals very marked gender differences with regard to the use of mouthings, with women consistently making greater use of English influenced mouthings than their male counterparts. In Chapter 4, we reported that Militzer found that for female signers aged 18–35, 75 per cent of lexical items were accompanied by mouthings, while the figure for men in this age group was 52 per cent. In the 40–55-year age group, 60 per cent of lexical items articulated by women co-occurred with mouthings, and for men, the figure was 39 per cent. For those aged 55 years and above, 45 per cent of lexical items produced by women co-occurred with mouthings, while men in this category produced mouthings in only 12 per cent of all instances.

We have seen that mouthings accompany mainly nouns, and we would add, these are forms that are firmly based in the established lexicon category, reinforcing the notion that the established lexicon has been influenced heavily by language contact (with other signed languages and with English). We also point out that mouthings are found in the gendered signs that were generated in the schools for the deaf following from the introduction of oralism in the 1940s (St Mary's School for Deaf Girls) and the 1950s (St Joseph's School for Deaf Boys).

In addition to lexical content words, the proponents of manually coded English created signs for function words like AND, OF, THEN, TO, FOR, HIS/HER, THEY, HE/SHE, AM, IS, WERE and WAS. Again, there is a tendency towards initialisation in these signs. Affixes were created for tense marking (for example, TALK+PAST = 'talked', TEACH+PAST = 'taught'), with regular and irregular past tense verbs being treated the same in this system (McDonnell 1997). As we shall see in Chapters 7 and 8, many of these forms have been incorporated into ISL usage, though their functionality may have shifted somewhat. Other lexical borrowings from English include the loan translation compounds that we discussed in Chapter 5.

Another subset of signs is those that have been influenced by English phonetics. Oralism and the use of a system known as cued speech have impacted on the lexicon of ISL, particularly the variety used by Deaf women. Cued speech is a mode of communication based on the phonemes of spoken languages. It aims to provide access to the basic properties of spoken languages through the use of vision.[1] Though never widely used in Ireland, some cohorts of graduates from St Mary's School for Deaf Girls still use elements which seem to have been influenced by cued speech, introduced in the context of speech training classes at the school. Examples include the use of the little finger at the lips to represent *k* sounds and the index finger at the lips to represent *sh* sounds. As a result, these gestures, accompanied by mouthed elements, are used by some Deaf women as the lexical signs for SHOE, CORK, etc. In Example 6.2, we see what might be considered the 'standard' form for the ISL sign SHOE (a) and the female variant, influenced by cued speech (b):

Example 6.2

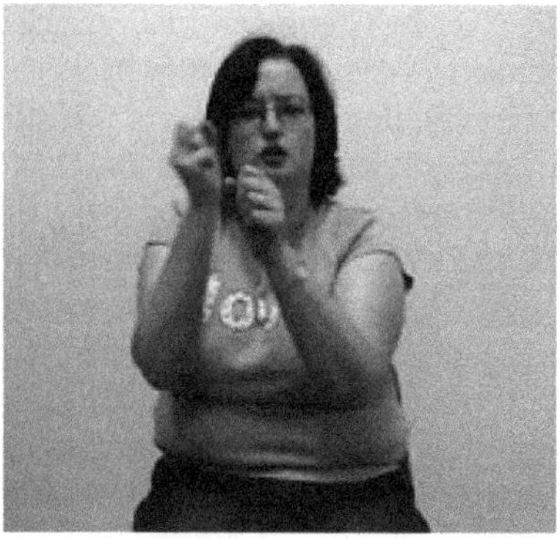

(a) SHOE (Citation)
Valerie (12) Personal Stories (Dublin)

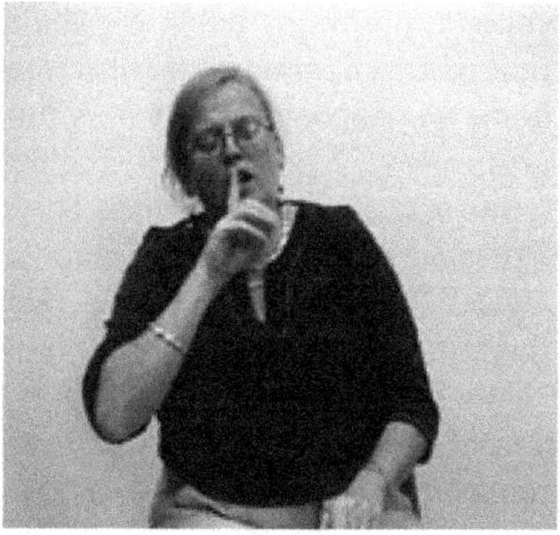

(b) SHOE (Cued speech influenced form (f))
Marian (16) Personal Stories (Dublin)

6.3.2 Borrowed signs

Some of the signs with a British or French Sign Language origin include GUINNESS (BSL-G-handshape), PROFESSIONAL (BSL-P-handshape), MEMBER (BSL-M-handshape), LOOK/SEARCH (C-handshape, from the French verb *chercher*, 'to look') and FRIDAY, (the ISL female variant for FRIDAY takes via LSF a V-handshape from the French word for Friday, *vendredi*). These are signs that have been borrowed into ISL in the nineteenth century. More recently, the influence of globalisation on signed languages has also been felt. Since the mid twentieth century, increased travel as a result of emigration, as well as shorter trips abroad for work, study and leisure purposes, has led to increased engagement with users of other signed languages in a wide range of domains. With the advent of new technologies, particularly in the past twenty years or so, the capacity for online engagement with foreign signed languages has increased, leading to increased potential for borrowing. A prime example is the use of name signs for countries: given increased participation at international meetings of organisations like the World Federation of the Deaf and the European Union of the Deaf, lexical gaps were filled and on occasion, pre-existing signs for countries were replaced by the indigenous sign. Sometimes a reason for phasing out the pre-existing signs was related to the fact that the older signs were considered pejorative in some way (for example, the signs for CHINA and JAPAN were originally signs associated with eye shape). More recently, signs for linguistics terminology, like LINGUISTICS, PHONOLOGY and PHONETICS, were borrowed from British Sign Language in the early 1990s, and then these signs underwent some phonological changes (handshape, movement) (Leeson 2005).

6.3.3 Iconic signs

We have made reference several times in this volume to the fact that iconicity permeates Irish Sign Language. We noted this particularly in Chapter 5 when discussing the role of size classifiers in the creation of verb predicates. We also saw how a cognitive iconicity underpins the clustering of related verbal concepts, for example verbs of cognition at the head and verbs of emotion on the torso. We can take this discussion a little further here by considering the range of iconic factors that impact on the formation of the established lexicon in ISL.

One of the most productive aspects driving lexical creation in ISL is metaphor. Mary Brennan (1990, 1992) describes the role of metaphor as a prime in the creation of the British Sign Language lexicon, and as we shall see, these underlying principles apply equally to ISL. Cognitive linguists such as George Lakoff and Mark Johnston argue that metaphor underpins human language, giving us an insight into how we conceptualise our world (Lakoff

1987; Lakoff and Johnson 1980, 2003). In this view, metaphor is not a special figure used to adorn language but an integral part of cognition. Lakoff and Johnson (1980: 3) claim that 'metaphor is pervasive in everyday life, not just in language, but in thought and action. Our ordinary conceptual system, in terms of which we both think and act, is fundamentally metaphoric in nature.' They argue that metaphor, as a form of analogy, is a cognitive process that we use to assimilate new concepts and fields of knowledge. Thus, the way we think is, as they put it, 'a matter of metaphor' (ibid.). A typical example in English is metaphor TIME IS MONEY, where time is conceptualised as a finite and concrete commodity. English speakers use expressions like those in listed in Example 6.3.

Example 6.3

(a) You're *wasting* my time
(b) That gadget will *save* you hours
(c) I don't *have* the time to *give* you
(d) How do you *spend* your time these days
(e) The flat tire *cost* me an hour
(f) I've *invested* a lot of time in her
(g) I don't have enough time to spare for that
(h) You're *running out* of time
(i) He's living on *borrowed* time
(j) I *lost* a lot of time when I got sick
(k) *Thank you* for your time
(Lakoff and Johnson 1980: 7–8)

While not all of these linguistic expressions arise in ISL, several do occur, in part, we suggest, as a result of the shared cultural reality of Irish Deaf and hearing people. ISL signers also use the TIME IS MONEY metaphor, with expressions like WASTE TIME ('I've wasted time'), LOSE TIME ('I've lost time'), THANK-YOU TIME ('thank you for your time') and TIME REDUCE / DISAPPEAR ('the time had run out').

Building on work like that of Lakoff and Johnson, Mary Brennan's detailed study of word formation in British Sign Language posits that metaphoric relationships play a significant role in the generation of new BSL signs (Brennan 1990, 1994). She suggests that visual metaphor is more immediately apparent in BSL, as opposed to say English, but that this does affect the working of the language itself. She points out that metaphors operate along with, and in some cases through, other features of the language, and must be taken into consideration when examining aspects of the lexicon and grammar of signed languages. Brennan argues that arbitrariness in form-meaning relationships at the lexical level is atypical for British Sign Language, and instead, the language exploits highly motivated relationships. She suggests that, while word formation operates on the basis of convention, in BSL:

> It is as if in developing a new word, the linguistic system operates according to a set of default commands of the following type:
> - match the selected meaning with an existing motivated morpheme or morphemes in the language;
> - combine, as required, two or more such meanings;
> - choose an appropriate morphological process by means of which the new form may be generated;
> - exploit the appropriate morph-phonemic primes for the realization of the new word (1990: 35).

In sum then, Brennan suggests that conventional does not equate with arbitrariness. In a similar vein, Wilcox et al. (2003) discuss the role of metonymy in American Sign Language (ASL) and Catalan Sign Language (LSC). Metonymy is an indirect referential strategy that exploits known associations of various types. One is the part-whole relationship, as, for example, when a nurse refers to a patient as 'the gallstones in bed 5', allowing the hearer to identify the intended referent, the patient. Wilcox et al. report that in ASL and LSC, the use of simple lexical metonymies is a common phenomenon, whereby a prototypical physical characteristic is used to represent the whole entity. Typical examples include the signs for BIRD, HORSE and COW in ASL and LSC, where prototypical physical properties of these animals are profiled in their lexical form, namely the beak, the ears and horns. In ISL, such simple metonymies are also widespread. Examples include a range of animal signs like BIRD (beak), BULL (shape of horns), CAT (whiskers), TIGER (stripes), LION (claw), GIRAFFE (long neck) and ELEPHANT (trunk).

A second kind of metonymy involves the use of the hands in interaction with some object to represent the instrument of action. Wilcox et al. give examples from LSC and ASL like TYPEWRITER, where the hands and fingers move in a way that represents the action of typing. In ISL, examples include many verbs of self-grooming (BRUSH-TEETH, WASH-BODY, PUT-ON-LIPSTICK, etc.).

A third category is that of prototypical action for activity. Wilcox et al. report that the hands and their movement can be used to represent a prototypical action taken with some object, and that this may come to metonymically represent the general activity. A prime example is DRIVE-CAR where the prototypical action of holding the steering wheel is profiled to mean 'drive a car' rather than 'hold the steering wheel' or 'steer a car' (145). ISL is rich in examples in this category, lending support to Wilcox et al.'s suggestion that 'The strategy of using a prototypical interaction with a specific component to metonymically express a whole activity is common across a range of objects and activities' (ibid.). ISL examples include DRINK-FROM-TEACUP (little finger extended, holding and raising a dainty teacup to mouth), DRIVE-CAR (moving steering wheel), DRINK-FROM-GLASS (hold cylindrical object and bring to mouth), TO-VACUUM (hold long narrow cylindrical object and move back and forth), TO-WASH-HAIR (action of rinsing shampoo from hair), SQUASH (hands grip and move a squash racquet) and TO-SMOKE-A-CIGARETTE (the movement of the hands to and from the mouth, the inhalation of smoke by the smoker).

Wilcox et al. also note the role that metonymy plays in the creation of some name signs, a topic we discussed for ISL in Chapter 5.[2] The iconic, gestural metonymy in which a salient characteristic of a well-known person is extended to stand for a more general quality runs beyond a direct part-whole relationship and metonymic chains arise. Taking CHARLIE-CHAPLIN as an example, they note that the LSC compounds an iconic depiction of Charlie Chaplin's moustache and the movement of holding a cane and moving it in circles as the referent did. They suggest that this combination draws on a PHYSICAL CHARACTERISTIC FOR PERSON (in this case, two characteristics) metonymy and they report that in the USA, this same sign is used to mean 'person moving fast' (145).

A final grouping of metonymically driven signs identified by Wilcox et al. is a group they call 'deviant behavioural effect for intensity of experience' (146). They define this category as arising in LSC when a 'visible, behavioural response to some experience stands not for the causing experience itself but for the intensity of the causing experience' (ibid.). An example in LSC is CRAZY-EYES, a sign that depicts eyes wide open and moving in wild circles to mean 'really good'. In ISL, there is a range of signs that could be considered to fall in this category. They include signs like TONGUE-ROLL-OUT-OF-MOUTH to mean 'drooling over something that is really good', STEAM-COME-OUT-OF-EARS to mean 'really angry' and EYES-POP-OUT-OF-HEAD to mean 'I couldn't believe what I saw, astonishment'. While we could not consider it as an example of a 'deviant' behaviour, the use of HAIRS-STAND-UP-ON-ARM to represent the negative feeling associated with something or someone might also be included here as a less prototypical member of the category.

6.4 The productive lexicon

We can address the role of the productive lexicon in word formation in ISL by continuing to look at the role of metaphor and metonymy. In Chapter 5 we introduced ISL classifiers, reporting on McDonnell's (1996) identification of four subcategories of classifier predicates, and outlined the ways in which these elements function morphologically. Here, we will look at how these items are both drawn on and embedded in a system where metaphor is pervasive and illustrate some of the ways in which classifier handshapes contribute to the development of new lexical items within this system.

Brennan (1990) outlines a range of prototypical[3] metaphors that arise in

BSL. Given the significant influence of BSL on 'Old ISL' and contemporary ISL, it is perhaps no surprise that there are many points in her description where identical or very similar examples arise in ISL. For example, Brennan describes the DROWN, MELT, DISAPPEAR and SUCK set of metaphors which she argues share strong links. She argues that many of these concepts share similar semantic elements which can be expressed by the same metaphor or metaphor set. She points out that in BSL, these metaphors share the same physical form allowing for the same action to be used when describing someone or something drowning or disappearing into thin air, and notes that these are akin to English phrases like 'melting into the darkness' or 'swallowed up by the mist' (Brennan 1990: 111). The BSL DISAPPEAR metaphor is identical in form, and it seems function, to the ISL signs DISAPPEAR and MELT in Example 6.4. She points out that this form can also be articulated at the head to mean MIND WENT BLANK, again, an extension also used in ISL. Related to this, Brennan notes that a one-handed version of the sign can be used in BSL to transmit meanings associated with 'suck', 'suck in' and 'suck out' where the sign is accompanied by a mouth gesture comprised of 'lip rounding and a sharp intake of breath at each repetition' (ibid.). Again, these descriptions apply to ISL in terms of both form and functionality.

Example 6.4

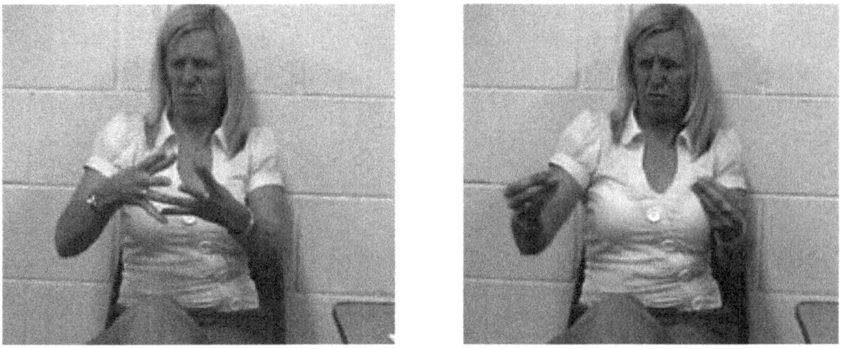

(a) DISAPPEAR
Rebecca (38) Personal Stories (Waterford)

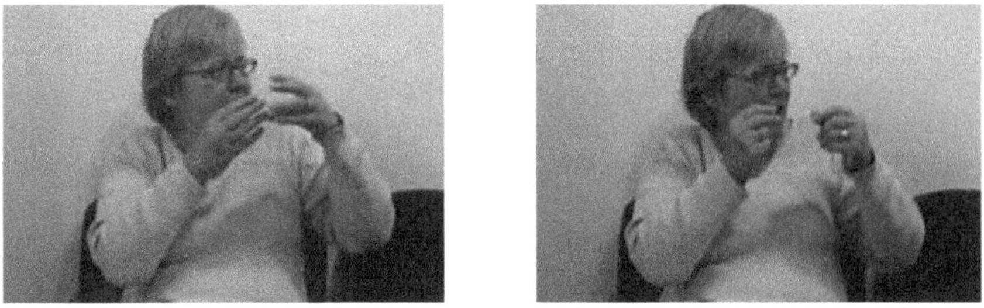

(b) MELT
Mary (33) Personal Stories (Galway)

Another set of metaphors that Brennan identifies for BSL, also clearly identifiable in ISL, is the EMANATE/EMIT set. She notes that these are most typically realised when the hand moves from a closed position to an open position, with the resulting meaning of 'emanating' or 'sending forth' (1990: 97). Brennan notes that while a traditional semantic analysis would not capture the relationship between the range of signs that are related via this visual metaphor, the unifying feature that prevails is the fact that all these signs make use of the same morpheme, and this morpheme is based on the underlying visual metaphor, EMANATE/EMIT, that is to flow forth or proceed from something as the source or origin, to give forth, to discharge (after Brennan 1990: 98). She also suggests that the closed handshape is aligned with concepts associated with the source element, while the opening action is associated with giving forth from that source. She illustrates with the BSL example of SUN, where the closed handshape may be influenced by the physical reality of the sun: the closed handshape symbolises the source of heat, light and power, and the opening action of the palm and spreading of the fingers is suggestive of the release of the sun's energy, suggesting rays of light which extend from the source.

Other BSL signs that draw on this underlying metaphor include LIGHT(S), SEND, TRANSMIT, MAGIC, PROGRAMME (TV), SPEND, BOMB, STRIKE, BLOOD, PERIOD, DISCHARGE, EMIT, SHOUT, FLOW, EJACULATION, MICROWAVE and DISHWASHER (Brennan 1990: 97–8). While not all of these signs make use of the EMANATE/EMIT form that Brennan discusses in ISL, many do. These include SUN-SHINING, LIGHT(S), TRANSMIT, MAGIC, SPEND, BOMB, DISCHARGE, EMIT, SHOUT, FLOW and MICROWAVE. Other signs in ISL which also make use of the EMANATE/EMIT form include DISTRIBUTE, SPREAD, FLASHLIGHT, HEADLAMPS, CAR-EXHAUST, STREETLIGHTS, FLASHING DOORBELL, POLICE-SIREN, AIRPORT-LANDING-LIGHTS, OVERHEAD-PROJECTOR and SHOWER. Brennan reports on the creative use of underlying metaphors in BSL in the creation of new signs which may over time become part of the established lexicon, or be used for creative effect. EMANATE/EMIT arises creatively, for example to illustrate FLOODS OF TEARS. This is a form also found in ISL and is widely used. Clearly, it is a highly utilised productive morpheme. (See Example 6.5.)

While we cannot in this section provide a comprehensive overview of how the productive lexicon combines with metaphoric morphemes in ISL, we note that it is a very pervasive process. The dynamism of this process also raises questions about categorical distinctions between the established lexicon and the productive lexicon. We can see in examples of the productive lexicon in ISL the combination of classifiers in conventional ways. The difference may be seen therefore in terms of compositional complexity rather than productivity. We can also note that over time, some items that begin life

Example 6.5

(a) SUN (onset)
Marian (16) Personal Stories (Dublin)

(a) SUN (offset)
Marian (16) Personal Stories (Dublin)

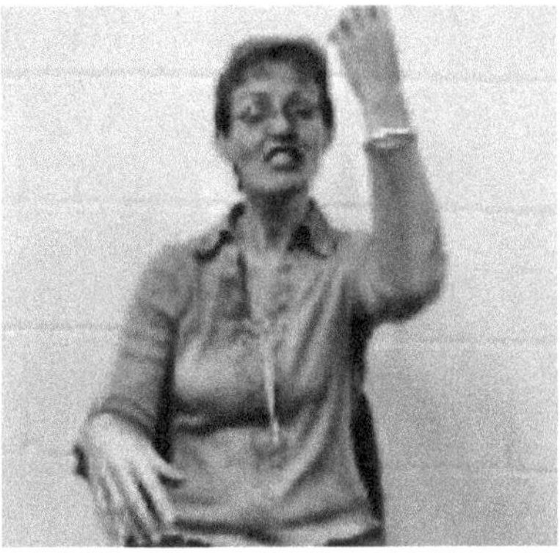

(b) SHOWER (onset)
Fiona (36) Personal Stories (Waterford)

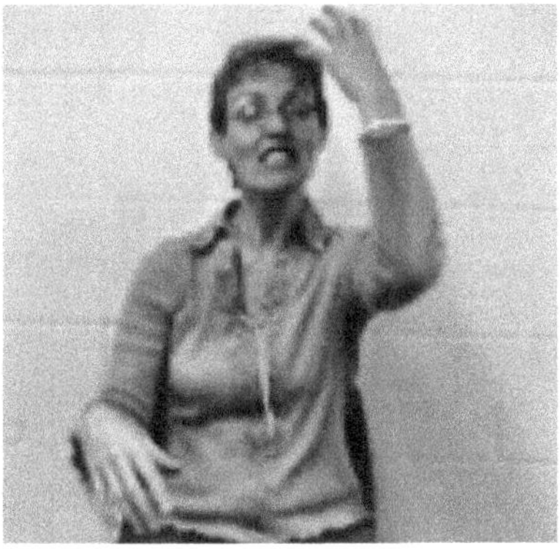

(b) SHOWER (offset)
Fiona (36) Personal Stories (Waterford)

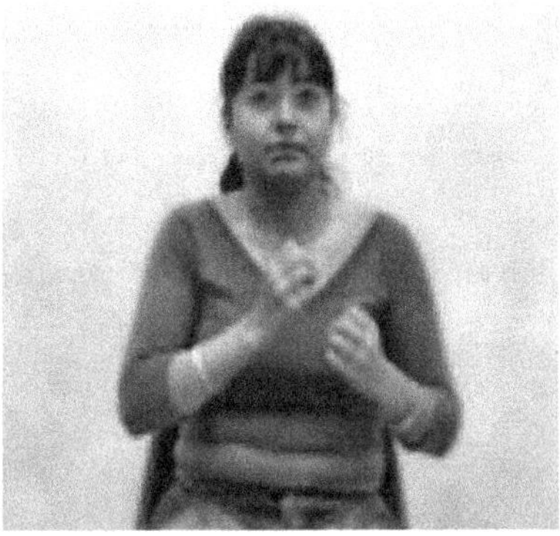

(c) BOMB (onset)
Lianne (14) Personal Stories (Dublin)

(c) BOMB (offset)
Lianne (14) Personal Stories (Dublin)

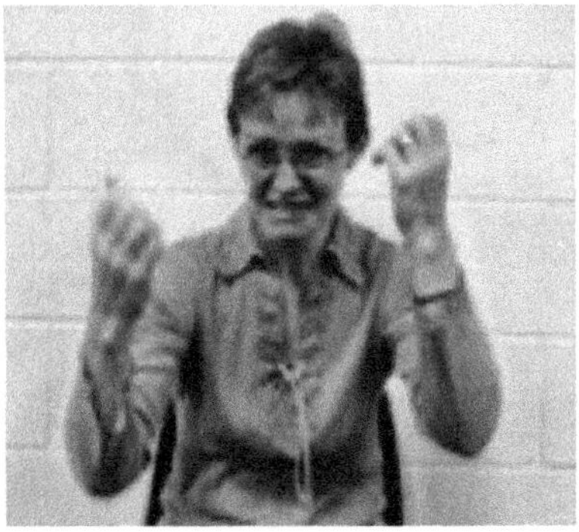

(d) TRAFFIC-LIGHTS (onset)
Fiona (36) Personal Stories (Waterford)

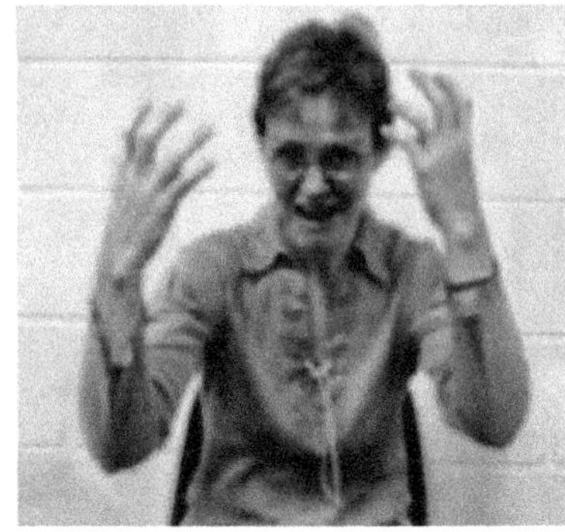

(d) TRAFFIC-LIGHTS (offset)
Fiona (36) Personal Stories (Waterford)

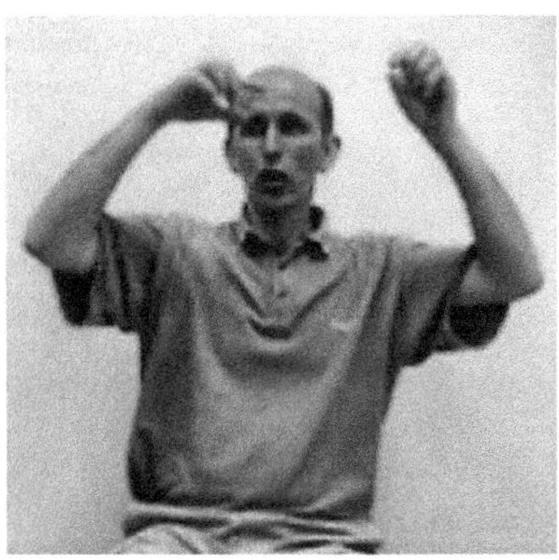

(e) CEILING-LIGHTS (onset)
Fergus D. (06) Personal Stories (Dublin)

(e) CEILING-LIGHTS (offset)
Fergus D. (06) Personal Stories (Dublin)

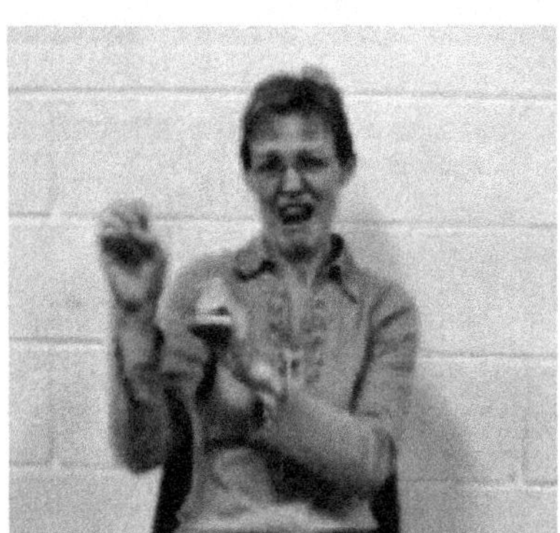

(f) (CAR)-HEADLAMPS (onset)
Fiona (36) Personal Stories (Waterford)

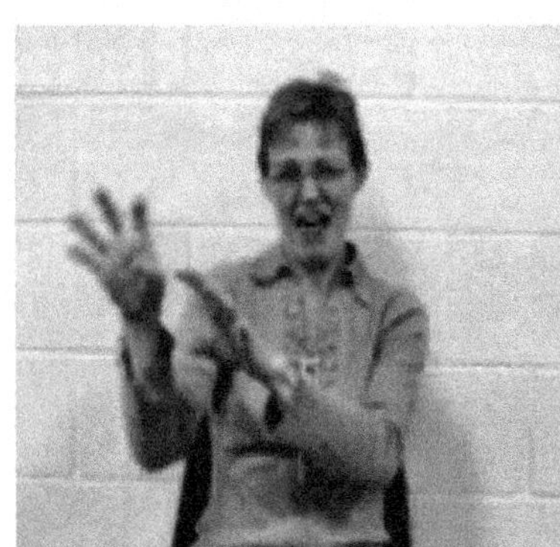

(f) (CAR)-HEADLAMPS (offset)
Fiona (36) Personal Stories (Waterford)

as wholly productive elements become conventionalised. This is particularly evident in the use of ISL signs like EURO (which trace the outline of the euro symbol) or in the signs for FAX and SCANNER, MOBILE-PHONE, LAPTOP-COMPUTER and COMPUTER-MOUSE. These are all items that have come into the established lexicon of ISL in the past twenty years via the productive lexicon.

6.5 Gestural substrate

It is difficult to say with certainty just how pervasive the gestural substrate is with respect to the formation of lexical and grammatical items in ISL, and even if this were possible, it is essential to note that identifying a gestural substrate for signs is not the same as saying that signed languages are mere gesture. Sherman Wilcox makes this case very clearly:

> Positing a gesture–language interface does not deny that signed languages are unique in important ways. Suggesting that signed languages are kin to gestures, or that developmental paths may lead from gesture to language, doesn't mean that signed languages are merely gestures. It simply means that the remarkable family resemblances between signs and gestures, and the tight integration of speech and gesture, point to a common ancestor. (Wilcox 2004b: 69)

At the simplest level, what we can say is that just like hearing speakers of a language, signers also use gestures. These include 'emblems' or 'quotable gestures': gestures that are culturally widespread like the holding up of a hand to indicate STOP, which differs from the lexical sign STOP, identical to the gesture that a police officer would use to stop traffic. Signers also use iconic gestures or 'illustrators', that is gestures that are closely aligned to speech and serve to illustrate what is said with respect to physical objects. For example, a speaker uses his or her hands to show the extent of an object (length, width, height, etc.) while talking about the subject, adding detail to the mental image that the speaker is attempting to convey. Further, these gestures give insight into the viewpoint (first person or non-first person) that the speaker is 'seeing things from the perspective of', so to speak. This makes them remarkably similar in form to the trace-path classifier forms we discussed in Chapter 5, and we consider this in more detail below.

Signers also make use of metaphoric gestures. These serve to explain a concept and can take the form of specific shapes such as finger pinches, or a more general waving of hands that symbolises the complexity of what is being explained.

Another widely used subset of gestural content is 'regulators', which are used to control turn-taking in conversation and include gestures associated with finishing a turn such as dropping of the arms, or seeking to start a turn, for example raising a hand or a finger in the air. In Chapter 8, we will see how turn-taking is managed in ISL discourse, and the functions of regulators like the raising of a hand in typical signed language discourse. Other gestural categories are 'beats' which accompany a point to create emphasis. A short beat, where, for example, a speaker might wag his or her finger in time to the prosody of his or her speech, or even bangs the table to emphasise a point, can mark an important point in conversation.

A good place to start in considering the relationship of gesture to sign is to consider a definition of gesture. We can agree that 'a gesture is a functional unit, an equivalence class of coordinated movements that achieve some end' (Armstrong et al. 1995; Studdert-Kennedy 1987). Sherman Wilcox builds on this definition and situates his work on gesture and language, with a particular focus on gesture and signed languages in cognitive grammar. Cognitive grammarians claim that:

> all of language, including lexicon, morphology, and grammar, is fully describable as assemblies of symbolic structures, pairings of semantic and phonological structures. These symbolic structures vary along several dimensions, including schematicity, symbolic complexity, and conventionalization. Although the gestures [examined here] [. . .] do not initially display internal complexity, as they are incorporated into the linguistic system they do begin to combine with other elements. Two corollaries must be noted. First, although symbolic complexity applies to unipolar structures: either form or meaning may vary from componentially simple to complex. Second, not only can individual symbolic components be combined to form a complex composite structure, but unanalyzed structures can be broken down into components. (Wilcox 2004b: 47)

Such decomposition includes analysis of the phonological elements of handshape, movement, location and orientation that we discussed earlier in this volume. It also includes analysis of things like manner of movement and movement type. Wilcox (ibid.) notes that once movement types become part of a linguistic system, they can combine to create composite forms, and he urges us to bear in mind that movement and manner of movement initially appear as unanalysed conceptual units. Wilcox describes conventionalisation as 'the measure of how much a structure is shared' (ibid.). That is, conventional structures are widely shared and known to be shared among a community of language users (Langacker 1987) though 'schematicity, symbolic complexity, and conventionality each vary along independent continua that apply both to form and meaning' (Wilcox 2004b). Moving forward from this theoretical point, Wilcox argues a strong case for two routes to the evolution of gesture to signed language:

> The first route begins with a gesture that is not a conventional unit in the relevant linguistic system. This gesture becomes incorporated into a signed language as a lexical item. Over time, these lexical items acquire grammatical function. [. . .] The second route proceeds along a different path. The source is not a free-standing gesture capable of being incorporated as a lexical item into a signed language. Rather the source gesture may be one of several types, including a particular manner of movement of a manual gesture or sign, and various facial, mouth, and eye gestures. (2004b: 48)

Examples of the first route take a quotable gesture that is borrowed into the linguistic system as a lexical sign. Over time, the gesture takes on a more grammatical function as a result of grammaticalisation processes. For American Sign Language, research has demonstrated that the morphological marker for future developed from the lexical morpheme GO, which in turn has a gestural basis (Janzen and Shaffer 2002; Shaffer 2000). This is described as being produced with the palm of the hand open and held edgewise, with a repeated upward movement (de Jorgio 2000) and is a gesture still used amongst hearing people in the Mediterranean region (Morris et al. 1979). This gesture also appears in French Sign Language as the lexical morpheme PARTIR 'depart' (Wilcox 2004b), which strongly resembles the ISL sign GO-OFF illustrated in Example 6.6.

Example 6.6

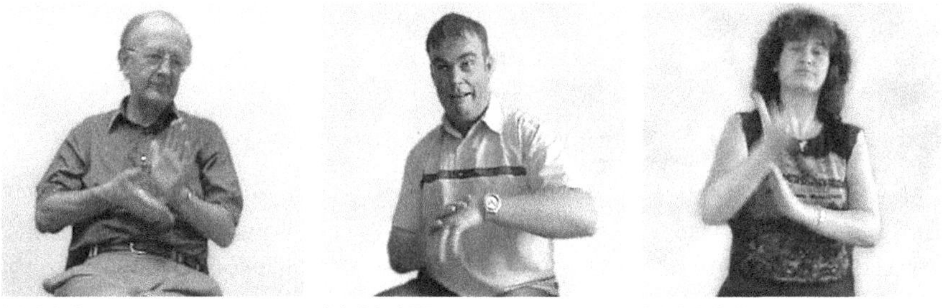

(a) GO-OFF
Peter (18) Personal Stories (Dublin)

(b) GO-OFF
Lawrence (19) Personal Stories

(c) GO-OFF
Helen (27) Personal Stories (Wexford)

Examples of the second route take an improvised gesture which is incorporated into the lexicon of the given signed language and over time, via grammaticalisation processes, acquires grammatical meaning. These gestures often begin the route to lexical or grammatical element as a gesture that enacts an actual or metaphorical object, a characteristic or a concept (Wilcox 2004b). Wilcox suggests that ASL evidential forms such as SEEM, FEEL and CLEAR/OBVIOUS have grammaticalised from the lexical morphemes MIRROR, FEEL (used in its physical sense) and BRIGHT, and that each of these lexical items can be traced back to a gestural source. He outlines the following developmental path for these ASL items:

1. [gesture enacting upper body strength] >STRONG>CAN
2. [gesture enacting looking in a mirror]>MIRROR>SEEM
3. [gesture enacting physically sensing with finger]>FEEL (physical)>FEEL (evidential)
4. [metaphorical gesture indicating rays of light]>BRIGHT>CLEAR/OBVIOUS (evidential). (56)

While linguists have not examined grammaticalisation processes in ISL or specifically analysed the gestural basis of signs in a systematic manner, we can point out that there are parallels to the process described for ASL in (3) above. As in ASL, ISL appears to use the lexical morpheme FEEL to represent both physical and evidential situations as in Example 6.7.

Example 6.7

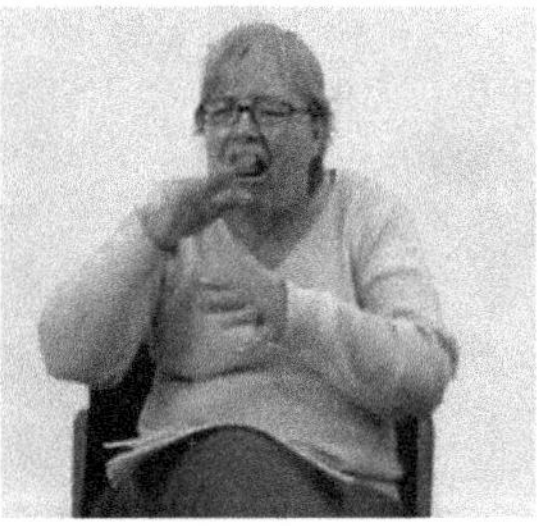

(a) FEEL-SNOW
(. . . and felt the snow . . .)
Mary (33) Personal Stories (Dublin)

(b) FEEL HOLD-LIFTING BRANCHES THERE STAG
(. . . and I felt that there was a stag there) Eric (32) Frog Story (Cork)

(c) FEEL FREE
(. . . and they felt free . . .)
Senan (01) Personal Stories (Dublin)

In Example 6.7(a) we see a physical touching of the snow, with the enactment of a situation where one physically reaches out to touch something. In (b) the lexical item FEEL is used and while this use could be interpreted as a literal experience of feeling a stag approach by, for example vibration, it is more likely given that an evidential reading is intended. In (c) no such ambiguity exists and the use of FREE here is purely about a mental state, the reported feeling of freedom.

This analysis seems to sit well with the third of the three tendencies that arise in the grammaticalisation process, described by Traugott: (1) meanings based in the external situation become meanings based in the internal, evaluative/perceptual/cognitive situation; (2) meanings based either in the external or internal situation become meanings based in the textual or metalinguistic situation; and (3) meanings tend to become increasingly based on the speaker's subjective belief, state, or attitude towards the proposition expressed

(Traugott 1989; Wilcox 2004b). As Wilcox points out, items that are based in speaker subjectivity are an indication of a greater degree of grammaticalisation of that item. This view on the grammaticalisation of gesture to sign language morpheme is one that has gained currency amongst researchers in the early part of the twenty-first century with some scholars noting the need to

> rethink assumptions about the relationship between signed languages and gesture and to seek further evidence of the extent to which movement and location in classifier constructions may be grammaticalised gestures, or whether they involve blends of linguistic and gestural elements. (Schembri et al. 2005: 287)

Others, like Vermeerbergen and Demey (2007), call for re-examination of the assumption that signed languages fall on one end of what some researchers call 'Kendon's Continuum' while co-speech gestures (that is, gestures that co-occur with spoken elements) and other kinds of manual activity occur at other points of the continuum (McNeill 1992; Vermeerbergen and Demey 2007) as follows: gesticulation>language-like-gestures>pantomimes>emble ms>signed languages. Instead, Vermeerbergen and Demey suggest that when studying natural languages, researchers need to take account of output from all channels, including manual and oral, considering how each channel may incorporate elements that are more language-like elements or less language-like elements.

To sum up, for ISL it is clear that gesture plays a role as a substrate influencing the formation of lexical and grammaticalised items, but also may appear in other forms and serve functions akin to those identified in spoken languages. It may be preferable, as Johnston et al. (2007) suggest, to correct the tendency to view languages as homogeneous systems and instead see them as more heterogeneous, combining elements such as gesture.

6.6 Male and female varieties

As we saw in Chapter 3, gender variants in ISL are a direct result of educational segregation (that is, the educational policy on segregation of the genders led to the separation of boys from girls) which, coupled with oralism, led to the development of male and female varieties of ISL, or more correctly, to St Joseph's and St Mary's variants of ISL, with additional in-cohort variants arising. In Chapter 3, we mentioned the pioneering work of Barbara LeMaster in documenting the extent of the lexical differences in gendered-generational ISL (LeMaster 1990, 1999–2000, 2002; LeMaster and O'Dwyer 1991). While LeMaster's work focused on the now elderly cohort of ISL, Leeson and Grehan (2004) explored (1) whether female variants still were used by younger Deaf women than those LeMaster described and (2) what the form and function of some of these might be. They focused specifically on documenting for the first time the female signs that emerged amongst cohorts of women who were educated orally. The signs they describe emerged organically, created by cohorts of female students who had very limited access to older signing role models due to the physical segregation of girls who signed from those who were branded 'oral successes', as discussed in Chapter 3. Leeson and Grehan describe some of the female signs that women who had attended St Mary's use. One of these is the sign glossed as FUNNY-ON (female), a compound that follows the general principles of compound formation in ISL (see Chapter 5 for discussion). They note that the sign co-occurs with a mouthed element that approximates a 'vun-on' pattern, probably derived from the English words 'funny' and 'on'. This sign means 'that an item of clothing or a suit of clothes does not look good on a person; that is, the person's clothes look funny (strange) on that person' (49). Another example from this genre is SPOIL (female), which co-occurs with the mouthing, 'spoil'. SPOIL is used in contexts where the signer has made a mistake, done something wrong, or said something they regret (52).

Other gendered signs that form part of the established lexicon include signs that do not take identifiably English mouthings, despite their proximity to oralism. This category includes signs like 'F' (traditionally a male sign, now widely used) which co-occurs with a close lipped mouth action (Leeson and Grehan 2004: 53–4), FOO (female) which co-occurs with the mouthing 'foo' (47), and DID-ON-PURPOSE (female), which has a 'buv-e' oral component.

Describing the form and function of 'F', Matthews notes that

> The distinguishing feature is the pace of movement, combined with various non manual features together with the head and shoulder movement. These combinations of features give rise to several explicitly different meanings such as 'oops – I made a mistake, I'm surprised at that, take that with a grain of salt (scepticism)' or it can also mean 'I was wrong' or be used as a response to news as 'fancy that' or 'I would not have expected that'. (1996a: 157)

FOO has two female variants which carry related meanings. Leeson and Grehan (2004: 47) note that FOO can be articulated with an ASL-T-handshape, which has its onset at the signer's body at chest level as shown in Example 6.8(a). The hand then travels forward, making contact with the non-dominant hand, which finds its position in neutral space. The non-dominant hand takes the same handshape as the dominant hand. The dominant hand then travels, palm facing the signer, back towards the onset point. The movement is rapid and smooth. The oral component is a lip pattern that resembles the pronunciation of the components 'a-vu'. FOO is typically used when a signer observes or learns that someone has told an interlocutor something that the person already knew, something that is hurtful to the person, or something that the interlocutor should not have known. FOO (female variant) can also be articulated to the side of the signer, as in Example 6.8(b). Here the handshapes of the dominant and non-dominant hands remain in an ASL-T-handshape, but the place of articulation is lowered and to the side of the signer, so as to be unobservable by a third party. When articulated at this location, FOO is used when the signer wants to quietly inform an interlocutor that what the interlocutor is saying is inappropriate and that the person should stop. Both of these variants differ from an existing male variant of FOO which serves a similar discourse function but has different articulatory parameters.

Example 6.8

(a) FOO (onset) (Female) Variant 1

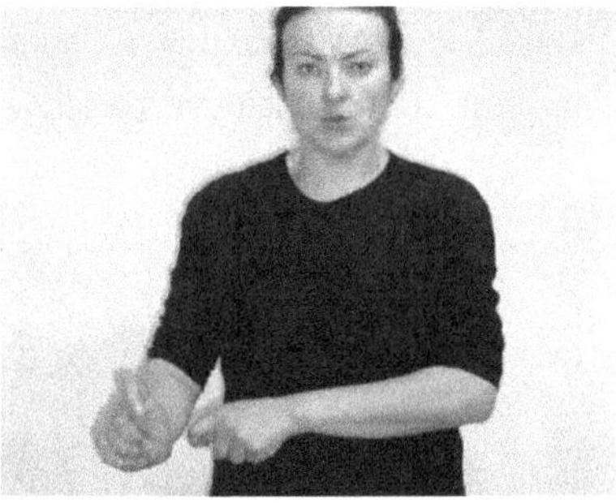

(a) FOO (offset) (Female) Variant 1

(b) FOO (onset) (Female) Variant 2
Sarah-Jane (09) Personal Stories (Dublin)

(b) FOO (offset) (Female) Variant 2
Sarah-Jane (09) Personal Stories (Dublin)

Leeson and Grehan (ibid.) describe DID-ON-PURPOSE as a two-handed sign, where the dominant hand takes an ASL-G-handshape, with the palm facing the signer. The tip of the index finger moves from a point of onset at the chin. As the hand moves, the palm rotates. The hand arcs forward and downward, and as it moves, the handshape changes, becoming an open-5-handshape. The palm at this stage faces downward. The non-dominant hand finds its position in neutral space, with a flat-B-handshape, palm facing upward. The dominant hand makes contact with the non-dominant hand and slides along its surface. DID-ON-PURPOSE can be used in a broad range of circumstances, for example a female signer can use it to refer to her own deliberate actions or to describe the wilful actions of another person, male or female (though male signers could not use this sign to refer to a woman in the same position: they would use the male variety of this sign). DID-ON-PURPOSE co-occurs with the oral component 'buv-e'. DID-ON-PURPOSE can be used when a signer's interlocutors have deliberately manipulated a situation. For example, if a student was supposed to have handed in an assignment on a certain date and deliberately did not bring it to class, the student might sign DID-ON-PURPOSE to a fellow student, making sure that the teacher did not observe the interaction. In other contexts, DID-ON-PURPOSE can be used when the interlocutor intended no manipulation but is nevertheless suspected by the signer. (See Example 6.9.)

Example 6.9

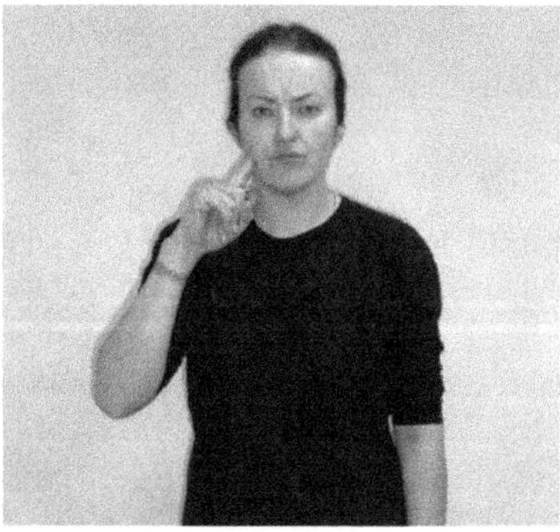

DID-ON-PURPOSE (onset)

DID-ON-PURPOSE (offset)

A sign that began life as a female variant, but which is now used by men in their 30s and 40s is WUF. Leeson and Grehan (ibid.) describe how WUF is articulated with a bent-5-handshape, palm facing sideways. The onset of the sign is parallel with the signer's cheek on the dominant side of the signing space. The hand moves across the signer's face, closing as it moves, until it becomes a closed-fist-S-handshape. The oral component is a 'wuf' movement, lending its name to the female signers' label for the sign. WUF is typically used when one finds out that someone (other than the signer) has decided that an activity is not permitted. WUF is a response to thinking that the decision is silly. For example, if a schoolgirl is told that she is not allowed to go to the local stores, she might sign WUF (that is, she thinks that the ban on her going shopping is unfair or stupid). Adult women also use WUF in response to a decision that they think is without merit. For example, if the Centre for Deaf Studies at Trinity College Dublin had decided to ban the use of ISL, we might expect female students and staff to respond with WUF. In the mid 1990s, Leeson and Grehan reported that while WUF is widely considered to be a 'strong' female sign, they had occasionally witnessed male signers aged 30–45 years using it. In the interim, WUF seems to have become more widespread in use amongst male signers under 45 years and it will be interesting to monitor the use of this sign over time.

One interesting aspect of the signs we have illustrated is the lack of iconic or gestural basis for them. In contrast, there are other signs which have an iconic basis. These include EYEBROW-RAISE (the index finger is placed at the eyebrow level and traces the raising of an eyebrow to mark surprise or fear at some suggestion; see Example 6.10(a)) and DON'T-ANNOY-ME (elbow used as if to push someone who is annoying the signer away from their side; see Example 6.10(b)).

Example 6.10

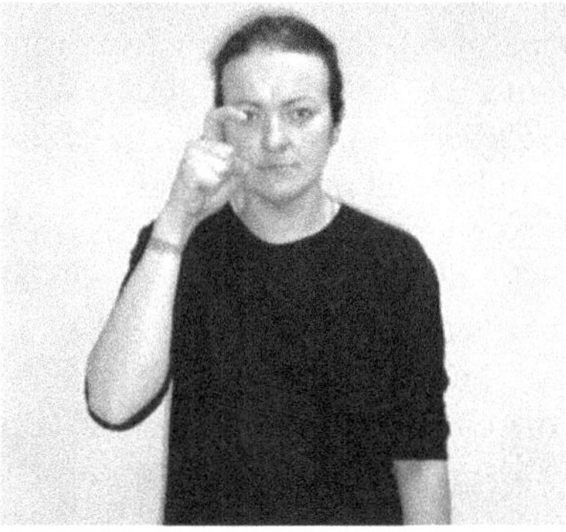

(a) EYEBROW-RAISE

(b) DON'T-ANNOY-ME

What this suggests is that an iconic base is not obligatory when generating new lexical items in ISL, with the potential for arbitrary (if contextually determined) signs emerging. It is also important to point out that while these signs have sometimes been dismissed as 'not real signs' by hearing educators, Deaf men and occasionally Deaf women themselves because of their distance from English, these gendered variants are just as much a part of the established lexicon of ISL as established signs like HOUSE or HOME.

6.7 Summary

In this chapter, we have explored the range of influences on the formation of the lexicon in ISL. We have seen that there are a number of internal and external forces that have been brought to bear on ISL. External forces include the language contact situation with BSL, LSF and other signed languages as well as English. We saw that this has led to the borrowing into ISL of morphemes from other languages that have, over time, undergone phonological changes. We also saw the significant role that gesture has played as a substrate for many signs. This role arises not just because gesture seems to be a universal feature of human communication, but also because of the atypical language transmission paths that most deaf children experience in the acquisition of ISL. Without Deaf parents, the majority scaffold their language development on conventionalised gestures that are often referred to in the Deaf community (and the literature) as HOME SIGN. This gestural root is often married to metonymic elements and when lexicalised, these metonymies remain identifiable. We considered the role of metaphor in the system and saw that it has a significant role to play in driving ISL conceptually. We noted that this applies at the level of underlying idealised conceptual models (ICMs) as in metaphors like TIME IS MONEY which generates a clustering of verbs around particular concepts. We also saw how ICMs operate to underpin the development of the productive lexicon, sometimes pushing towards the lexicalisation of what were probably originally productive forms. These include BODY IS A CONTAINER and IDEAS ARE LIQUID. When such metaphors are nested, we can arrive at very complex patterns of language use, an issue that we have simply scratched the surface of here.

Finally, we noted that when generating new lexical items in ISL, it seems that while iconicity plays an important role, it is not obligatory, and this allows for the emergence of arbitrary signs even in contexts where they are less anticipated as is the case for the girls from St Mary's and St Joseph's who generated several arbitrary signs in the context of suppression of their language and a focus on oral language use.

Notes

1. See <http://www.cuedspeech.org/default.asp> (accessed 25 November 2011).
2. But see Wilcox et al. (2003) for further analysis of the metonymic basis for name signs.
3. We discuss prototype theory in more detail in Chapter 9.

7 Syntax

7.1 Introduction

In this chapter we look at how ISL sentences are constructed. In comparison with some other signed languages there has been relatively little investigation of syntactic structure and our discussion remains at a fairly preliminary level. We begin by looking at the basic building blocks of sentences, the syntactic categories. We saw in Chapter 5 the morphological behaviour that distinguishes the two basic grammatical categories of noun and verb. They are also distinguished by their syntactic behaviour, that is the other elements they combine with to form sentences. For example, nouns may be modified by determiners and adjectives; verbs are modified by adverbs. The main grammatical categories of ISL, identifiable by their morphological and syntactic behaviour are: noun, verbs, pronouns, adjectives, determiners, prepositions and conjunctions. These may be further subdivided into classes, for example a subclass of verbs is auxiliary verbs, which unlike main verbs cannot form sentences by combining with nouns, as discussed below. The classes of noun, main verb and adjective are in general open classes, in that new members can be added by signers creating, or coining, new words, or as loans. However, the system of classifier handshapes described in Chapter 5 imposes a closed system on a subset of verbs. The classes of pronoun, auxiliary verb, determiner, preposition and conjunction are closed classes in that their membership changes only very slowly over time and generally cannot be added to by an individual act of coining. The question of whether there is a unitary syntactic category of adverb is problematic. There are lexical signs such as THEN, which are used to modify predicates, and intensifiers like VERY, which modify adjectives. However, as we saw in Chapter 5, verbal signs may also be modified by changes in their articulation, for example by speed and iteration. They may also be modified by non-manual features produced during the sign, as with the feature 'mm' described in Chapter 5, which provides the adverbial information that the action occurred 'in the normal way' or 'normally'. Thus these various forms share the same type of function but do not make up a discrete formal class.

7.2 The building blocks of syntax: nouns, verbs and other categories

7.2.1 Noun phrases

Noun phrases are the syntactic units that can act as arguments of a verb to form a sentence. At their simplest they consist of a single item, which may be a name, noun or pronoun. Of these three types, nouns may combine with other elements like determiners and adjectives to form complex noun phrases. We look at each type of nominal in turn.

7.2.1.1 Names

Members of the Irish Deaf community use name signs as personal names. These are distinct from official names, recorded in English and Irish. Given their longevity and generality amongst the community, name signs are unlike nicknames in the surrounding spoken language communities. As has been noted for name signs in American Sign Language, names in ISL can be categorised into different types, including initialised sign-names and sign-names associated with the physical characteristics, personality or actions of a person. If we look at the first type, many Irish signers have sign names that take the initials of their first name and surname and combine them with the mouthed English name. In some instances only their first name is used, while in other instances both first and surname are used. This may involve the simultaneous production of both elements, so for example if someone were called Kevin Smith, he might have a sign-name where the dominant hand articulates a K-handshape against a non-dominant hand that takes an S-handshape. Typically such signs involve a repeated movement. In other instances, both initials may be articulated only on the dominant hand. For example, someone called Peter O'Malley might have a sign-name that sees the dominant hand articulate a transition from P to M, or indeed, this might result in a fingersigned P-O-M. In other cases, only the initial of the first name along with the mouthed English name (either first name only or both name and surname) may be used. Thus someone called Patricia O'Reilly might have a sign-name that is a P-handshape that has a movement attached to it. Other sign-names are initialised but articulated on the body. Frequently used parts of the body for sign-names include the non-dominant arm, the cheek and the side of the head.

Another group of sign-names take a physical characteristic of the signer, sometimes originating in childhood, that typically becomes the signer's name-sign for life. Examples from ISL include PIG-TAILS (for a woman who wore her hair in pigtails as a child), HAIR-QUIFF (for a man who wears his hair in a quiff), BALD-HEAD, RED-CHEEKS, BUSHY-BEARD, GOATEE-BEARD, LONG-HAIR, CURLY-HAIR, FLAT-NOSE, WEARS-GLASSES and WEARS-SEVERAL-EARRINGS. Other name groups reflect perceptions of the signer's personality, such as the sign-names PATIENT and SWEET; or something that they characteristically do, like RUB-JAW, WEAR-OVER-EAR-HEARING-AID, DANCES, PLAY-PIANO or PUSH-GLASSES-UP-NOSE (Supalla 1992; Wilcox et al. 2003). For some signers – and anecdotally, this seems to be truer for younger signers than older signers – it is possible that they may know another Deaf person's sign name but not their English name. What is important to note is that signers do not select their own sign-names: they are given sign-names by the community, and typically have the opportunity to reject a proposed sign-name before an agreed sign is adopted. Given this, it is very rare that someone changes their sign-name, even when it may refer back to a characteristic of their childhood experience, for example someone who is now bald will still carry the sign-name CURLY-HAIR, and someone who now uses a digital hearing aid may be known as WEARS-BODY-RADIO-AID.

There are some similarities in the categories of names for places. Some places have lexicalised signs such as DUBLIN, BELFAST, KERRY, MONAGHAN and DONEGAL. While none of the former signs have any initialised element associated with them, other lexical signs do: an example is the K-handshape articulated at the ipsilateral chest area, which, depending on which mouthed element it co-occurs with, can mean either Kildare or Kells. Yet others are based (at least partially) in calques, for example WATER-F 'Waterford', LONG-F 'Longford' and rather amusingly, BALLS-BRIDGE 'Ballsbridge' for the Dublin suburb. Other place names may have originally been fingerspelled in full, but over time, phonological deletion rules have applied and today a reduced number of letters are articulated, and this, together with an identifiable movement pattern, suggest that the formerly fingerspelled items have lexicalised to a greater or lesser degree. As we saw in Chapter 6, examples include C-O-R-K ('Cork'), T-I-P-P ('Tipperary'), L-K ('Limerick') and G-W-Y ('Galway'). We also saw in Chapter 6 how cued speech, which attempts to provide visual access to the phonemes of spoken languages, has occasionally been used in word formation among some cohorts of graduates from St Mary's School for Deaf Girls. An example is the use of the little finger at the lips to represent 'k' sounds. This gesture has stabilised to mean CORK and is used by some female signers.

7.2.1.2 Nouns

Common nouns denote classes of items, as we have seen in many examples in this book, such as MAN, CAR and CINEMA. We looked at some aspects of the morphology of nouns in Chapter 5: we saw, for example that some nouns may be pluralised by reduplication. Nouns may combine with determiners, which help hearers identify the intended referent by giving specific information to distinguish entities in the context, such THIS and THAT; quantity, such as LOT (many); or possession relations, such MY and YOUR. The manual form of THIS and THAT is identical with an INDEX-handshape pointing into the neutral space ahead of the signer. In Example 7.1(a), the signer signs THIS YEAR, situating the relative proximity of the intended win in basketball on the mixed timeline. In (b) the signer is referring to another point in time when she went to Belfast.

Example 7.1

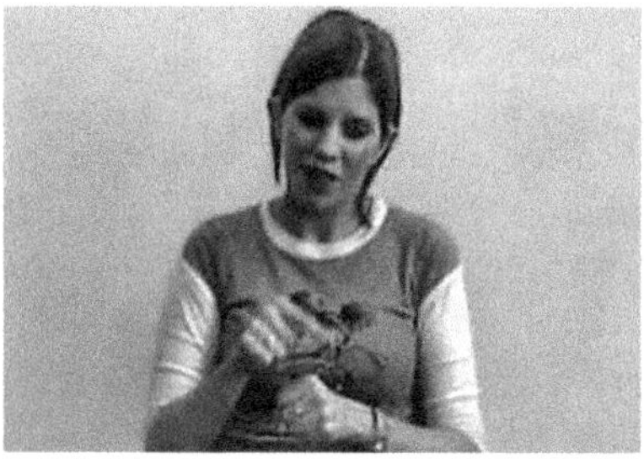

(a) THIS
Caroline (15) Personal Stories (Dublin)

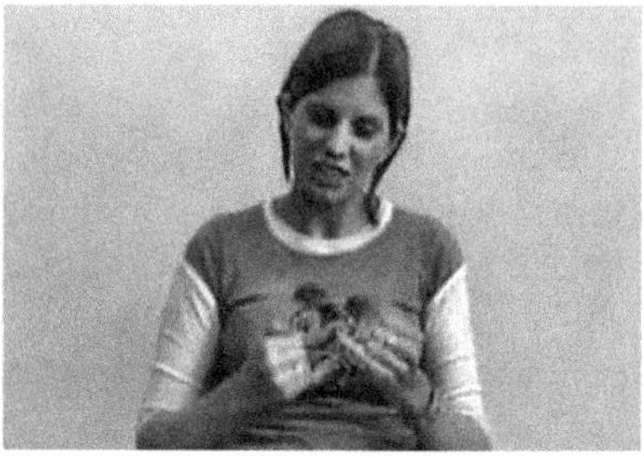

(a) YEAR (Atypical Handshape)
Caroline (15) Personal Stories (Dublin)

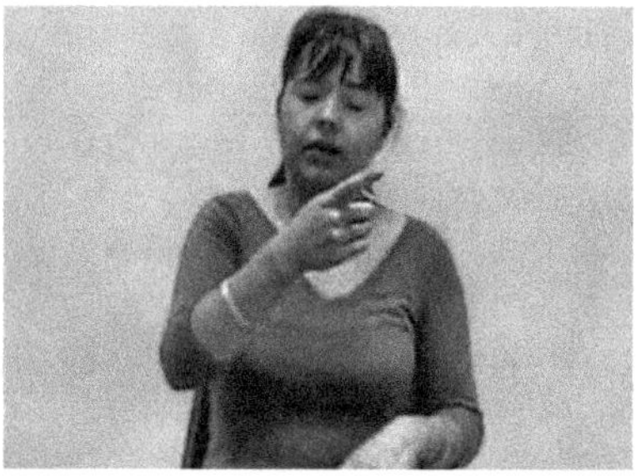

(b) THAT
Lianne (14) Personal Stories (Dublin)

(b) TIME
Lianne (14) Personal Stories (Dublin)

Nouns may also be modified by adjectives, such as BIG, SMALL, NEW, OLD and SMALL, and by colour terms, with the adjective typically occurring pre-nominally as in Example 7.2.

Example 7.2

(a) THINK BIG HEAD
'(I) thought (he was) big headed'
(Laurence (19) Personal Stories (Dublin))

(b) MEAN BIG LADDER
'meant the big ladder'
(Michelle (05) Personal Stories (Dublin))

(c) BIG CELEBRATION
'big celebration'
(Bernie (02) Personal Stories (Dublin))

(d) STOP RED TRAFFIC-LIGHT
'(He) stopped at the red traffic light'
(Fiona (36) Personal Stories (Waterford))

(e) SMALL HANDBAG
'(It was a) small handbag'
(Marian (16) Personal Stories (Dublin))

(f) SMALL GIRL
'a little girl'
(Helen (27) Personal Stories (Wexford))

(g) SMALL BOY
'a little boy'
(Sean Frog Story (Dublin))

(h) OLD WOMAN
'a (nosey) old woman'
(Valerie (12) Personal Stories (Dublin))

(i) OLD FASHION
'old fashioned'
(Annie (26) Personal Stories (Wexford))

All of the examples in 7.2 illustrate the general tendency for adjectives to precede nouns in ISL. There are occasions where the noun comes before the adjective, but while we might normally expect these instances to arise in topic-marked clauses, there is no evidence of non-manual marking for topic for TREE-IN-BRANCHES in Example 7.3. This suggests that in ISL, signers have the option of producing adjectives pre- or post-nominally, but that the typical case is for adjectives to come before the noun. Interestingly, only adjectives quantifying size (BIG and SMALL) were found in post-nominal position, as in Examples 7.3 and 7.4.

Example 7.3

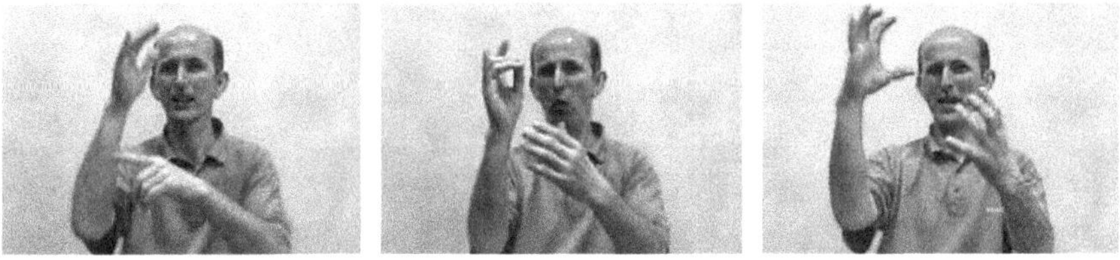

(a) (SEE TREE) IN-BRANCHES h.o.l.e. BIG
The boy saw a tree, and in the branches of the tree there was a big hole'
Fergus D. (Dublin) Frog Story

Example 7.4

(a) BUY SELF OWN SHOVEL SMALL-ONE
'You had to buy your own small shovel'
(Kevin (17) Personal Stories (Dublin))

(b) WHEN JASON SMALL
'When Jason was small'
(Catherine (31) Personal Stories (Cork))

(c) TWO MAN SMALL SLIM
'Two men, (both of whom were) small and slim'
(Michael (34) Personal Stories (Galway))

When quantifiers and numerals are used as determiners the noun is not normally pluralised, for example ALL BOY 'all (the) boys', or, as in (c) above, TWO MAN (the two men).

As shown in many examples in this book, ISL, like some spoken languages such as Japanese or Russian, does not routinely employ articles, such as English *a* and *the*, although some signers do use a lexical sign THE as in Example 7.5. This is not used in any way approaching the frequency of English: indeed, there is only one instance of THE in the annotated section of the SOI corpus. These words in English signal the accessibility of referents in the discourse, for example distinguishing between a first mention and subsequent references to the same entity. In Chapter 8 we discuss some ISL strategies to achieve similar discourse goals.

Example 7.5

IN THE KITCHEN
Peter (18) Personal Stories (Dublin)

7.2.1.3 Pronouns

Pronouns function in ISL quite differently from spoken languages because they map referents to locations. It is useful to make a distinction between the deictic and anaphoric uses of pronouns. The deictic use relies on the physical presence of the referent in the context of communication. Deictic pronouns are formed with pointing signs: the direction of pointing allows three-fold distinction between signer, addressee and others, each identified by their real-world location. We can gloss these as INDEX+c (first person reference), INDEX+f (YOU/HE/SHE – as determined by context or previously established locus at that point in space).

Example 7.6

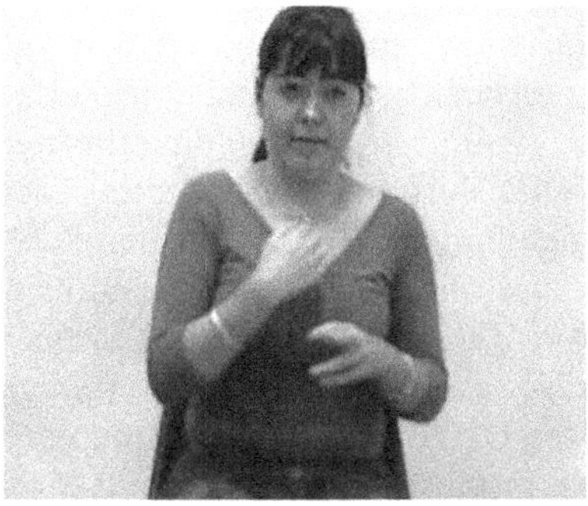

(a) INDEX+c BEGIN DECIDE GO-OFF BELFAST* INDEX+fl INDEX+c* FOR* SHOPPING*
'I began by deciding to go to Belfast to do some shopping'
Lianne (14) Personal Stories (Dublin)

(b) INDEX+f (you)
Michelle (Dublin) Frog Story

(c) INDEX+f (HE/HIM/SHE/HER/IT)
Louise (35) Personal Stories (Galway)

It is important to note that the forms in Examples 7.6(b) and (c) are identical in form, and the means of identifying the intended referent lies with understanding how the signers have conceptualised their signing space, where they have established referents in that space and how they have tracked movement of referents across the signing space, including through the use of surrogates (also known as reference shifting or 'role shifting' devices). We will discuss some of these strategies in more detail in Chapter 8.

In addition to the use of INDEX as a pronominal referential device, it is worth noting that in ISL, there are lexical forms for HE, SHE, THEY and WE which are also used by some signers, though these are used much less frequently than the INDEX form. For example, in the Signs of Ireland corpus, there are eight instances of the lexicalised form of HE, two instances of SHE (both by the same signer), nine instances of THEY and five instances of lexicalised WE in a total of more than 46,000 glossed tokens (see Example 7.7). In contrast, there are 1,527 instances of INDEX (INDEX+c, INDEX+f, INDEX+sl, etc.) across the corpus, suggesting that the most frequent means of indicating pronominal relationships is via use of indexical forms, mapped onto signing space. Further research to explore the relative distribution of such forms in context would add to our understanding of how emphasis may be marked through choice of lexicalised pronominal forms over indexical forms.

Example 7.7

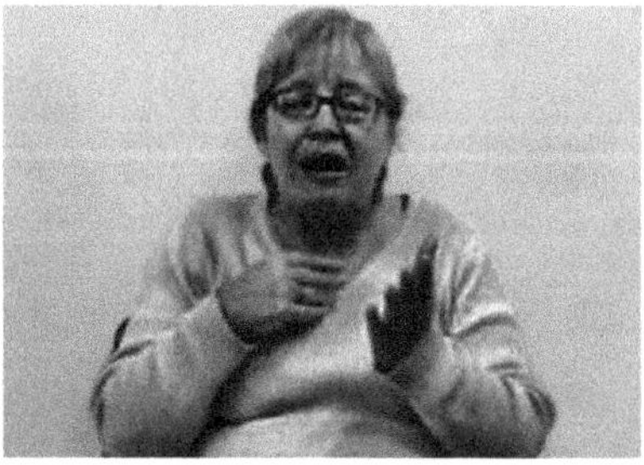

(a) WE (Lexical)
Mary (33) Personal Stories (Galway)

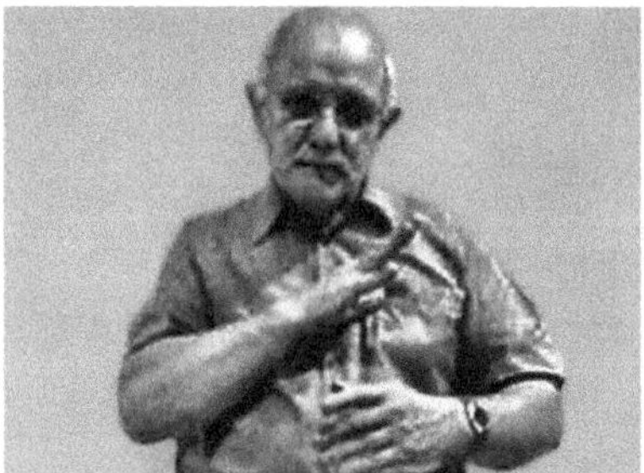

(b) HE (Lexical) (Onset)
Fergus M. (07) Personal Stories (Dublin)

(c) HE (Lexical) (Offset)
Fergus M. (07) Personal Stories (Dublin)

(d) SHE (Lexical) (Onset)
Alice (29) Personal Stories (Cork)

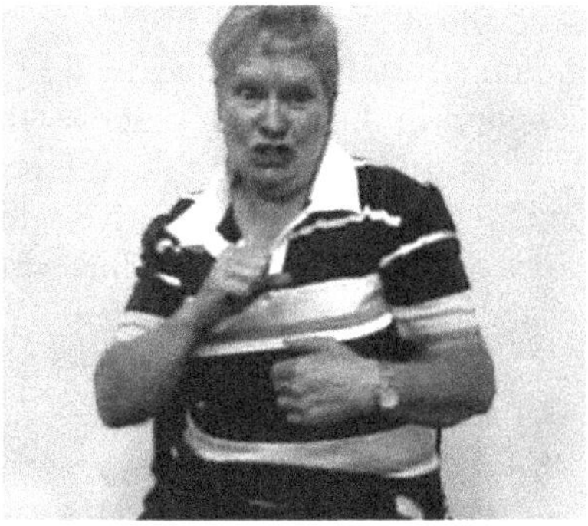

(e) SHE (Lexical) (Offset)
Alice (29) Personal Stories (Cork)

Plural non-first person forms are formed by moving the pointing sign though a horizontal arc in the direction of the referents, as in Example 7.8.

Example 7.8

(a) HE OFTEN TELL-ALL
'He often told everyone'
(Fergus M. (07) Personal Stories (Dublin))

(b) ALL-OF-THEM FUNNY
'All of them thought it was funny'
(Mary (30) Personal Stories (Cork))

An inclusive first person plural pronoun WE/US is formed by a downward-pointing sign moved in an arc or circular motion between the signer and addressee(s). We note that where number is specified (for example, TWO-OF-US, THREE-OF-US or FOUR-OF-US), then the INDEX-handshape is replaced by a numerical handshape but the arced or circular motion is maintained, as in Example 7.9.

Example 7.9

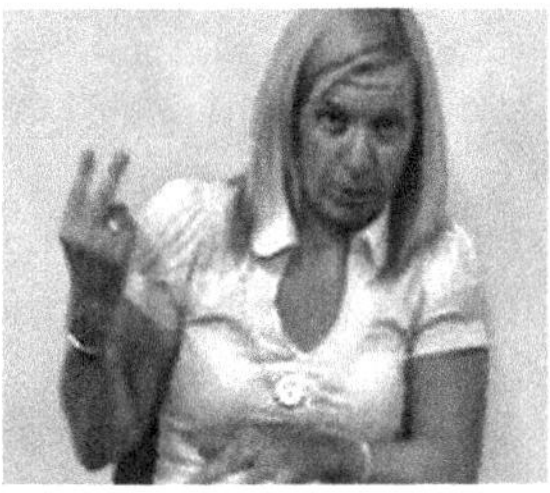

(a) TWO-OF-US (onset)
Rebecca (38) Personal Stories (Cork)

(b) two-of-us (offset)

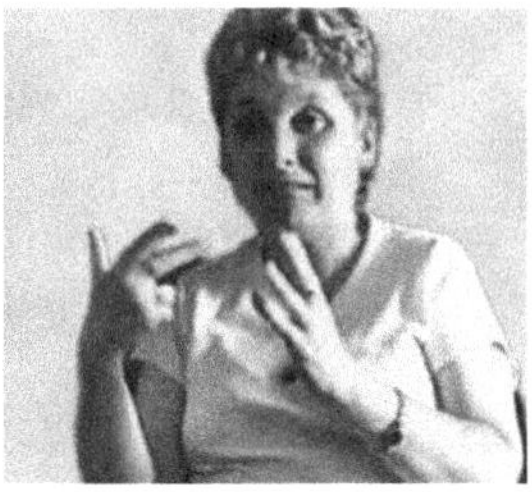

(c) THREE-OF-US
Margaret (21) Personal Stories (Wexford)

The anaphoric use of pronouns is dependent on the prior establishment of nominal referents. Typically a nominal is introduced and associated with a location in the signing space by the use of a deictic determiner. Thereafter a pointing sign directed to that location acts as a pronominal reference to that entity. The occurrence of these deictic pronouns interacts with the morphological class of the verb. Thus with plain verbs they may be the only marker of the arguments, as in Example 7.10.

Example 7.10

INDEX+fr KNOW INDEX+f+lo WAS INDEX+f ENGINE
'He (the mechanic) knew that the problem (with the car) was engine related'
(Fergus (06) Personal Stories (Dublin))

In Example 7.10, the signer has established his friend, a mechanic at +fr in signing space. His car, which is giving him trouble is at +f+lo. Here, the signer layers information associated with the car so that the +f+lo locus is co-referential for the car, the car's bonnet and all parts of the engine.

In person agreement verbs information about the arguments, for example actor and undergoer, is incorporated into the articulation of the sign itself, as we saw in Chapter 5, and independent pronouns are less common. However, while in principle it is possible for independent pronouns to co-occur with morphological agreement markers for emphasis, this does not seem to be a commonly occurring feature.

7.2.2 Verbs

We saw in Chapter 5 a number of different morphological classes of verb. In syntax, we distinguish between main verbs, which combine with nouns to form sentences, and auxiliary verbs, which combine with verbs and therefore are not independent. ISL auxiliary verbs convey distinctions of tense, modality and aspect and include CAN, FINISH, MUST, NEED, SHOULD and WILL. Auxiliary verbs occur before the main verb, as in Examples 7.11 and 7.12.

Example 7.11

(a) DAUGHTER SAID WILL BACK HOME CL:L (ISL)+sl+fl ('Sometime-after') IN *JUNE
'(My) daughter said that she would be home at some point in June'
(Peter (18) Personal Stories (Dublin))

(b) KNOW FUTURE TWO ZERO SIX WILL SET-UP f+CAMERA+c gesture 2xCL5 palms-up
'I know that in future, in 2006, we will be able to use video-based (interpreting services)'
(Annie (26) Personal Stories (Wexford))

Example 7.12

(a) INDEX+c LOVE IT BECAUSE CAN SIGN
'I love it because I can sign (there)'
(Noeleen (03) Personal Stories (Dublin))

(b) CAN+++
'(He really) can (do it)'
(Fergus (06) Personal Stories (Dublin))

(c) . . . FEEL SHOULD NOT WAR . . .
'. . . felt that there should not be a war . . .'
(Senan (01) Personal Stories (Dublin))

(d) NEXT TIME PREPARE MUST MAKE SURE TAKE-NOTES DETAIL LIKE WALL NAME WALL NAME PLASTER . . .
'Next time, in preparation, (I) must make sure to take note of things like what kind of a wall is involved, what kind of plaster is used . . .'
(Annie (26) Personal Stories (Wexford))

Some morphological classes of main verb were discussed in Chapter 5, where we saw that main verbs may be intransitive (LAUGH), transitive (IGNORE) or ditransitive (GIVE). We also saw that the mode of marking arguments differs across types. So agreement verbs carry inflectional marking of arguments while plain verbs do not.

7.2.3 Adjectives and adverbs

As noted above, certain lexical signs may function as either adjectives or adverbs. Adjectives may occur as predicates in ISL, without a linking or copula verb, as in Example 7.13.

Example 7.13

(a) SHE ALWAYS HAPPY WITH ME
'She is always happy with me'
(Alice (29) Personal Stories (Cork))

(b) EVENING COLD+
'The evening was very cold'
(Patrick (33) Personal Stories (Wexford))

As described in Chapter 5, and shown in Example 7.13(b), adjectives and adverbs can be modulated in their articulation to convey graded distinctions of manner, intensity and other qualities, such as size.

7.2.4 Prepositions

ISL generally draws on the capacity to utilise signing space to represent locations and spatial relations in the real world, such as are marked in English by prepositions like *on*, *under*, *in*, *over* or *beside*. That said, ISL also has lexical items that are also used in lieu of or in addition to spatially represented locative relationships. In a study focused on cross-linguistic analysis of data, Johnston et. al (2007) analysed locative utterances (and reversible and non-reversible utterances) in three signed languages (Auslan, Flemish Sign Language and ISL). For ISL, they report that eight of the twelve locative examples analysed made use of a lexical preposition like ON and UNDER in the verb slot (for example, CAT ON CHAIR or Argument 1 PREP Argument 2). In some responses the use of a preposition was clearly influenced by English grammar (for example, TABLE WITH BALL UNDER i.t.). Ten of the ISL locative responses consisted of at least two clauses or more. In nine of these, the subsequent clause(s) involved a simultaneous construction. Forty-five per cent of the responses for locative situations in the ISL data set included simultaneous constructions, with only one respondent not making use of any simultaneous constructions to mark out locative relationships. Looking at the SOI corpus, we can say that simultaneous constructions are the most typical means of marking out locative relationships with a small number of lexical prepositions used. For example, while ON is used as a preposition in Example 7.14(a), in the corpus it is more typically used in phrasal constructions like GO ON and ENGINE ON. The same applies to UNDER, with non-locative uses of UNDER found in phrases like YEAR UNDER FULBRIGHT ('spent a year funded under the Fulbright programme'). Example 7.14 illustrates some uses of lexical prepositions in ISL while Example 7.15 provides some examples of simultaneous encoding of prepositional relationships via use of classifier constructions to represent the relative location of the positioned entity vis-à-vis a landmark. In Example 7.15(a) the frog is positioned relative to the glass jar holding him (he is contained within it). In (b), the location for 'under the jumper' is discernable only with respect to the position that the classifier handshape representing the sweater takes, while in (c) the boy's position is situated with respect to the landmark of 'the stag'.

Example 7.14

(a) WALK ON COURT
'walk onto the (basketball) court'
(Caroline (15) Personal Stories (Dublin))

(b) LOT UNDER TREE
'[a lot of baby frogs] under the tree'
(Fergus D. (06) Frog Story (Dublin))

(c) AT LAST FIND UNDER CLOTHES
'At last, [I] found it under some clothes'
(Catherine (31) Personal Stories (Cork))

(d) INDEX+c WORK BESIDE WINDOW
'I work beside a window'
(Peter (18) Personal Stories (Dublin))

(e) SIDE PARENTS HOME
'At the side of [my] parents' home'
(Fiona (36) Personal Stories (Waterford))

Example 7.15

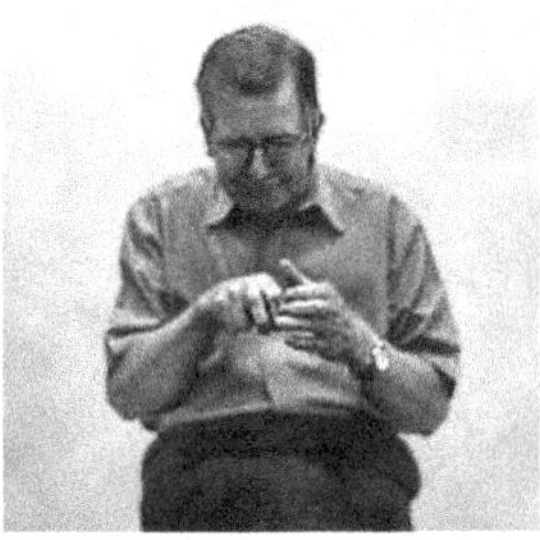

(a) FROG-MOVE-AROUND-IN-JAR The frog moved about in the jar'
Kevin (Dublin) Frog Story

(b) UNDER-THE-TOP '(He thought the frog was) under/ in the jumper'
Marian (Dublin) Frog Story

(c) BOY CAUGHT-ON-STAG'S ANTLER 'The boy was caught on the stag's antler'
Fiona (Waterford) Frog Story

7.3 Sentence types: statements, questions and imperatives

We can identify the default or basic sentence type in ISL as declarative, used to make statements, since this type can be described in terms of the absence of the required and overt markers of other sentence types. So, for example, the main markers of interrogative sentences, used to make questions, are non-manual features, especially movements of the signer's head and body, that are absent in declarative sentences. One basic type is polar questions, which are requests for confirmation or denial of a proposition and hence often called yes–no questions. This sentence type in ISL is marked by the non-manual features of raised eyebrows, widened eyes and the head tilted forward, as in Example 7.16.

Example 7.16

________________________________br
YOU AWAY HOLIDAYS SUMMER YOU
'Are you going to go away during the summer holidays?'
(Leeson 2001: 23)

A declarative version of this sentence, that is 'You're going to go away during the summer holidays', would include the same lexical signs but without the brows raised. In such a declarative a head-nod may co-occur with the manual signs.

A further sentence type is content questions, which can be seen as a request for information missing from, or needed to complete, a proposition. Since in English the type of information required is identified by question words beginning with *wh*, for example *who*, *where*, *why*, these are sometimes called WH-questions in the English grammatical literature. ISL too has question words that are signed manually; some of these are shown in Example 7.17. These signs are accompanied by non-manual features, which typically (but not always) include a forward tilt of the head, together with a lowering of the eyebrows and, in some cases, a narrowing of the eyes.

Example 7.17

(a) WHAT
Derek (28) Personal Stories (Cork)

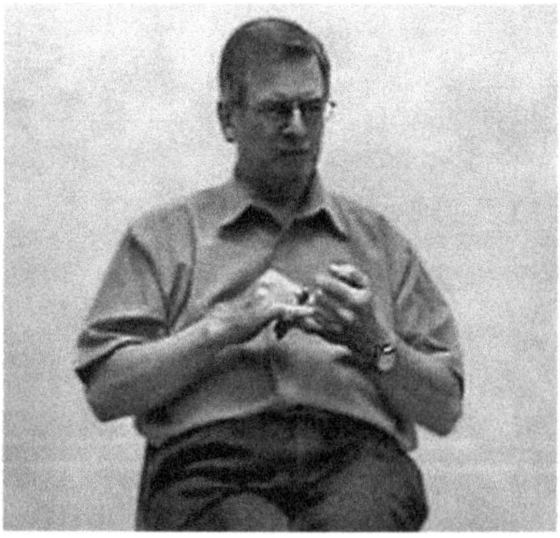

(b) WHO
Kevin (17) Personal Stories (Dublin)

(c) WHERE (onset)
Louise (35) Personal Stories (Galway)

WHERE (offset)
Louise (35) Personal Stories (Galway)

(d) WHEN
Fergus D. (06) Personal Stories (Dublin)

A third major sentence type is the imperative, typically used to give commands or make requests or strong suggestions. In ISL, lexical items like MUST and HAVE-TO frequently occur in such contexts as in Example 7.18.

Example 7.18

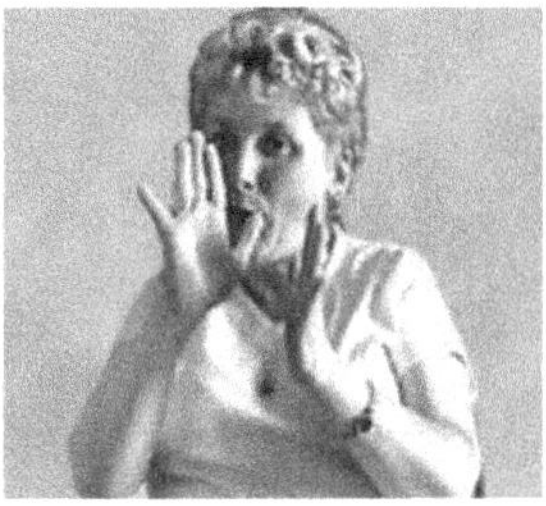

(a) INDEX+c **MUST** TOGETHER DEAF
'(My mother said that) I must stay with the (other) Deaf (people)'
Margaret (21) Personal Stories (Wexford)

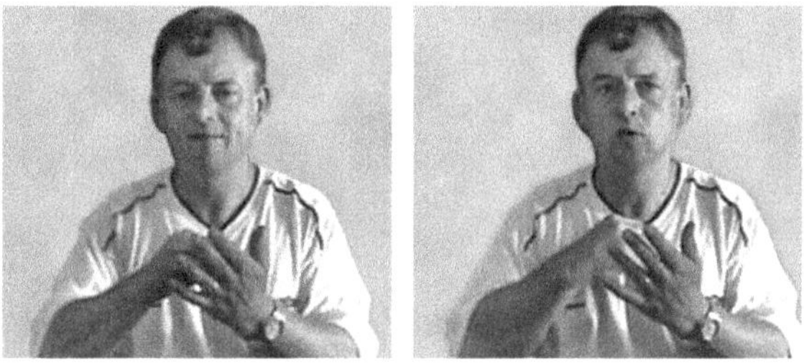

(b) HAVE-TO TELEPHONE ENGLAND+f+hi FOR INSURANCE
'(The Police said that I) had to phone England regarding my insurance'
Nicholas (22) Personal Stories (Dublin)

7.4 Negation

Sentences may be negated in two ways: by inserting a negative word, such as NOT, NEVER or NOTHING; or by the simultaneous use of a non-manual sign through the clause. The non-manual sign is a headshake, or side-to-side movement of the head. We can see these two strategies for negating a statement in Examples 7.19 and 7.20.

Example 7.19

(a) IF NOTHING LET INSPECTOR EXAMINE . . .
'If they don't let the (UN) inspector carry out his examination . . .'
(Senan (01) Personal Stories (Dublin))

(b) DON'T-WANT PLAY
'. . . but [the dog] didn't want to play'
(Louise (35) Personal Stories (Galway))

(c) INDEX+c NEVER THINK
'I never thought . . .'
(Annie (26) Personal Stories (Wexford))

(d) INDEX+c CANNOT STOP THINK++
'I cannot stop thinking [about it]'
(Rebecca (38) Personal Stories (Waterford))

(e) DISAPPOINT NOT FINISH
'[I was] disappointed [that it] was not finished'
(Fergus (06) Personal Stories (Dublin))

(f) INDEX+c WILL-NOT DRINK
'[The dog] would not drink'
(Eilish (10) Personal Stories (Dublin))

Example 7.20

(a) headshake
EXPLAIN DEAF
'I tried to explain to those Deaf people, but they wouldn't accept what I said'
(Geraldine (20) Personal Stories (Dublin))

(b) headshake
LATER-ON THANK PARENT DECIDE* MOVE-OUT BECAUSE INDEX+sl FATHER RETIRE
'Later on, thankfully, my parents had decided to move not because of that (previously discussed incident) but because my father retired'
(Geraldine (20) Personal Stories (Dublin))

(c) headshake
INDEX+c WATCH MAKE INDEX+c
'I didn't want to be a watch maker'
(Fergus M. (07) Personal Stories (Dublin))

In Example 7.20(a) above, we see a negative headshake marking a response from a non-first party interlocutor (other Deaf people) without any lexicalised element being produced. Here, the non-manual negation is the negative utterance, providing meaning of 'they didn't accept what I said'. In contrast, in (b), the same signer negates the lexical items MOVE-OUT BECAUSE with a negative headshake, changing the potential meaning from 'My parents moved because of that . . .' to 'My parents decided to move but not because of that . . .'. In (c), the signer presents a wholly declarative sentence which he negates only by non-manual means, with the headshake occurring towards the offset of the sentence final INDEX+c, giving some overlap to this lexical component, but serving to influence the scope of the sentence. Questions may be negated in the same way, for example negative polar questions can combine the non-manual features for a question and for negation.

7.5 Time in the sentence

As noted in Chapter 5, tense is not marked morphologically on ISL verbs. Time references are given by a range of strategies at the sentence level, with the main verb uninflected. One strategy is to include time adverbials such as NOW, TOMORROW and YESTERDAY, as in Example 7.21.

Example 7.21

(a) . . . NOW WANDER-ROUND . . .
'. . . and then I wandered round . . .'
(Lianne (14) Personal Stories (Dublin))

(b) NOW LIVE WATERFORD
'Now I live in Waterford'
(Fiona (36) Personal Stories (Waterford))

(c) TOMORROW MORNING WAKE-UP GET-OUT-OF-BED
'The next day, he awoke and got out of bed'
(Fergus D. (06) Frog Story (Dublin))

(d) TOMORROW MORNING MY BROTHER (SIGN NAME) DEAF INDEX+f (SIGN NAME) BEFORE GO-OFF JOB EAT SEE D HAVE TWO OTHER (gesture) *DOG EAT
'The next morning, my brother, (name), who is deaf, before he went to work, he checked that the other dogs (we had two other dogs) had eaten'
(Louise (35) Personal Stories (Galway))

(e) NIGHT THROUGH INDEX+fl IN-BED-TOGETHER SLEEP TOMORROW MORNING NIGHT INDEX+fl FROG FROG-CLIMB-OUT-OF-JAR-AND-RUN-AWAY DISAPPEAR BOY AND *DOG TOMORROW MORNING WAKE-UP GET-OUT-OF-BED . . .
'During the night, while the boy and dog slept together, the frog crept out of the jar and ran away. The next morning, the boy and the dog woke up and got out of bed . . .'
(Fergus D. (06) Frog Story (Dublin))

Time references may be deictic, relating to the immediate context, or anaphoric, parasitic on an earlier specification of a time reference. In the contextualised version of Example 7.21(b), reproduced here as 7.21(f), the signer sets the time as 'a long time ago' in the first clause and then uses a pointing sign anaphorically in the second clause to refer back to that time. The adverbial NOW in the third clause operates deictically: picking up the time specification from the context of the act of narration.

Example 7.21(f)

PAST PAST HAVE FUNNY STORY TOPIC SMALL INDEX+c TIME LIVE DUBLIN INDEX+c NOW LIVE WATERFORD

'I have a funny, short story from a long time ago. At the time I was living in Dublin. Now I live in Waterford'

(Fiona (36) Personal Stories (Waterford))

A second strategy employs zones of the signing space that conventionally express time distinctions. Points in time may be mapped onto locations on time lines (Brennan 1983) around the signer's body, where the past is conceptualised as a line extending backwards from the signer's dominant shoulder while the future extends forward. The general past tense sign BEFORE, which carries the meaning 'in the past', is shown in Example 7.22.

Example 7.22

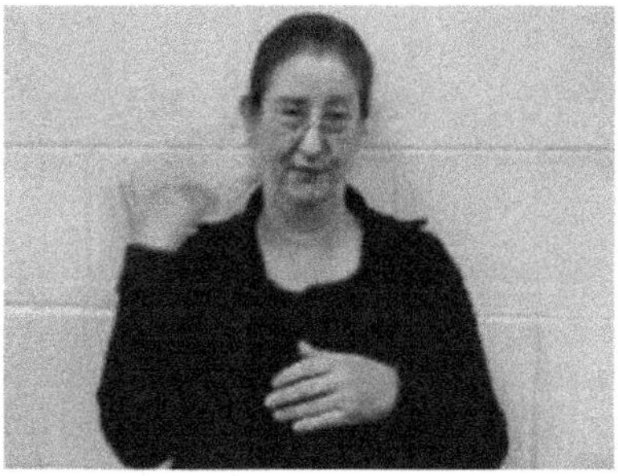

BEFORE (past)
Linda (40) Personal Stories (Waterford)

Deictic distinctions about relative distance in the past, for example, may be made by indicating distance on the time line. That is, a relationship holds where physical distance equals relative temporal distance. However, articulatory constraints operate to make it impossible physically to produce signs that are longer than arm's length into the signing space in front of the signer. Similarly, as Example 7.23 demonstrates, when discussing the distant past it is not possible physically to move the arm very far beyond the signer's head. Instead, signers tend to tilt their bodies forward when indicating future events and lean backwards when establishing time frames that have a 'past-tense' reading. We see this in Example 7.23, where the signer is leaning backwards, and further, has squinted eyes, which serve to reinforce the temporal distance under discussion.

Example 7.23

LONG-TIME-AGO
Senan (01) Personal Stories (Dublin)

This conceptualisation of time as location in space is lexicalised in time words which incorporate movement forward like TOMORROW or FUTURE; or backwards like YESTERDAY as illustrated in Example 7.24. The modal verb WILL is another example of a sign where a forward movement functions as a metaphor for future time. The forward movement of the sign is sometimes accompanied by a forward lean of the signer's torso, as can be seen in Example 7.24(a).

Example 7.24

(a) TOMORROW (onset)
Louise (35) Personal Stories (Galway)

(b) TOMORROW (offset)
Louise (35) Personal Stories (Galway)

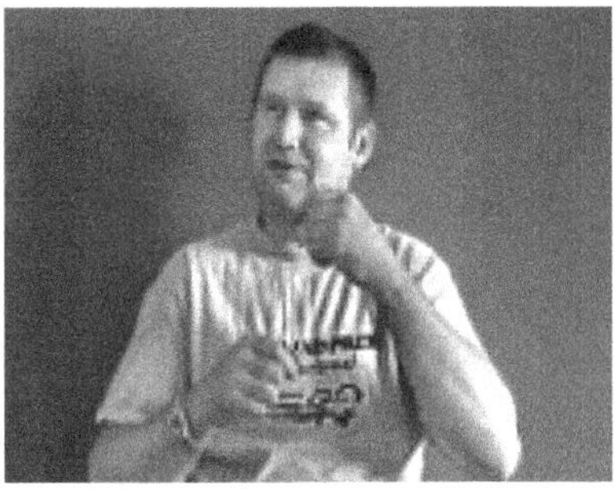

(c) YESTERDAY (onset)
James (23) Personal Stories (Wexford)

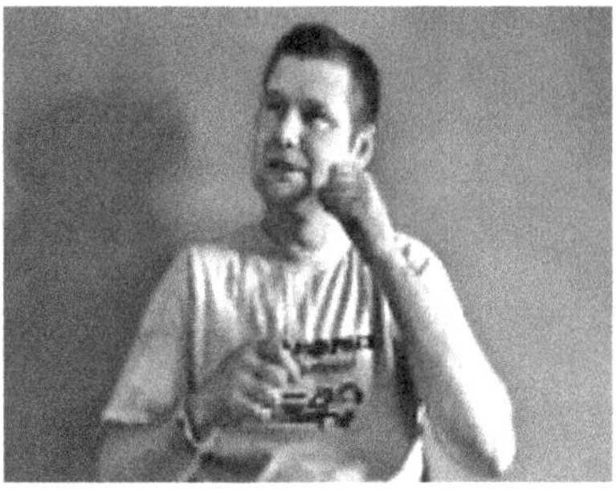

(d) YESTERDAY (offset)
James (23) Personal Stories (Wexford)

(e) **FUTURE**
Annie (26) Personal Stories (Wexford)

(f) **WILL**
Peter (18) Personal Stories (Dublin)

7.6 Constituent order and simultaneity

Word order in ISL is determined by the interaction of a number of interlocking principles. Two of the most important are a topic-comment structure at the level of information structure and a subject-verb-object order at the level of grammar. These two principles may coincide to produce the same order since, as in many languages, the selection of topics and of subjects is influenced by similar principles of animacy, empathy and viewpoint. As when discussing agreement morphology in Chapter 5, it is useful when discussing word order to distinguish between types of verb, for example between person and location agreement verbs. In the former, the verbal arguments represent the range of semantic roles that may be grouped into the two macro-roles of actor and undergoer (Dowty 1991; Foley and Van Valin 1984). Typically the actor role includes the roles of agent and experiencer; while the undergoer role includes patient, recipient and stimulus. The default mapping between semantic and grammatical roles in ISL transitive clauses is for the actor role to be subject and the undergoer role to be object. This is realised in the basic order of subject-verb-object, as in Example 7.25.

Example 7.25

(a) YOUNG GIRL HUG GRANDMOTHER
'The little girl hugs grandmother'
(ISL elicited sentence 14)
(Leeson 2001: 86)

(b) GIRL WATCH TV
'The girl watches TV'
(Leeson 2001: 160)

As discussed in Chapter 2, the use of two signing hands means that simultaneous constructions are employed in a range of contexts. This process means that information about constituents can be distributed across the signed sentence. For instance, in Example 7.26, the object nominal 'string' is introduced before the verb and recapped by a classifier handshape during the articulation of the verb. In an example like this, linear order is only part of the syntactic construction.

Example 7.26

GIRL WOMAN STRING s.t.r.i.n.g. d **CUT-WITH-SCISSORS**
nd CL.G. string_________

'The woman cut the string'
(Leeson 2001: 88)

In location verbs the verbal arguments represent a different range of semantic roles, including source, path, goal and the moving item which is variously called theme or figure (Foley and Van Valin 1984; Talmy 1985, 1988). Here one typical mapping between semantic and grammatical roles is for the theme role to be subject and the goal role to be object, once again giving a basic order of subject-verb-object as in Example 7.27.

Example 7.27

DRIVE+f HOME+f
'(I) drove home'
Fergus D. (06) Personal Stories (Dublin)

These basic orders are flexible and may be altered by a range of discourse-based processes, as in Example 7.28 where a goal argument, SHOP, occurs first because the signer has for discourse reasons identified it as a topic.

Example 7.28

SHOP (-sl) MAN V-CL+(c+MOVE+sl+fingers move)
'The man walked to the shop'
(Leeson 2001: 89)

Topics are marked by non-manual features. The main features arising in prototypical topic marking are a slight head tilt back, raised eyebrows during the articulation of the topic sign, followed by a head nod. However, these non-manual features do not appear in all instances and it seems that it is male signers that are more likely to mark topics in this way (Leeson 2001; Leeson and Grehan 2004). It is also possible for the topic to be followed by a slight pause (Leeson 2001; Leeson and Grehan 2004). Topics may be any argument of the verb or an adjunct external to the main predication, as shown in Example 7.29.

Example 7.29

(a)

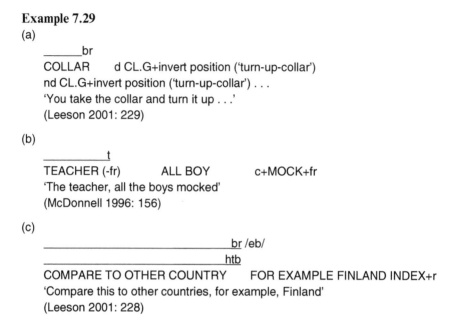

______br
COLLAR d CL.G+invert position ('turn-up-collar')
nd CL.G+invert position ('turn-up-collar') . . .
'You take the collar and turn it up . . .'
(Leeson 2001: 229)

(b)

__________t
TEACHER (-fr) ALL BOY c+MOCK+fr
'The teacher, all the boys mocked'
(McDonnell 1996: 156)

(c)

________________________________br /eb/
______________________________htb
COMPARE TO OTHER COUNTRY FOR EXAMPLE FINLAND INDEX+r
'Compare this to other countries, for example, Finland'
(Leeson 2001: 228)

The role of topics in discourse is discussed in Chapter 8.

Passive constructions also involve a change in basic word order, along with other features. In the passive sentence in Example 7.30, the actor argument is omitted while the undergoer argument occurs in initial position. The foregrounded undergoer is co-referential with the signer's locus (the 'c-locus'). The signer's averted eyegaze signals lack of volition or co-operation on the part of the undergoer.

Example 7.30

ME BEFORE-BEFORE BEAT-Upc. (eyes averted)
'I was beaten up'
(Leeson 2001: 301)

Simultaneous constructions are particularly common with location verbs, especially where a spatial relationship links two entities. Here a number of factors including animacy, viewpoint and empathy motivate the selection of one entity as more prominent and thus represented on the dominant hand, while the less prominent or backgrounded entity is signed by the non-dominant hand. Often the backgrounded entity is introduced as a topic, before the spatial relationship is depicted. For instance, in Example 7.31, a location, the bridge, is first established by the dominant hand. Thereafter in the portrayal of their interaction, the dynamic entity, the car, is represented on the dominant hand while the more static item, the bridge, is signed on the non-dominant hand.

Example 7.31

ROAD BRIDGE-extend-from-sl-to-sr CAR
d. CL.B-vehicle+go-under-bridge
nd CL.B. (be-located-at-c.+hi.)-bridge
Theme 1/ Location Agent/ Agent-Verb-Location/ Location
'The car goes under the bridge'
(Leeson 2001: 108)

Finally, ISL sentences when connected in discourse are frequently characterised by the omission of contextually available arguments; thus a nominal argument may be introduced and thereafter be understood over a sequence of clauses, especially if the argument occupies the same semantic slot in the clauses, as in Example 7.32.

Example 7.32

sobs
GIRL LOOK NOT HAPPY/ WANT BEAR r/s CL.V.+ LOOK-AT
eyes on rabbit
CL.B EXAMINES RABBIT
'The girl did not seem happy. (She) wanted (her) bear. (She) looked at the rabbit, examining him while crying'
(Leeson 2001: 99–100)

Here a single occurrence of GIRL is the subject of a string of successive verbs: LOOK NOT HAPPY, WANT, LOOK AT and EXAMINE. Simultaneously, information about the girl's action is given by non manual features.

7.7 Complex sentences

7.7.1 Co-ordination

ISL has the lexical connectives AND, OR and BUT, although as we will see in Chapter 8, these linking devices are often replaced in discourse by other strategies, involving simultaneous constructions. When clauses are conjoined by AND there may be omission of repeated elements, for instance in Example 7.33 we can identify three clauses, where the second clause AND WHITE BEAR is interpreted as 'and the white bear was asleep', and the third clause, also elliptical, is simply adjoined in what we can call parataxis.

Example 7.33

LITTLE GIRL ASLEEP/ AND WHITE BEAR/ IN GIRL HOUSE
'A little girl was asleep along with a white bear. (They slept) in the girl's house'
(Leeson 2001: 171)

Parataxis, the juxtaposing of clauses without subordinating one to another or using overt connectives is a common strategy in ISL as in Example 7.34.

Example 7.34

ME ARRIVE+a / JOB gone // SOMEONE sr +GO-TO +a. COMPLETION JOB
'I arrived. The job was gone. Someone went there and got the job'

7.7.2 Clause combining

Clauses can be combined by subordination when a clause appears as the object of a verb in another clause, as in Example 7.35, where INDEX+sr. GROW-UP IN AMERICA is the object of KNOW just as a nominal might be.

Example 7.35

. . . MY FATHER KNOW INDEX+sr. GROW-UP IN AMERICA . . .
'. . . My father knew that he (his grandson) was growing up in America . . .'
(Leeson 2001: 89)

This kind of clausal subordination commonly occurs in spoken languages with verbs of communication, such as English *say*. This is much less common in ISL because, as will be described in Chapter 8, reported talk is commonly depicted using surrogacy, where the signer's body is a surrogate for another character. Here the third person becomes first person and can communicate directly.

Clauses may also be combined by a process of fusion where two clauses share the same argument, for instance in Example 7.36 where the object 'him' of the first verb is the unexpressed subject of the second verb, producing an 'overlapping' argument.

Example 7.36

________ee
FATHER sl+TEACH+**sr** TALK+
'My father taught him (his grandson) to talk'
(Leeson 2001: 97)

ISL has lexical signs that function as subordinating conjunctions like BECAUSE (Example 7.12 earlier), BEFORE and UNLESS. However in many cases the linking relation is implied rather than stated, as in Example 7.37.

Example 7.37

____________________sl
BOY EAT+sl ALL+sl FINISH+sl sl+GO-TO+fr
'When the boy had eaten everything, he went outside', lit. 'The boy ate everything. He went outside'
(McDonnell 1996: 327)

When clauses are combined there may be formal signs of subordination. So, for instance, in Example 7.38, the subject of the subordinate clause 'she' is downgraded by being held on the non-dominant hand, rather than signed by the dominant hand.

Example 7.38

dh: sl+TELL+c GO-HOME
nd: INDEX+sl___________
'(She) told me that she was going home'

A complex ISL construction that consists of a sequence of a question and answer has counterparts in other signed languages, such as Australian Sign Language (Auslan: Johnston and Schembri 2007), that have been identified with spoken language pseudo-clefts, like English *What I've come here for is my money*. This English sentence contains a partition between assumed or presupposed information (*I've come for something*) and new asserted information that is the focus of the sentence (*the something = my money*). An ISL example using a question-answer exchange is given in Example 7.39.

Example 7.39

(a) YOU COME HERE WHAT FOR
'What are you doing here?'

(b) I COME HERE WHAT-FOR I TEACH A CLASS
'What I'm here for is to teach a class'[1]
(Ó Baoill and Matthews 2000: 184–5)

The non-manual features associated with the apparent question part of this construction are raised eyebrows and a backward tilt of the head, together with a slight pause. Since these features resemble the features marking topics, as we shall see below, and also since this construction is not interpreted as a question, it seems reasonable to follow Johnston and Schembri's analysis for Auslan of a complex sentence rather than a sequence of sentences.

7.8 Conclusion

In this chapter we have described some important aspects of ISL sentence structure. While, as we noted, the study of ISL syntax remains at a preliminary phase, we have outlined the main syntactic categories and seem something of how phrases and clauses may be combined. We looked at how negation is marked and how pronominal and temporal references are signalled in sentences. It is clear that constituent order is significant both for signalling the default mappings between semantic arguments and syntactic positions and for variations on these to reflect the discourse functions marked by topic and passive constructions. As the discussion of topic shows, the investigation of sentence structure can only ever be partial in the absence of consideration of the discourse context. In the next chapter we look at discourse level structures and processes, and in particular examine the important roles played by simultaneous constructions.

Note

1. Ó Baoill and Matthews (2000: 185) give the translation 'I have come here to teach class'. They use the term 'rhetorical question' for this ISL construction, as do Baker-Shenk and Cokely (1980) for similar constructions in ASL. However, it seems clear that these sentences are functionally dissimilar to standard rhetorical questions, which, roughly speaking, have the effect of asserting the negation of the question apparently being asked.

8 Discourse

8.1 Introduction

This chapter discusses discourse features at both the macro, interactional level and the more micro, discourse-internal level. For the former we concentrate on the participants' processes of managing conversational interaction: the signalling of turn-taking, topic maintenance and politeness. For the latter we are concerned with discourse cohesion. Picking up on topics from earlier chapters, we discuss the use of space, of deictic systems and of discourse connectives in the maintenance of the common ground of the conversation. Finally we broaden the discussion to consider forms of talk in ISL, and spend some time looking at the establishment and maintenance of cohesion across stretches of discourse.

8.2 What we know about discourse in signed languages

Relatively little has been written about discourse structure in any signed language. Work includes material on American Sign Language (Dudis 2004; Janzen 1998; Liddell 2003; Roy 1989). For British Sign Language, Morgan (1998) has looked at aspects of adult discourse and used this to compare and contrast for child language acquisition pathways of certain structures (for example, role-shifting mechanisms). More recently, there has been work that has looked at a range of features occurring in Swedish Sign Language (Nilsson 2007, 2010), including the use of the non-dominant hand to maintain referents through use of fragment buoys and theme buoys (following Liddell 2003). Nilsson also looks at instances where the non-dominant hand mirrors an activity on the dominant hand, termed 'mirroring', or where the non-dominant hand remains in the signer's lap, labelled 'in-lap'.

Work on discourse in Irish Sign Language is still in its early stages, but some research exists, which we draw on here. Leeson (2001) looked at how discourse topics are used in a range of ISL data and made a first inroad into exploring aspects of simultaneous patterning in the language. Saeed and Leeson (2004) looked more closely at the interaction between discourse functionality and information structuring, identifying tendencies for the distribution of more or less animate entities on the dominant and non-dominant hands. Later work built on this and looked at the signer's representation of conceptual space in signing space, and particularly, the development of megablends through layering of event spaces on signing space, with a great deal of inferencing required of the interlocutor in order to track the intended referents across the discourse (Leeson and Saeed 2007). Other discourse-level analyses include consideration of the functionality and distribution of theme buoys and fragment buoys in ISL (Leeson 2010; Leeson and Saeed 2010). These are issues we return to below.

8.3 Managing conversational interaction

Given that signed languages are visual languages, it comes as no surprise that in order to engage in conversation, there is a need to ensure that the interlocutor is looking at the addressee. Around this basic requirement, a number of rule-governed behaviours have developed that underlie gaining attention and turn-taking.

8.3.1 Gaining attention

One of the strategies for gaining a desired interlocutor's attention is via use of waving. In Example 8.1(b), the signer waves to an (off-screen) interlocutor to get her attention. Having presumably gained the eye contact desired, she begins to tell her story. Other acceptable means for gaining attention include tapping the person on the shoulder, arm or knee (but never on the head) or gaining a person's attention by tapping the table or stamping on the floor so that the vibrations of the movement will cause them to look up, and identify their would-be interlocutor. Other allowable means include asking another person to function as an intermediary in getting someone's attention, because you have their visual attention and they are nearer to the intended interlocutor. This can be done by asking them to tap the desired addressee and direct their attention to you or using the same 'tap on shoulder' gesture to gain an interlocutor's attention, as illustrated in Example 8.1(a)–(c).

Gorbet and Wilcox (2010) note that for American Sign Language (ASL) and Italian Sign Language (LIS), there is a process in play that has led to nonverbal communication that is gestural in nature becoming linguistic. Discussing the shoulder-tap, they speculate that the gestural origins foreshadow the articulation of signs used to gain attention. We can see this pattern in ISL where, for example, the sign ANNOY (or BOTHER) in Example 8.1(d) shares the same handshape and movement as for GET-ATTENTION-OF, but the location for articulation is on the surface of the non-dominant hand, though, as in the example below, this can also move upwards to the location associated with TROUBLE. The use of the arm as a semantic field for concepts associated with 'trouble' stems probably from the action of police (and in former times, also teachers) physically taking someone by the arm when they are doing something they are not supposed to do. Hence, the signs for ARREST, TROUBLE, PROBLEM, POLICE and PRISON are all articulated at the same location on the upper part of the arm on the ipsilateral side of the signer's body.

Example 8.1

(a) GET-ATTENTION-OF
Fergus D. (06) Personal Stories (Dublin)

(b) GET-ATTENTION-OF+sr
Marian (16) Personal Stories (Dublin)

(c) GET-ATTENTION-OF+f
Helen (27) Personal Stories (Wexford)

(d) BOTHER/ANNOY
Valerie (12) Personal Stories (Dublin)

Matthews (1996b) notes that the creation of vibration is used as a means of getting attention: as noted above, this can include tapping or banging on a table or a banister, or stamping one's foot on a wooden floor. Where the attention of a larger group of people is required, mechanisms such as flashing lights on and off are frequently utilised (for example, in classrooms with deaf/hearing students or at Deaf community events). Flashing lights are also used to gain the attention of a single person working in an office environment (ibid.), with a function more or less equivalent to knocking on the door of a hearing person's office, that is the flashing light signifies that someone is present and has entered the person's space.

The context of communication also impacts on turn-taking in conversation. Turn-taking is quite formalised in ISL, especially in groups, where signers signal a wish to participate by gesture and tend to wait for compliance, predominately signalled by eyegaze. Van Herreweghe (2002) discusses turn-taking in Flemish Sign Language and contrasts sign language meetings with those involving spoken language users. The differences can cause difficulties when signers and speakers interact in meetings, using interpreters. Deaf signers are impeded in gaining turns by speakers' willingness to over-lap and self-select without tacit approval. Describing sign language meetings, she notes:

> eye gaze proved to be an extremely important and powerful regulator by which the current speaker selected the next speaker. A person could self select in all-sign meetings by waving a hand, indexing, lightly touching the current speaker on the arm, rapping the table, stretching out a 5 classifier handshape (with the palm away from the speaker and the fingers up, just above the table), or asking another participant to warn the current speaker that the person wants the next turn. However, whoever self-selected as next speaker got the floor only when the current speaker (and not the chairperson) looked at him rather than at any of the other participants. So self-selection in all-sign meetings was never pure self-selection because the current speaker still had the power to allocate the next turn by means of eye gaze. (Van Herreweghe 2002: 98–9)

This characterisation fits meetings between ISL users equally well.

8.3.2 Cultural and linguistic politeness

Lane et al. (1996) note that the rules of politeness in the American Deaf community differ from those of the hearing community. Examples include what they call 'the requirement for frank talk' (73). They note that

> hinting and vague talk in an effort to be polite are inappropriate and even offensive in the DEAF-World [. . .] A principle of etiquette in the DEAF-World seems to be 'always act in a way that facilitates communication'. Hence, blunt speech is not rude, but sudden departures, private conversations, and breaking visual contact are. (73–4)

This also holds true for Irish Deaf people. Matthews (1996b: 15) notes that 'The style of conversation may appear very direct', with conversation aimed at distinguishing deaf people from hearing people, identifying the schools attended by participants (traditionally, the deaf schools, and contemporaneously, whether one attended a school for the deaf, mainstream school or something in-between), establishing who has Deaf relatives, and for hearing signers, who taught them to sign. Foley-Cave (2003) likens the Irish Deaf community to a small town where Deaf people take an interest in the detail of events in their community, and this links also, we suggest, to another feature of Deaf culture: the requirement for reciprocity which holds that individuals help others in their community, to the point where if they consistently make themselves unavailable, they will not be party to assistance from the community as a result (Mindess 1999). This principle may, we suggest, include the expectation that interlocutors reveal personal information about themselves. For interpreters, Mindess suggests that signed language skills are seen as coming from the Deaf community, and as a consequence, interpreters are expected to 'give back proportionally to the community' (115). Thus Mindess suggests that Deaf communities are collectivist cultures, and as such, impose tight boundaries on membership of the community, are fiercely loyal to that community and invest a great deal of time in the community. Identification with the group is valued highly, and ostracism is the worst punishment for a group member. While signed language use is a necessary condition of group membership, it is not sufficient in and of itself. Some degree of hearing loss is necessary for full membership, though the degree of hearing loss is considered irrelevant (Matthews and Foley-Cave 2004). A key requirement is 'attitudinal deafness', which entails self-identification as a member of the Deaf community and recognition of that membership from other members of the community (Baker and Padden 1978). This social context underlies notions of politeness in ISL conversation.

For Irish Sign Language another consideration for polite behaviour includes knowing the difference between public signing and private signing: if the articulation of signs is faster than normal or the signing space is smaller than usual, then the probability is that a private conversation is ensuing and it is considered rude to eavesdrop (Matthews 1996b). Signing while chewing gum, eating sweets, or having something in one's mouth (for example, a pen) is considered rude, particularly by older signers, at least in part because such behaviour interferes with use of NMFs. Matthews and Foley-Cave (2004: 81) list behaviours that are considered to be impolite in Irish Deaf communication. They include:

- 'Listening in' on a signed conversation without joining in.
- Staring.[1]
- Poking someone with an object such as a pen to gain their attention.
- Signing while someone else is signing. Appropriate turn-taking is highly regarded.
- Placing your hands on someone to stop that person signing, which they compare to placing your hands over someone's mouth whilst that person is speaking.

- Holding an object such as a cigarette, knife, fork or pen in your hand while signing. This is also distracting as it interferes with clear communication.
- Averting eyegaze from the signer whilst participating in a signed conversation: it denotes lack of interest in what the person has to say.
- For hearing signers to speak while there are Deaf people present, thereby excluding the latter from the conversation.

8.4 Discourse cohesion

Discourse is of course more than a sequence of well-formed sentences. Pragmatics research in various theoretical approaches has revealed how language users cooperate in establishing and maintaining shared conversational goals and a common ground (Stalnaker 1974) of shared assumptions. Every language, it appears, offers its users resources to distinguish between shared assumptions and new information; to vary perspective on events; to structure a narrative; and to show empathy with certain participants in scenes. In this section we look at some of these resources in ISL. These include the use of the signer's body to alter perspective on an event, the use of simultaneous constructions to background or foreground aspects of a piece of discourse (for example, through use of buoys), the use of body-partitioning, as well as the discourse use of conjunctions such as BUT, AND, THEN, etc. We begin by considering the role of embodiment in ISL discourse management.

8.4.1 Embodiment and perspective: signer's viewpoint is privileged

Cognitive linguists, for example Johnson (1987) and Lakoff and Johnson (1999), have emphasised the role of the human body in the formation of linguistic concepts. In this view, embodiment – the physical experience of being in the world – underpins a range of linguistic systems such as spatial prepositions, and the metaphorical mappings between, for example upright stature and success, moral strength, etc. We can see a discourse example of this in ISL where signers exploit a relationship between narrative perspective and the position of the signer's body: signers present what is before them at c. locus as the most focused elements in a discourse (Leeson 2010). Other less salient information is presented more distantly from the signer's body. Janzen (2010) describes similar behaviour in ASL as a form of metaphor: 'spatial distance is conceptual difference'. In such instances, signers present items that are considered to be conceptually distant from each other as being physically distant in signing space, and those that are considered to be conceptually similar or identical at adjacent points in space, or the identical point in space.

The privileging of signer perspective can be identified in the tendency to encode actor-led activity on the signer's body (that is, signer = actor), where the action is led by the signer (as him- or herself, as narrator or, as we shall see, as a character in a role shifting). It can also be identified in the privileging of the undergoer role in functional passive constructions. In such instances (as discussed in Chapter 7), the signer's body is that of the undergoer of an action (as opposed to the more typical signer's body = actor in an event) and this serves to foreground the experiencer of the event, and background the actor for a range of purposes. The actor may be unknown, presumed to be shared knowledge, or not required or desired to be made explicit.

What is true at the level of the clause or sentence also holds across discourse. We find that ISL signers encode events from their own perspective, and use role-shifting devices to create surrogates for other protagonists whose perspective on the event is to be encoded and privileged. For example, we can consider how characters are presented in Fiona's (Fiona (36) (Waterford)) version of the Frog Story in Example 8.2. The Frog Story is a picture sequence story. Signers were shown the sequence and asked to sign the story in their own time. The story is about a boy who has a frog that he keeps in his room in a jam jar. He also has a pet dog. Overnight, the frog escapes, and in the morning, the boy and his dog set out to find the frog, encountering adventure along the way. Here, we find the following characters' perspectives encoded via use of the signer's body as surrogate: Fiona as storyteller/narrator, the boy, the dog, the frog, an owl and a deer. However, not all animate entities in the story are embodied via a surrogate. For example, the swarm of bees that chase the boy and the dog are never embodied, though formally this could be done: one bee could be associated with the signer's body via a surrogate blend and that bee could stand for all bees in the swarm, as an instance of metonymy. Instead, the swarm of bees is seen from the point of view of the boy, who is chased by the bees. Thus, the discourse strategy reflects the signer's decision to foreground the experience of the most human-like entity, in this instance the boy.

In other parts of the story, this is not the case. In escaping from the swarm of bees, the boy and his dog literally run into a deer. The deer has large antlers and the boy becomes entangled with them. The deer is embodied (that is, encoded on the signer's body), and the event is momentarily viewed from the perspective of the deer who now has the boy caught on one antler (presented by a CL-Legs-handshape on the dominant hand, articulated at the side of the signer's head, commensurate with the location for the deer's left antler). Indeed, in this case, there is a two-fold view on the event. First, we have the deer's view on the event: the signer's body now equals the deer's body. Body partitioning is also in evidence. The signer's body is the deer's body; the signer's face is the deer's face; the signer's non-dominant hand is the deer's antler and the signer's dominant hand represents the relative position of the boy on the deer's inferred left antler. It is the fact that the signer uses a CL-Legs-handshape to represent the boy that shifts the coding of perspective here. While the deer surrogate gives us an 'on-stage' view of the event, a life-sized rendering of the situation, the classifier handshape presents a miniature-sized view on the position of the boy vis-à-vis the deer. The boy is down-sized momentarily:

his experience of the event is downgraded for now, until the signer's body is again equated with his experience in a subsequent surrogate.

Example 8.2

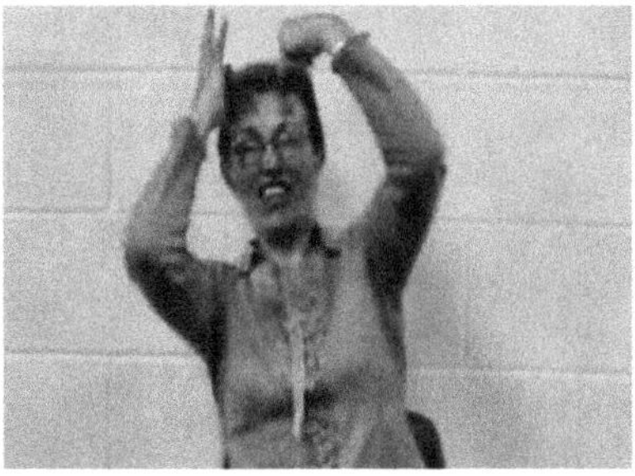

Deer surrogate blend. Deer surrogate is 'on stage' view; boy on antlers is 'off-stage' view. Fiona (36) Frog Story (Waterford)

8.4.2 Event spaces

One way of describing the narrative techniques discussed above is to say that signers establish event spaces and that these spaces function as the realisation of conceptual space: how the signer conceives the event conceptually is mapped onto the signing space. Signers introduce referents within these spaces and track them across discourse through a variety of devices including the use of space to represent physical or abstract relationships between entities and concepts, pronominal referencing, the use of surrogates and inferential relationships. As we shall see, signers also build on spaces: event spaces are layered, with inferential links between them, and these links contribute to discourse complexity, and, as suggested by Nilsson (2010), text density. Further, signers present different views of events, which Liddell (2003) talks about as 'on-stage' and 'off-stage' views. That is, when the signer presents a view on an event from his or her core perspective, that is as narrator, or through use of the signer's body as a surrogate for another (typically animate) entity, he or she is selecting a particular viewpoint and 'forcing' the viewer to see the event from that perspective. It may also be the case that there is a link between evidentiality and point of view, with a stronger commitment to the truth of a described event being associated with the use of surrogates. That is, it might be the case that a signer chooses to use a surrogate when he or she is committed to or has first-hand experience of the event being described.[2]

The sophistication of signers' use of event spaces can be seen in the short section of narrative shown in Example 8.3, an excerpt from a rendition of the Frog Story. In 8.3(a) we see the signer introduce a participant, an owl, by using a lexical item. In (b), she embodies the owl via a surrogate, thus promoting the owl's viewpoint on this event at that point in the narrative. A shift back to the perspective of the boy occurs in the next clause (c), where the signer lexically reintroduces the boy. She then presents a surrogate of the boy. From this viewpoint, we see a 'life-sized' enactment of the boy falling backwards. The boy is startled and steps backwards, and in (d), the boy is embodied, and looks upwards at the (inferred) owl's locus. Here, it is also interesting to note that the signer rotates signing space 360 degrees: the position of the owl is the same as that of the boy. The cue to interpreting the rotated positions of the owl and boy is eyegaze. The owl looks forward when flying out of the hole in the tree while the boy looks upwards towards the previously established position of the hole that the owl has emerged from. Thus, as in Example 5.2 on the war in Iraq that we looked at earlier in the volume, we see further evidence of layering spatial information or 'mental spaces', where interlocutors have to be able to manage multiple levels of information that when combined, create what has been termed a megablend (Fauconnier and Turner 2002).

Example 8.3

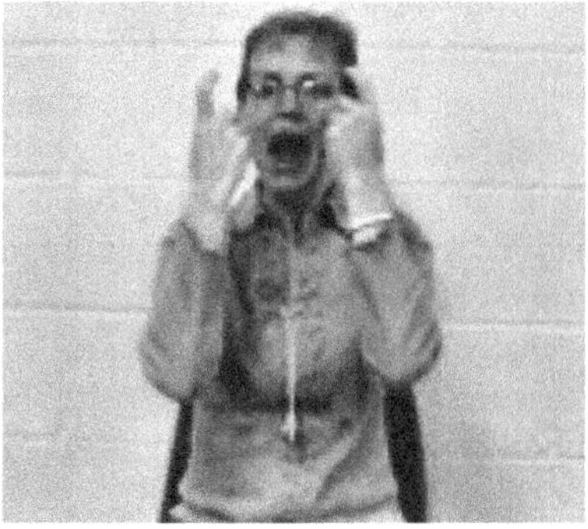

(a) OWL
Fiona (36) Frog Story (Waterford)

(b) Surrogate-OWL
Fiona (36) Frog Story (Waterford)

(c) BOY
Fiona (36) Frog Story (Waterford)

(d) Surrogate-BOY-LOOKS-UP (toward owl)
Fiona (36) Frog Story (Waterford)

8.4.3 Deictic systems

We have seen that signers may describe the actions of others by representing them through the medium of their own body, that is, as if they are representing the action or perspective themselves. Another way of stating this is to say that the signer can, through use of a surrogate blend, present other viewpoints in an embodied way. In other words, the world is viewed through the eyes of signer and presented through the signer's body. This narrative strategy can be seen as one of a range of devices that alter or switch the default deictic devices of the language, to reflect the signer's discourse goals.

8.4.3.1 Reference shifting in action and dialogue

As we have seen, in Irish Sign Language the signer locus may be used to refer to a non-first person referent. This feature has been reported for a variety of signed languages and has been referred to as role-playing (Meier 1990), role-shifting (Padden 1990), role-switching (Mandel 1977) and referential-shift (Poulin and Miller 1995). More recent work from within a cognitive linguistic framework has referred to such shifts in foregrounding of characters associated with the signer's body as instances that make use of what is termed surrogate space and in turn, contribute to surrogate blends. In doing this, the signer, adopting the role of a character in an event, engages in displaced action or dialogue, which has also been termed constructed action and constructed dialogue (Metzger 1995, 1999; Tannen 1989).

When a surrogate is used, the signer typically breaks eye contact with the addressee and in addition non-manual features may change, though this seems not to be obligatory. Sometimes body position is adjusted, with the signer rotating the shoulders to the left or the right. This seems to be more marked in certain settings, particularly those where there are a larger number of participants. In such instances, the signer's torso can rotate to mark a referential shift, probably a function of the fact that he or she may need to be visible to a larger audience, for example at a conference. In less-populated settings, eyegaze along with a slight inclination of the head can mark such a shift. These differences in usage may or may not have so much to do with the formality of the event as with the number of participants by whom a signer has to be clearly viewed. It may be that instead of being a corollary of formality, a highly visible referential shift may be a function of the fact that the signer wishes to have his or her differentiation of characters more clearly viewed by the interlocutors in large-scale multi-party interactions than in smaller-scale events.

Engberg-Pedersen's (1993) analysis of Danish Sign Language reveals three distinct 'reference shifting' structures that may have different functions. She notes that these structures can co-occur, but equally, they can occur in isolation:

1. **Shifted reference**: pronouns are used from a quoted sender's point of view. This term is reserved for reported speech.
2. **Shifted attribution of expressive elements**: the signer uses his/her body and face to express the mood or attitude of a referent other than the signer. This structure is not limited to a reported speech function, but can also be found in reports of a person's thoughts, feelings or actions.
3. **Shifted locus**: this structure is unique to signed languages because of their spatial parameters. This structure is used when signers use their own locus (c-locus) to represent someone other than the signer's thoughts/actions, or where they use a locus other than the c-locus to represent the signer.

In these instances, signers can manipulate use of pronominal referencing systems to foreground another referent's perspective; they can manipulate non-manual elements to add an affective (and sometimes humorous) dimension to their discourse, and signers can also rotate their body toward the locus associated with the intended referent in order to inhabit their locus and 'become' the other person. In this way, a signer can present the views of another person as first person rather than reporting their speech as occurs in English. Another way of saying this is that the signer embodies the perspective of the intended referent by inhabiting their locus for the duration of their contribution in the discourse.

In Example 8.4(a) we see a constructed dialogue: here the signer is recounting an interaction with her young daughter who is looking for something. The story teases out what the hearing toddler daughter is trying to ask for, and the difficulty the mother has in figuring that out. Here, she presents a surrogate for her 3-year-old, who gestures something that looks like BICYCLE while mouthing 'big ladder'. (It turns out that she has seen the back of an old chair and thinks of it as her 'ladder'.) The discourse works through the signer's dialogue with her daughter, with the signer also representing herself in the time frame of the event via a surrogate. Taking an Engberg-Pedersen analysis, we can say that this is example shows shifted reference (that is, reported speech), shifted attribution of expressive elements (the facial expression and mannerisms of a 3-year-old), and shifted locus (identified primarily via shoulder shift towards +sl in signing space and eyegaze towards +sl, where +sl is the locus for the mother in this discourse, as indicated in Example 8.4(b).

In Example 8.5(a) the signer is describing how some ex-mainstreamed deaf people might volunteer to participate in committee work in the Deaf community. An 'ex-mainstreamer' is a term used in the Deaf community to refer to deaf people who spent part of their educational lives in mainstream education programmes rather than attending a school for the deaf. Some ex-mainstreamers engage with the Deaf community and learn ISL, but their position within the community is sometimes marginal/ised, sometimes as a result of attitudes held towards them by some members of the Deaf community.

Example 8.4

(a) Constructed dialogue.
A surrogate for Michelle's young daughter

(b) Constructed dialogue.
A surrogate for Michelle's response

In 8.5(a), we see a surrogate for an unspecified person, who represents any ex-mainstreamed deaf person who is involved in the Deaf community. In terms of constructing action, the signer puts her hand in the air, a gestural representation of the act of volunteering. As in all discourse, she had a range of choices to draw from, including options that would have lexically reported on the action (for example, SOME VOLUNTEER), but instead opted for constructed action which serves to foreground the perspective of the ex-mainstreamed person. If we were to apply Engberg-Pedersen's analysis, we could note that there is no evidence of shifted reference here: there is no reported speech in this instance. We do find shifted attribution of expressive elements (the affect is that of the unspecified actor(s)) and shifted locus (the signer shifts towards +sr to represent the views of the ex-mainstreamed deaf people, which contrasts with the +sl locus associated with the Deaf community viewpoint).

Example 8.5

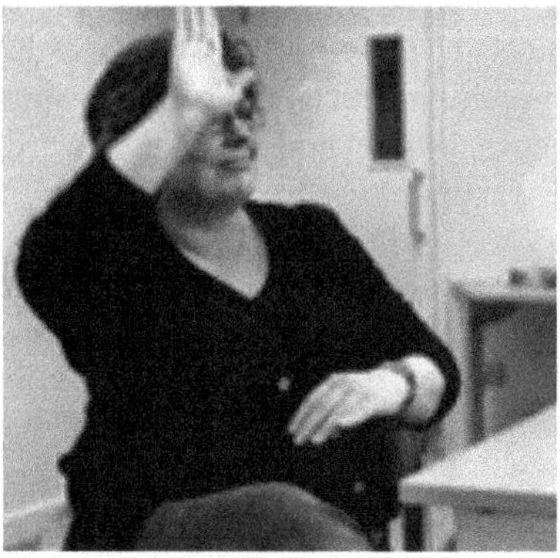

(a) Constructed action. A surrogate for a potential ex-mainstreamed deaf volunteer

(b) Constructed action. A surrogate for a potential Deaf community response

8.4.3.2 Body partitioning

Paul Dudis (2004) has described the processes that ASL signers employ to use simultaneous constructions that, from an articulatory perspective, subdivide the body (including eyegaze and mouthing) to represent a number of different actors at the same time and from a cognitive perspective, create 'megablends' combining previously established blends in discourse. He shows how a signer's narrative goals interact with the physiological limits of signing to affect the construction and flow of a signed language narrative. Dudis suggests that signers frequently establish simultaneous blends by assigning different body parts to separate blends in order to overcome such constraints, leading to a range of narrative strategies that signers can draw on.

Example 8.6 provides an example of body partitioning in ISL. Here the signer, recounting the Frog Story, makes use of surrogate space to embody the perspective of the boy, who is asleep in bed. His non-dominant hand is the boy's, holding the bed covers to his chest. The 'invisible surrogate' (Liddell 2003) here is the bedcover. His dominant hand presents a different element: through use of a CL-Legs-handshape, the signer represents the relative position of the dog lying on the bed. Not only does his dominant hand represent a different entity, but he also combines a token space, mapping it onto surrogate space. That is, while the surrogate presents a real-world-sized representation of a human in an imagined bed (signer's body, non-dominant hand), the dominant hand presents a miniature representation of the relative size of the dog vis-à-vis the boy. This instance of body partitioning thus presents both an on-stage (boy) and an off-stage (dog) viewpoint.

Example 8.6

Body partitioning: BOY (in bed) and DOG (CL-Legs (on bed))
Sean (Dublin) Frog Story

Later in this chapter we will look at further instances of body partitioning and its role in discourse. First, we will look at more general features of discourse structure.

8.4.4 Explicit establishment of discourse topics

Discourse level topics serve to introduce the theme of the discourse and establish the major focus for discussion and in this sense, we could say that these topics really are 'what the discourse is about'. In the stories in the SOI corpus ISL, there is a strong tendency for signers to explicitly introduce a discourse topic. This may be an artefact of how the data were collected: signers were asked to tell us a story about a topic of their choosing, so given this condition, it is perhaps not surprising that many of them open their personal stories by explicitly giving an indication of discourse topic. It is probable that in extended discourse streams, where signers shift topics, not every new discourse topic would be overtly marked in this manner. Having said this, explicitly referenced discourse topics are a feature of ISL. Before we go on to look at some ISL examples, we should say a little about the term 'discourse topic'. Brown and Yule (1983) criticise early definitions of discourse topicality as over-generalised and over-simplified. They instead adopt a hypothesis that 'there is a specific connection between "discourse topic" and "discourse content". The former can be viewed, in some sense as consisting of the "important elements" of the latter' (107). An explicit discourse topic streamlines the addressee's task of identifying this relation. For instance, in Example 8.7, the signer introduces his monologue about a car that needed some extensive repairs by saying that he will tell us about his car, while in Example 8.8, the signer introduces a current affairs piece about the war in Iraq in the same manner: he explicitly states that he is going to talk about that topic.

Example 8.7

INDEX-me ABOUT MY CAR CAR
BEFORE YEARS-AGO
dh: ABOUT FIVE YEAR AGO INDEX-me BUY SECOND h.a.n.d. CAR
INDEX-me
nd: (Theme buoy)
INDEX-me LOVE CAR INDEX-me DRIVE FOR FAMILY
HAVE SEVEN SEAT ONE-BEHIND-THE-OTHER
DRIVE YEARS
OVER-A-PERIOD-OF-TIME-TO-NOW DAY
DRIVE-AROUND
UNTIL RECENTLY
ABOUT TWO THREE MONTH AGO . . .

'I'm going to tell you about my car. About five years back, I bought a second-hand car. I loved this car and used it as the family car. It was a seven-seater. I drove the car for years without any problem until recently. Then about two or three months ago . . .'
(Fergus D. (06) Personal Stories (Dublin))

Example 8.8
ME EXPLAIN ABOUT i.r.a.q.
RECENTLY A-LOT-OF WAR
INDEX+f START WAR REALLY HAPPEN BEFORE-BEFORE
AROUND 1990 1991
i.r.a.q. JUST ONE DAY c+cl-5-OPEN+F 'GRABBED'
dh: Cl-b + SMALL-CIRCLE-ON-MAP-AT-SOUTH –OF-LOC.
nd: CL-C ______________________________________
k.u.w.a.i.t. 'GRAB' TAKE-OVER
WEST WORLD AMERICA ENGLAND u.k. LIST ANGRY 2h CL-5 'CONFLICT'
THAT TIME k.u.w.a.i.t.
'I'm going to talk about Iraq. There has recently been significant outbreaks of war in Iraq, but to understand the crux of the issue, one must look back to circa 1990–1 when Iraq, without warning, invaded Kuwait. At that time, the Western powers (including America and the United Kingdom) responded by entering into a war over Kuwait'
(Senan (01) Personal Stories (Dublin))

Leeson (2001) also notes that explicit discourse topics do not only occur at the outset of a narrative: they also seem to serve as signposts to the addressee that the signer is about to change the focus of the story somewhat. It may be that such markers are pragmatic and more typical of narrative monologues that are signed to camera for an unknown audience in order to maximally clarify the ordering of the discourse. Further research is needed to explore this point. Examples 8.9 and 8.10 show the explicit marking of topic shift.

Example 8.9
NOW EXPLAIN FOUR POINT VERY IMPORTANT
'Now I want to discuss four points which are very important'
(Informant B: conference presentation: 'IDS Archives')
(Leeson 2001: 238)

Example 8.10
LOOK FOR BICYCLE
'(We arrived on the Aran Island) and began to look for bicycles'
(Informant N: *Horizon* footage)
(Leeson 2001: 238)

Example 8.9 occurs in the middle of a presentation to a Deaf audience. The presenter is discussing the grammatical features of ISL, and draws the audience's attention to the fact that she will next introduce four salient points for their consideration. She does this through use of what we will describe below as list buoys, introducing each element through use of an ordinal number on the non-dominant hand (FIRST, SECOND, etc.) and then discussing the element on the dominant hand; if we adopt Janzen's (1999) thesis, these ordinal number signs function as discourse-cohesion topics.

Discourse topics frequently occur at the outset of narrative monologues, but they are not obligatory there. Leeson (2001) also identifies narrative monologues that do not begin with the explicit establishment of discourse topics, but which rather set some of the background contextualising conditions of an event or set of events that will be recounted. These include Examples 8.11 and 8.12.

Example 8.11
LITTLE GIRL ASLEEP
'A little girl was asleep'
(Informant G: narrative)
(Leeson 2001: 240)

Example 8.12
ME COME FROM DEAF FAMILY MOTHER-FATHER DEAF . . .
'I come from a Deaf family. My parents are Deaf . . .'
(Informant C: *Angry Silences* footage)
(Leeson 2001: 240)

However, the use of discourse topics at the outset of narrative monologues does seem to be more typical in the ISL data examined. Another important point to consider is the information status of discourse topics. Unlike sentence topics discussed in Chapter 7, explicitly stated discourse topics do not introduce given or old information, or information that is backgrounded as opposed to foregrounded (Givón 1984). Nor do they follow the given-new pattern described by Chafe (1994). Janzen (1999) suggests that such explicit discourse topics include the kind of information that is not within the consciousness of the signer at the time of utterance, but is accessible: 'that is, the signer must assume that the addressee can identify the information in these topics as accessible to ground the information contained in the comment' (277).

Such information can be pragmatically derived. It can, for example, draw on presumed shared knowledge of a shared culture or worldview. This is clearly what the signers in the examples above are doing: grounding the information they are about to share in an accessible manner before discussing the details or elaborating on the issue in the comment.

8.4.5 Specific time reference in discourse

Structurally time phrases may act like explicit discourse topics. It has been suggested that ISL utilises 'specific time reference' (Leeson 1996), following Jacobowitz and Stokoe (1988) (for ASL), recognising the fact that ISL does not mark tense on the verb, as is the case in languages like English. Instead, a signer marks the time period that contextualises the discourse at the outset and this time frame remains in place until the signer explicitly changes it. Generally discourse unmarked for time is interpreted as being located at speech act time. This can be considered the default setting for present time reference. Examples 8.9–8.12 illustrate this default setting.

Specific time references parallel discourse topics in a number of ways, for example both serve to establish the context for the discourse that follows. Furthermore, when a topic or specific time reference has been introduced, both remain until the signer explicitly alters them. Returning to Example 8.7, we can see that the signer follows the introduction of his discourse topic by setting the time frame for the purchase of his car (ABOUT FIVE YEAR AGO), and then tells us that he has been driving the car for some time (YEARS-GO-BY // DRIVE // UNTIL RECENTLY // ABOUT TWO THREE MONTH AGO . . .). Then, we find that all information subsequently presented is relative to the discourse time established, in this case the unfolding of the story from two to three months ago when he started experiencing problems with his car. In Example 8.8, we find the same kind of nesting of specific time reference occurring after the establishment of the discourse topic. Here, the signer tells us that while there had recently been an outbreak of war in Iraq (circa 2003), the root of the current situation could be traced back to a previous war, in the early 1990s. The rest of the segment about the invasion of Kuwait by Iraq, and the response of the Western nations to the crisis, all occur in the same time frame that the signer has established. That is, if we did not interpret the text subsequent to the introduction of 1990, 1991 as occurring in that time frame, we would assume that the default time frame is unmarked time and interpret this as something happening 'now' or, given our access to world knowledge, might infer that the events reported were associated with a current war in Iraq.

8.4.6 Discourse use of connectives

Irish Sign Language makes use of lexical conjunctions and connectives such as AND, BUT, IF, SO, THEN and NEXT. These connectives guide the addressee in making the intended connections in the discourse. Example 8.13(a) shows how AND is used to group related concepts (three men, in this instance), while 8.13(b) shows how AND is used to link sentences (how a group of friends did something the next day). The use of BUT in ISL is demonstrated in Examples 8.13(c) and (d). In (c) we find BUT used to make a contrast, and focus emphasis on the post conjunctive element: '. . . but of my seven sisters . . .'. In (d) we see the same kind of structure arising, with BUT used to signal the contrast in 'all three of them were hearing but I was the only deaf person amongst them'. In ISL, the use of BUT in both instances seems to identify the contrast in order to convey the signer's attitude to the situation described. Examples 8.13(e) and (f) illustrate use of IF in ISL. In (e) the signer notes that if hearing people experience problems with their houses (that is, electrical problems), then they can phone someone. Here the Deaf signer's experience of house-building issues is contrasted against a possible world and the differences experienced by deaf and hearing people when faced with difficulties. Example 8.13(f) also sets up a possible scenario, this time the situation is a description of past experience: the signer suggests they liked it when (IF) lots of visitors came by. In 8.13(g) and (h) we see instances of the use of THEN, a connective that marks a temporal sequence, cause–effect relationships between segments of discourse, and may signal topic shifts. In (g) we see the sequence interpretation of THEN: Rebecca tells a story about how her dog, Polo, went missing. After much searching, she decides to tell her parents that they must call a radio station and THEN (when they get through on the phone), tell them the dog's name etc. In the run-up to 8.13(h) Frankie signs that she and two other women and four nieces and nephews went shopping. She notes that they were strolling along, with a buggy in tow, and THEN (or subsequently) looked into a shop. The THEN marks both temporal sequence and a shift to a new episode in the story: she enters the shop and tells how the children wanted to hold everything, especially fragile items, in the shop, and how ultimately she ended up buying the children decorative butterflies.

Example 8.13

(a) . . . e.a.m.o.n. AND s.e.a.n. **AND** MY HUSBAND . . .
(b) INDEX+sr FRIEND INDEX+f **AND** NEXT DAY INDEX+f
(c) BROTHER ALL HEARING **BUT** SISTER SEVEN SISTER . . .
(d) ALL-OF-THEM THREE HEARING **BUT** ALONE DEAF CL-ISL-L-bent ME
(e) FOR EXAMPLE HEARING PHONE **IF** PROBLEM HOUSE . . .
(f) USE TO LIKE **IF** LOT VISITOR INDEX+fr+c 'COME HERE'
(g) TELL MOTHER^FATHER HAVE TO RING RADIO **THEN** TELL INDEX+fr+hi NAME DOG . . .
(h) 2 x CL:A 'PUSH-PUSHCHAIR-BRISKLY' **THEN** LOOK IN TO SHOP

It is worth noting the relative frequency of connectives in the SOI corpus: of 46,499 tokens, there are only eight instances of THEN, forty-eight instances of AND, ninety-three instances of BUT, fourteen instances of IF and no instances of SO (though this lexical sign is also used in discourse in ISL). This suggests that while lexical signs do function to mark discourse relations there must be other devices that perform the range of functions that lexical connectives serve in a spoken language like English. In the coming sections, we look at some of these.

8.5 Simultaneous constructions and discourse structure

Simultaneous articulation is a hallmark of signed languages, and this is especially true of discourse level phenomena. In this section, we focus specifically on the functionality of the non-dominant hand in creating and maintaining discourse structure. Early work on simultaneity in signed languages included work by Chris Miller (1994: 8) who discusses the variety of simultaneous strategies, including:

1. Two hands producing two different lexical items simultaneously
2. Preservation of one sign on one hand while the second hand articulates a series of other signs
3. Production of the 'topic' on one hand while the 'comment' is articulated on the second hand
4. Placing a sign articulated on the dominant hand on or in relation to an enumeration morpheme, which is expressed by the non-dominant hand (we might refer to this as a 'listing' strategy).
5. One hand represents the locative position of one argument while the second hand represents the relative locative position of the second argument.

This range of strategies is also found in ISL discourse (Leeson and Saeed 2007; Saeed and Leeson 2004), and we have outlined some of the clausal or sentential level simultaneity that occurs in ISL in Chapter 7. Here, we want to consider more closely the more macro-level instantiations of simultaneity that arises. To do this, we will draw on Scott Liddell's (2003) categorisation of the range of functions of the non-dominant hand. These include (1) list buoys, (2) fragment buoys, (3) theme buoys and (4) pointer buoys. We will also look at the use of signer strategies to 'stage' (following Grimes 1975) or create episodes within discourse by returning their hands to their laps (Nilsson 2008, 2010). Following Anna-Lena Nilsson, we call this simply, 'in-lap'.

8.5.1 Foregrounding and backgrounding strategies

Leeson and Saeed (Leeson and Saeed 2007; Saeed and Leeson 2004) looked at the role of simultaneity in foregrounding and backgrounding elements in discourse. This work proposed a general principle for simultaneity in ISL: that the dominant hand marks foregrounded material while the non-dominant hand marks backgrounded material. Another way of stating this is that the choice of what to articulate on which hand is based on principles of the windowing of attention (Talmy 1996). Talmy notes that 'Language affords the speaker alternatives of attentional windowing upon essentially the same event frame, with the addressee feasibly able to infer the different gapped portions for each alternative so as to reconstruct back to the same single event frame' (260). Thus signers can choose to place focus on one element in isolation while gapping certain information. They can establish a chronological relationship between one element and the next, and, like speakers of any language, place greater focus on one element than on others. But compared with speakers of a language, signers have access to a wider range of simultaneous strategies. The outcome seems to be that information that could be gapped in spoken discourse is maintained, though often backgrounded, in ISL in line with Talmy's suggestion.

A number of tendencies follow from the general principle of simultaneity, for example that the dominant hand will be used to mark the most animate element while the non-dominant hand marks a less animate element; or, for example, that the dominant hand will mark the most active element while the non-dominant hand represents a less active or dynamic element. We can see some examples of these by looking in some detail at Example 8.14.

Example 8.14

(a) AREA-OF-SMALL-LAND-UNDER-IRAQ
'Kuwait is a small country situated to the south of Iraq'

(b) WHOLE-AREA-OF-IRAQ
'Iraq itself'
(Senan (01) Personal Stories (Dublin))

(c) HALF-AREA-OF-IRAQ
'partitioned Iraq'
(Senan (01) Personal Stories (Dublin))

(d) A-PART-FROM-RIGHT-SIDE-OF-IRAQ-TO-LEFT-SIDE-OF-IRAQ
'the partitioned zone'

(e) PLANE-FLY-FROM-WEST-SIDE-TO-EAST-SIDE-OF-IRAQ 'the area where planes could not fly (or 'the no-fly zone')'

(f) ENTER-IRAQ-SIMULTANEOUSLY-FROM-TURKEY-AND-KUWAIT '(The plan) was to invade Iraw via Turkey, from the north, and Kuwait, from the south'

In Example 8.14(a) we see the signer introduce the relative geographical position of Kuwait vis-à-vis Iraq from the point of view of someone looking at a map. Here, his non-dominant hand is functioning as a placeholder for Iraq's position while the dominant hand foregrounds the position of Kuwait. In the piece, the signer holds the nd hand in place while locating and introducing Kuwait.

In Examples 8.14(b)–(d), the signer's non-dominant hand is again a placeholder for Iraq. At this stage in the story, the United Nations has declared the northern territory a 'no-fly zone'. Here, the signer does several things. First, his non-dominant hand is in the space that has previously been established as co-referential with Iraq from the point of view of one looking at a map, in this case, the signer's viewpoint. We see that his non-dominant hand represents the extent of Iraq's geographical terrain so that his fingers are commensurate with the most northerly tip of Iraq and the base of the hand is commensurate with the most southerly part of the country. In Example 8.14(c), his dominant hand partitions off the top portion of the non-dominant hand using a B-handshape. This serves to function as a representation that the northern part of the country was conceptually partitioned and named as a no-fly zone, dividing the hand in two parts which equate with the two sections of Iraq – the north and the south. The signer subsequently refines the extent of the partitioned zone in Example 8.14(d) where he traces a path across the perseverating non-dominant hand with the thumb and index finger of his dominant hand. This serves to demarcate the mid-hand area as being the no-fly zone and maps onto the geographical domain from a topographical viewpoint. In 8.14(e), the signer reinforces the fact that in this partitioned area, Iraqi planes were not allowed to fly. In this case, we see that a layering of inferential information comes into play: the non-dominant hand continues to maintain the

B-handshape, representing the whole of Iraq. However, the audience now has to map-in mentally the information from the last piece of discourse, the fact that the central zone was a no-fly area. The signer's dominant hand now is active, tracing the area where planes could not fly. In 8.14(f) we see that the non-dominant hand no longer perseverates a B-handshape to maintain the position of Iraq. While the point of view remains that of a person viewing a map of the situation, here, we have to again mentally map-in the position of Iraq, and also access previously established information about the geographical positioning of Turkey and Kuwait with respect to Iraq. With these notions activated in the discourse, we can make sense of the information in (f) which tells us that the allied forces planned to invade Iraq via the northern and southern borders (via Turkey and Kuwait) simultaneously.

This close analysis of Example 8.14 shows both the sophistication and fluidity of the simultaneous strategies and the important role of inference in the interpretation.

A second general principle at work is iconicity. The choice of what is represented on the dominant and non-dominant hands may be dictated by the actual positioning of entities in the real world, modelled in topographic signing space. This is very clearly evidenced in the 'war in Iraq' narrative, and further, it is clear that there is a relationship between how signers conceptualise these relationships and then demonstrate these relationships in signing space. We could add that because of the visual nature of signed languages, the relationship between conceptualisation of space and articulation of how things are related to each other in space is perhaps more readily identifiable than for speakers of languages.

In the next sections we look at two other important other roles of the non-dominant hand in discourse, in-lap and mirroring, using two monologues from the SOI corpus, both presented by the same signer (SOI-36). We can call the first the Motorbike Story;[3] the second is a version of the Frog Story, as outlined earlier in this chapter.

8.5.2 Marking episodes: in-lap

While the position of the signer's non-dominant hand in the signer's lap has been considered for Swedish Sign Language (Nilsson 2010), there does not seem to have been much attention given to date to the functionality associated with both of the signer's hands in the lap position. In ISL, monologues typically commence and end with the signer's hands in the in-lap position, and some signers seem to mark episodic boundaries by returning their hands to the lap position. Thus in this example of the Frog Story the signer opens her narrative with her hands in the in-lap position. She then introduces the main protagonists in the Frog Story: the boy, the dog and the frog. She establishes the scene in the boy's bedroom, locating the relative positions of the boy (in his bed), the dog and the frog. Then she tells us that the boy is a pet lover, enacts the boy petting the dog and then brings her hands to the in-lap position again. This opening sequence thus introduces key referents and gives us some context for the opening scene of the story. Following this second use of in-lap, the signer recounts the story of how the frog escapes and the ensuing adventures of the boy and his dog as they seek to find the missing frog.

Example 8.15

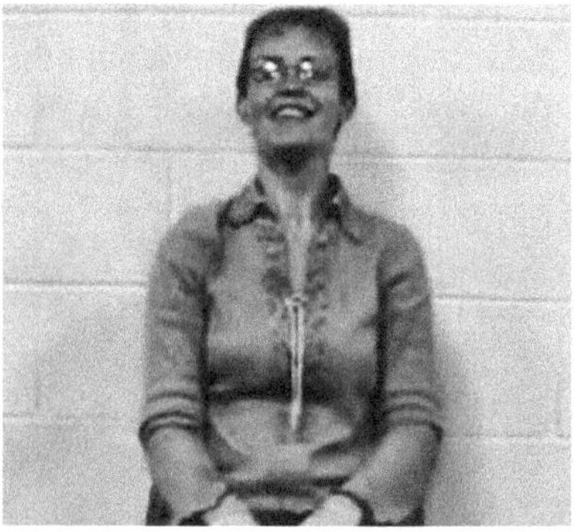

'In-lap'
Fiona (36) Frog Story (Waterford)

A number of factors may contribute to the use of in-lap as an episodic marker in some contexts but not others. These include the proximity of the topic to the signer's own experience, for example whether the story being told is about his or her own experience or an event he or she personally witnessed. Conventionality is also a factor, where a clear episodic structure may trigger the in-lap marker as a delimiting device.

8.5.3 Marking emphasis: mirroring

Mirroring occurs when a normally one-handed sign is 'mirrored' or repeated on the non-dominant hand (Liddell 2003). In ISL, we see many instances of mirroring that seem to function as markers of emphasis. For example, in the Motorbike Story, the signer signs WHAT-IS-THIS, a normally one-handed, informal sign (and historically, also a male sign) on both the dominant and non-dominant hand at an early stage in her story when she is leaving her parents' house with the motorbike and something seems wrong, but she cannot see any problem (Example 8.16(a)). What is interesting here is not just the doubling of hands, but the fact that the non-dominant hand (her right hand – she is a left-handed signer) remains at the locus associated with one of the motorbike handles. In her previous utterance, she has signed DRIVE MOTORBIKE. She then maintains the non-dominant hand in position while she signs INDEX-ME. In the next section we will describe this action of the non-dominant hand as a fragment buoy. This is followed by WHAT-IS-THIS on both the dominant and non-dominant hands. What we might have expected is that the non-dominant hand would have maintained the fragment buoy as a placeholder for her position on the motorbike at this point, but instead, we see a doubling of the hands, which serves to mark that she is really giving due attention to the fact that something seems awry. We can compare this with 8.16(b) where the signer retells the interaction she has with her inspector at work who asks what she is doing with a dirty hosepipe. Here, again, we see mirroring on the non-dominant hand, but here the sign is echoed with the same orientation, which is a more expected outcome. In Example 8.16(c) we see the 'typical' one-handed rendition of the sign, for comparative purposes.

Example 8.16

(a) Mirroring – reversed palm orientation on non-dominant hand
Fiona (36) Personal Stories (Waterford)

(b) Mirroring – same orientation of palm on non-dominant hand

(c) One-handed articulation of WHAT-IS-IT (OR WHAT-FOR) with a fragment buoy on the dominant hand

8.5.4 Buoys

Liddell (2003) describes buoys as signs produced by the non-dominant hand that are held in a stationary configuration as the dominant hand continues to produce signs. Buoys typically represent discourse entities and can be pointed at and have verbs and pronouns directed towards them (that is, they can be referential). Semantically, buoys 'help guide the discourse by serving as conceptual landmarks as the discourse continues' (223). Thus they can function as discourse markers. Liddell identifies a range of buoys for ASL discourse including fragment buoys, theme buoys, list buoys and pointer buoys, which we discuss in turn.

8.5.4.1 Fragment buoys

Liddell (ibid.) suggests that when a one-handed sign follows a two-handed sign, it is common for the weak hand to maintain its configuration from the preceding two-handed sign, and these are known as fragment buoys.

For ASL then, perseveration of the weak hand into the succeeding one-handed sign is reported (248). Fragment buoys are created by associating the meaning of a sign with all or part of its final state of production. In ASL, the signer can point at the fragment buoy to refer to the entity is stands for or to reactivate it in the discourse. In ISL, fragment buoys also serve to guide the interlocutor with respect to the signer's perspective. The fragment buoy held on the non-dominant hand is less-focused information (or 'old' information) than whatever the signer is discussing on the dominant hand (Leeson and Saeed 2007; Saeed and Leeson 2004). As the material held on the non-dominant hand is backgrounded while the material on the dominant hand is profiled, we can suggest that the distribution of information on the dominant and non-dominant hands also tells us something about the salience of the distribution of material from the signer's perspective: we suggest that fragments also tell us something about embodiment. In these stories, fragments are of physical entities or entities that are held or handled, which may of course be a function of the genre of the material considered here. The fragment buoys that arise represent physical appendages – arms, hands, paws, antlers, etc. Often the intended referent is not the physical appendage that the fragment represents, but an inferred item associated with it, typically previously explicitly introduced in the discourse: for example, we see instances as in Example 8.17(a) where the fragment is the signer's arm, but the intended referent is the (invisible) hosepipe that is held wrapped around her arm. Another example comes from Fiona's rendition of the Frog Story where her hand is the fragment which, by association, stands in reference for the frog who is now in a glass jar that the boy holds in his hand – Examples 8.17(b) and 8.17(c).

In 8.17(b) we see the signer provide a profile of the glass jar that holds the frog. She outlines the size and shape with the dominant hand while the

Example 8.17

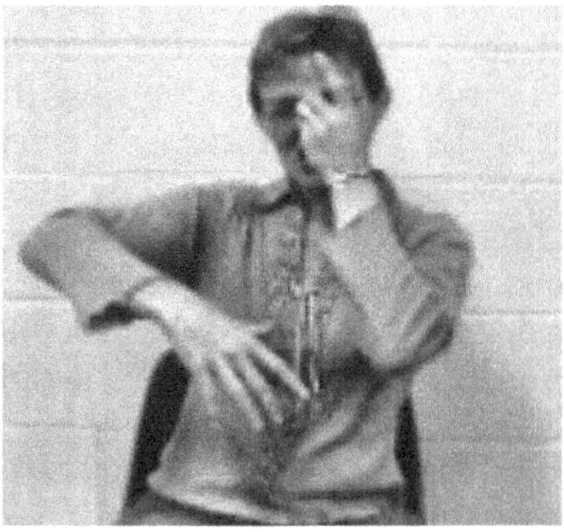

(a) Signer's non-dominant hand is a fragment that stands as a placeholder for the hosepipe on her arm
Fiona (36) Personal Stories (Waterford)

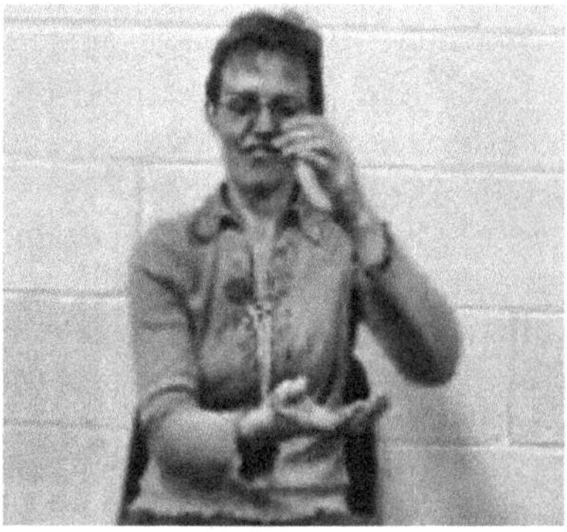

(b) Signer's non-dominant hand is a fragment that provides a profile of the glass jar holding the frog
Fiona (36) Frog Story (Waterford)

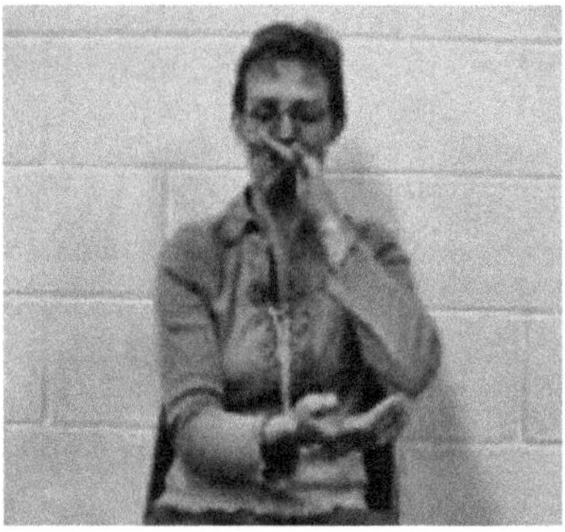

(c) Signer's non-dominant hand maintains the fragment profiling the glass jar holding the frog
Fiona (36) Frog Story (Waterford)

(d) Signer's non-dominant hand holds a fragment of the two-handed sign, DEER
Fiona (36) Frog Story (Waterford)

non-dominant hand serves as a landmark for the profiled event as well as serving as the boy's physical hand in surrogate space (that is, the signer takes the point of view of the boy here). In (c), the non-dominant hand is serving as a fragment buoy, a place-holder which, through the process of holding, also evokes the associated inferred referent, the glass jar (which is held in the boy's hand). It is also part of a partitioned surrogate here (it is the boy who is holding the glass jar). It is also worth noting that the glass jar is introduced using the productive lexicon (size and shape specifiers) rather than the established lexicon. Thus it is not possible to suggest that this is a normally two-handed sign in ISL.

In 8.17(d) we see a more expected form of fragment buoy arising: the non-dominant hand holds a fragment of the two-handed sign DEER, represented via the metonymic sign which represents the deer's antlers. This sign arises as part of a surrogate buoy: the signer is presenting this part of the story from the point of view of the deer. At the same time, an 'off-stage' view is also presented: the dominant hand represents the boy, caught on the deer's antler. Here, the boy is represented by the CL-Legs-handshape, held against the deer's head. Clearly the boy is not 'life-sized' here, in contrast with the 'on-stage' view associated with the deer, presented in surrogate space. Further, we can point out that this example of a fragment buoy is embedded in an instance of body partitioning: the non-dominant hand and body are associated with the deer's perspective while the dominant hand is associated with the boy's position. Here it is ambiguous as to whether the signer's mouth gesture and eyegaze are to be read as co-occurring with the deer or the boy's perspective, though Dudis (2004) suggests that the mouthed elements are typically associated with the point of view of the non-surrogate element, which in this case would be the boy's perspective, while the eyes are associated with the referent represented in the surrogate.

In ISL, while we find that more commonly fragment buoys may be the remnants of two-handed signs, one-handed signs can also be held. Typical candidates for fragment buoys in ISL are articulators that represent real-body parts (human or animal) in fragment buoys, for example fragments representing how something is handled. Such use of fragments may offer us some insights into how body partitioning is arranged and the constraints that operate. These elements, which are 'fragments' of the conceptual picture that perseverate, are often embodied in relation to a surrogate, for example a hand. These might be crucial markers of focus from the signer's perspective. An example is the hosepipe in the Motorbike Story, which 'disappears' while the signer's hand functions as a placeholder for it. Such instances demonstrate that the fragment is presenting backgrounded, old information, but that this is not redundant information: the ongoing discussion is predicated on the presence of the hosepipe on her arm. Given this, we can say that in ISL fragment buoys may be either the maintenance on one hand of a two-handed sign (as where the MOTORBIKE is maintained on one hand as a fragment) or, perhaps less frequently, one-handed signs may be articulated on the non-dominant hand and maintained in a backgrounded manner for the same purpose.

8.5.4.2 Theme buoys

A theme buoy signifies that 'an important discourse theme is being discussed' (Liddell 2003: 242). In such instances, the non-dominant hand (or 'weak hand' in Liddell's terminology) maintains a one-handed configuration with the index finger elevated horizontally as the other hand produces an independent sign. Typically, the signer produces a sign related to the description of a theme of the discourse with the dominant hand while the non-dominant hand maintains the elevated index finger. Thus theme buoys can extend across a number of signs, but there are also instances of theme buoys that last for shorter instances, which as we shall see below also seems to have significance.

We might also see a signer point while introducing a character in a story to identify this character as a significant discourse theme.[4] Liddell (ibid.) notes that ASL signers who say they do not use the theme buoy themselves understand it and explain that 'it means that this is what the signer is talking about; that one must not forget', 'keep to it' and that 'this is the theme'. Given this, theme buoys help us to identify the essential aspects of discourse.

In ISL, theme buoys have two main functions: (1) to introduce and establish certain elements in discourse and (2) to introduce some new information where new referents are articulated by one-handed signs; or, as in Examples 8.18(b) and (c), a theme buoy can occur in some two-handed signs where signers can still process the intended meaning of the sign despite the degraded phonology of the non-dominant hand arising because the non-dominant hand takes on the phonology of the theme buoy with the result that the produced sign differs quite markedly from the citation form. In contrast, the theme buoy is not maintained to introduce two-handed referents like REINDEER, where the articulation of the two-handed sign could not be recovered together with maintenance of a theme buoy.

Example 8.18

(a) Theme buoy on non-dominant hand (right hand) and BEE introduced on dominant hand
Fiona (36) Frog Story (Waterford)

(b) Theme buoys maintained in discourse on non-dominant hand and MOTHER articulated with dominant hand
Fiona (36) Personal Stories (Waterford)

(c) Theme buoy maintained in discourse on non-dominant hand (left hand) while articulating a variant of IN
Fergus D. (06) Personal Stories (Dublin)

In Example 8.18(a), we see that BEE is introduced on the dominant hand (and subsequently a swarm of bees), while the theme buoy is articulated on the non-dominant hand. In (b), the signer signs MOTHER – which is normally a two-handed sign, articulated here on the dominant hand while the non-dominant hand maintains the theme buoy handshape. In the discourse, this is immediately followed by a similar articulation of FATHER (mother-father frog . . .), a seeming breach of Battison's (1978) symmetry principle, discussed earlier in Chapter 4. However, it seems that the breach of this phonological principle is permitted by the language because the place of articulation and the orientation of the palms remain as in the intended sign. This would also account for why two-handed signs like DEER cannot be modified to integrate a theme buoy in the same way.

However, it is not just symmetrical two-handed signs that can co-occur with a theme buoy in ISL. In Example 8.18(c) the signer signs IN, a normally two-handed sign where the dominant hand takes an I-handshape and the non-dominant hand takes a U-handshape. However, here the non-dominant handshape is not as expected. The signer maintains a theme buoy, but as with MOTHER, FATHER in (b), this does not seem to render impossible interpretation of the intended lexical item. As noted, IN does not usually have a symmetrical production of dominant and non-dominant hands, suggesting that it is also possible in certain circumstances to breach Battison's (ibid.) dominance constraint. This suggests that discourse requirements can, in certain contexts, supersede certain phonological requirements. Equally, it could be that there are no other signs like IN that are articulated with these handshapes in this space that could be confused by this alternative articulation. Either way, we can see clearly that in ISL, where the place of articulation of two-handed signs is in neutral space, and where the palm orientation of the non-dominant hand in the articulation of sign is downward, a theme buoy can be maintained, replacing the expected non-dominant handshape associated with the sign. This seems to be in line with Liddell's (2003) findings for ASL where the theme buoy can also serve as the base hand in an asymmetrical sign. However, it differs from the situation described for Swedish Sign Language (Nilsson 2007, 2010) where theme buoys disappear when the signer produces a two-handed sign.

In considering the duration of theme buoys in discourse, we find many examples where the theme buoy is maintained across a body of discourse. For example, in the Motorbike Story, the signer's non-dominant hand holds the theme buoy across the establishment of context for the Motorbike Story. It remains in place while she tells us that she used to get up at 5.30 a.m. and had to travel some distance to work. This is crucial in setting the scene for the story.

Another Example (8.19) comes from the Frog Story, where the signer maintains the theme buoy across a piece of discourse while signing. All of this is occurs in the search for the frog, and arises as the penultimate encounter prior to discovering the frog. The use of the theme buoy here seems to serve to keep us on track; this information is relevant to the final outcome of the story's theme.

Example 8.19

DOG FACE BREAK GLASS CROSS GIVING-OUT-TO-DOG CAREFUL/ LOOK FOR FROG WALK-OVER TO FIELD FAR-AWAY *DOG STARING-AT BEE *HIVE

'The dog broke the glass with his face. The boy was cross with the dog and gave out to him (chastised him), and told him to be careful. They continued to look for the frog. They walked quite some distance to a field. There, the dog stood staring at a bee-hive'

(Fiona (36) Frog Story (Waterford))

While the extension of an index finger is typically understood as being anaphoric, representing (depending on the direction of the pointing) first or non-first person referents or indeed a locative point, the theme buoy does not seem to be anaphoric in nature despite sharing the characteristic of extended index finger. Instead, it seems that while the dominant hand takes responsibility for anaphoric referencing to track pronominals in the discourse, the non-dominant hand's theme buoy does something else, or something in addition to this. In Example 8.19, the signer's dominant hand produces an anaphoric pointing sign, which is co-referential with the +sr space, while the non-dominant hand maintains the theme buoy position. The theme buoy then is maintained in neutral space, regardless of the referent tracking activities mapped by the dominant hand. This serves to reinforce our understanding of the theme buoy as serving to bring attention to the importance of the current discourse for the overall discourse topic.

Example 8.20

Dominant hand produces anaphoric pointing sign while non-dominant hand maintains a theme buoy in neutral space
Fiona (36) Frog Story (Waterford)

To summarise, we can say that when theme buoys have a shorter life in terms of articulation time, they seem to be associated with the introduction of new information. Where theme buoys are extended, co-occurring with longer stretches of discourse, they are associated with the theme or topic of an utterance. We also note that, unlike some other signed languages, it seems that theme buoys in ISL can perseverate across subsequent two-handed signs as long as the phonological status of the two-handed sign can be reconciled with the maintenance of the buoy. This seems to entail that the two-handed sign is articulated in neutral space and that the orientation of the palms is downward.

8.5.4.3 List buoys

Saeed and Leeson (2004) describe the use of listing strategies (Miller 1994) for ISL, which have been more recently described for ASL as 'list buoys' (Liddell 2003). Miller (1994) describes listing strategies as involving a sign articulated on the dominant hand on or in relation to an enumeration morpheme, which is expressed by the non-dominant hand. Liddell (2003) describes list buoys as being produced by the non-dominant (or in his terminology, 'weak hand'), which serves to provide a physical presence to ordered sets. The signer lists entities on his or her non-dominant hand. Further, list buoys are generally produced with the same hand configuration as the corresponding numeral sign, but they are produced on the non-dominant hand and are oriented differently than numeral signs, with a more horizontal orientation of fingers (Liddell et al. 2007: 189). In Example 8.20(a), we see the signer present a list buoy. Listed entities are typically identified by pointing or touching the non-dominant hand with the dominant and providing a lexical sign or fingerspelling. Saeed and Leeson (2004) suggest that such list buoys function as an episodic marker. List buoys are found in several signed languages, though in some they may be a feature of more formal discourse (Ingram 2000 for ASL). In ISL, such listing strategies also occur, though, as can be seen in Examples 8.20(a)–(c). List buoys do not seem to be obligatory, but instead provide another means to signers for considering how to frame discourse.

Example 8.21

(a) List buoy
Sean (13) Personal Stories (Dublin)

(b) d HAVE HOT d.o.g. CHICKEN BURGERS HAVE
nd FIRST _________ SECOND _________THIRD
'They have hotdogs, chicken and burgers'
(Informant data: female informant aged 25–35 years, deaf siblings and partner; dialogue: *The ABC of ISL* footage)
(Leeson 2001: 47)

(c) d IF ANYTHING CROP-UP CAN USE f.l.a.r.e.s. o.r. e.p.i.r.b.
nd SECOND_________________
INDEX f.+hi. LINK WITH s.a.t.e.l.l.i.t.e. trace-with-index-finger-f.+hi.-to-s.l.+lo TO
r.e.s.c.u.e. CENTRE
'If there is an emergency you can use flares or an E.P.I.R.B. This is linked by satellite to a rescue centre'
(Informant data: male aged 45–55 years, deaf sibling/s and spouse; *Hands On* footage)
(Leeson 2001: 47)

In Example 8.21(b) we see an example taken from *The ABC of ISL*, a series of short scenes with a language teaching aim (IDS and RTÉ) (Leeson 1997). In this scene, the signer and her interlocutor are at a barbeque. She explains to her friend what is available to eat. We note a very straightforward alternation between the listing strategy and the introduction of the 'new' item. The list is held on the non-dominant hand, suggesting that this information is functioning as a 'scaffold' for the new information, in this case, the foods available at the barbeque, which are foregrounded through articulation on the dominant hand. In (c) we see a signer presenting another list, this time a range of strategies open to Deaf sailors in emergency situations. He 'holds' the strategic point that is under discussion on his non-dominant hand while outlining what the strategy entails with the dominant hand. Again, we might suggest that the 'holding' of the list seems to function as a scaffold. In this instance the 'hold' seems to function as a reminder to the audience that the point under discussion is just one of a series of strategies that are available to them in emergency situations. The emergency strategies are introduced as new information, supported by the scaffolding. Emphasising the optionality of list buoys, Saeed and Leeson (2004) note that what we are now calling fragment buoys may also serve to maintain reference to backgrounded information. The list buoy can clarify the scope of the discourse since it can serve to enumerate the number of points that will be discussed, offering the interlocutors a well-defined frame of reference for understanding where the discourse is going.

8.5.4.4 Pointer buoys

Liddell (2003) describes the pointer buoy as pointing towards an important element in the discourse. This buoy differs from the list, THEME, and fragment buoys because it points *at* an element in real space or in a real space blend and thus does not represent the entity but points at it. The pointer is not a blended entity and other signs like pronouns and verbs do not point at it, which is possible with all the other buoys described thus far.

In Example 8.22, we see the signer use a pointer buoy to indicate towards IRELAND, which he has situated on the left-hand side of signing space. He follows this with a pointer buoy towards the right-hand side of signing space, a space co-referential for the UK. Here, we find a number of things happening. In 8.22(a), the signer simultaneously articulates IRELAND on the dominant hand while articulating the pointer buoy on the non-dominant hand. He is pointing towards the left-hand side of signing space, which maps the signing space to the real-world locations of Ireland versus the UK, from the perspective of someone looking at a map. Thus there is conflation of real-world locations with conceptual uses of space. The point of view presented is that of someone who is in-between these locations. This is interesting because the account is of a group of young deaf people who came to a summer camp for deaf youths, which took place in Ireland. The way the signer later talks about the bonds developed during the youth camp, and the fact that the participants were upset when they had to return to the 'hearing world', suggests that he conceptualises the physical signing space associated with discussion of the youth camp as being a place in-between, or another country: a 'Deaf world'.

In this instance, the pointer buoy is not anaphoric since it is not referring back to a previously established item: it co-occurs with the establishment of a referent, IRELAND. Instead, it positions IRELAND conceptually in signing space, and any subsequent reference to Ireland, or activities associated with coming from or returning to Ireland, are typically associated with that location.

Example 8.22

(a) IRELAND+sl
Pointer buoy towards IRELAND (+sl)
and the UK (+sr)
Sean (13) Personal Stories (Dublin)

(b) UK + sr
Pointer buoy towards IRELAND (+sl)
and the UK (+sr)

8.6 Summary

In this chapter we have discussed some important features of ISL discourse. We discussed politeness and noted that there are culturally established rules of engagement that govern the gaining of attention, engaging in signed conversations, observing conversations and turn-taking. We have seen that signers use a range of mechanisms to structure discourse including explicit discourse topics, specific time references and lexical connectives. We saw that the relative infrequency of lexical connectives is balanced by other devices, involving in particular the signer's uses of the non-dominant hand. These uses act in various ways to guide the addressee through the discourse. We considered the role of the theme buoy in introducing new information, and maintaining focus on the discourse topic across extended pieces of text. We saw that the fragment buoy serves to maintain and background old information while the dominant hand brings the text forward. List buoys function to structure and list-off subordinate elements associated with superordinate concepts – for example barbeque: chicken, burgers; or children: naming each in their birth order – as well as listing new subtopics that will be expanded on in the subsequent discourse stream. We looked at the role of the pointer buoy in directing attention to the positions of entities in real-world space.

We saw something of the strategies signers use to maintain reference to entities in discourse and to shift viewpoint in a narrative. Signers exploit the deictic resources of the language to move characters back and forth across the stage set by the story. They employ a range of shifting devices, most notably surrogacy, to privilege the perspective of characters other than the narrator. Looking over these various discourse strategies reveals that, as in all languages, ISL participants cooperate in identifying conversational goals and establishing background assumptions. Signers rely on their addressees' ability and willingness to make inferences in order to flesh out the explicit content into the signer's intended meaning.

Notes

1. This of course poses some difficulty for hearing people seeking to acquire ISL and concentrating on sign formation.
2. Thanks to Prof. Terry Janzen and his class at the University of Manitoba, Canada, for raising this possibility.
3. The Motorbike Story presents the signer's experience of going to work by moped in the midwinter. She tells how she prepared to leave home while it was still dark. She turned the moped's engine on to warm it up, and when she went to leave, she felt that something was not quite right, but as everything seemed fine, she proceeded with her journey. As she made her way to work, she found herself being followed by a truck driver. She feared she was going to be abducted or that there was something untoward about the truck driver's persistence. He frequently flashed his headlights at her, but she did not know what he was trying to achieve with this act. At a set of traffic lights, the truck driver stopped beside her, rolled down his window and told her to look behind her. She turned to find that there was a 20-foot garden hosepipe attached to her rear wheel; she had not seen it in the dark.
4. Note that this use does not mean that the character is at an indicated location in space.

9 Towards a Cognitive Account of Signed Languages

9.1 Introduction

In this chapter we return to the ideas of cognitive linguistics, which we have touched on at several points in this volume. We will examine what light the study of ISL can throw on important notions in this paradigm. Looking the other way, we shall see how useful these notions are for bringing out key features of ISL. We have, for example, touched on the role of metaphor and metonymy in the ISL lexicon. We have also seen something of the spatial mental models by which signers keep track of entities in discourse. Similar spatial cognitive strategies are seen in signers' manipulation of temporal references. A marked feature of ISL is the extent to which the signer's body plays a role in a whole range of semantic and pragmatic processes, including mappings between body partitions and elements of the discourse. Each of these characteristics follows naturally from cognitive linguistics' views of how human languages work. We look at some of these in more detail in the following sections. We hope that this discussion will give us a chance to look back and summarise some general features of ISL that have been described in the chapters dealing with specific linguistic levels, and thus act as a conclusion to this volume.

9.2 Embodiment

A cognitive approach to language description views linguistic knowledge as part of general cognition where there is no separation of linguistic knowledge from general thinking or cognition (Lakoff 1987). In this way, the distinctions between literal and figurative language, linguistic knowledge and encyclopaedic knowledge are blurred or ignored. Language behaviour is seen as a part of the broad spectrum of human cognitive abilities that allow for learning, reasoning, etc. to occur. This differentiates the cognitive approach from, for example, generative linguistics, which argues that language and the general cognitive processes differ to such an extent that a separate model is hypothesised for language.

Cognitivists suggest that an explanation of grammatical patterns cannot be given in terms of abstract syntactic principles, but only in terms of speakers' intended meaning in particular contexts of language use; they propose cognitive models which structure thought. Such models, they argue, are used in reasoning and in the formation of categories. Depending on the level of use, concepts characterised by cognitive models are 'embodied' (Johnson 1987). Embodiment is the idea is that language users' physical experience of being and acting in the world, of perceiving the environment, moving bodies, exerting and experiencing force, etc., allows them to form basic conceptual structures which then are used to organise thought across a range of more abstract domains. This, Lakoff argues, contrasts with the classical view of concepts existing independently, removed from the 'bodily nature and experience of thinking beings' (Lakoff 1987: 13). We saw in Chapter 7 that ISL's temporal concepts are rooted in the body of the signer: time is conceived as a line relative to the shoulder of the dominant signing hand: the line stretches forward into the future and backwards into the past. We also saw that signers tend to tilt their bodies forward when indicating future events and lean backwards when establishing time frames that have a past-tense reading. The signer's body also plays an important role in information structure in discourse. In Chapter 8 we saw the relationship that exists between narrative perspective and the position of the signer's body. Signers present what is before them at c. locus as the most focused elements in a discourse while other less salient information is presented more distantly from the signer's body. Thus proximity to the forward orientation of the body is equated conceptually to the focus of attention in discourse.

In Chapter 8 we saw a further way in which the signer's body embodies narrative viewpoint: signers may describe the actions of others by representing them through the medium of their own body. This strategy has been given various labels, including surrogacy or constructed action. Normally of course the world is viewed through the eyes of the signer and presented through the signer's body. Surrogacy allows the signer to present other viewpoints in an embodied way. The signer's body becomes a device to make the audience adopt a new viewpoint for the purposes of narrative dynamism. A more complex version of this is body partitioning, where the signer subdivides his or her body to represent a number of different actors at the same time and from a cognitive perspective, simultaneously maps whole sections of the narrative onto his or her body. We will discuss partitioning a little later when we look at conceptual blending.

9.3 Lexical concepts and real-world knowledge

As mentioned earlier, cognitive linguists have re-examined the distinction between linguistic knowledge and ordinary, real-world knowledge. One area of investigation is at the lexical level: the extent to which knowledge of a word's meaning, for example a noun like *computer* or *whale*, is related to real-world knowledge about its possible referents. Cognitivists Evans and Green (2006) have argued that meaning does not reside in words themselves but in the structured contextual integration of lexical concepts and real-world knowledge. Words, in this view, have only a potential for meaning, which is activated in particular contexts by the process of composition from the resources available to the participants from their lexical and encyclopaedic knowledge. This account responds to the problem of the plasticity of word meaning by suggesting that any one word meaning derives from a unique nexus of various inputs. This view of online integration of lexical concepts and real-world knowledge, following conventional procedures, gives a useful view of the items described in Chapter 6 as part of the ISL productive lexicon. An illustration of this is Example 5.30 from the discussion of classifier predicates in Chapter 5, repeated in Example 9.1.

Example 9.1
'blah-blah'
. . . c.+CL.C.+move-to-mouth . . .
'. . . I can use the radio . . .'
(Informant T: interview, *Hands On* footage)
(Leeson 2001: 48)

Here we see the composition of a lexical item from a number of sources. The classifier is a type of handle entity-CL, classifying entities according to how they are manipulated by the human hand; here it is what we described as a CL-C-handshape. The contextual information includes the movement to the mouth and the accompanying mouthing gestures. The integration of these with knowledge of the context, a story about Deaf sailors, and its related real-world knowledge allows the communication of a lexical sign 'radio'. This view that word meaning is a compositional and one-off phenomenon fits very well with the use of words in ISL.

9.4 Metonymy and metaphor

Metonymy and metaphor are from the cognitive perspective both instances of analogical mapping. Metonymy maps within a domain of knowledge, while metaphor maps between distinct domains of knowledge. We saw in Chapter 6 how important metonymy is in ISL lexical semantics. A number of taxonomies have been suggested for the types of association that can produce metonymy, for example by Lakoff and Johnson (1980), Fass (1991), Nunberg (1995) and Kövecses and Radden (1998). Some typical associations are part for whole, traditionally called synecdoche; producer for product; and action for agent. We saw examples of lexical signs for animals, where part for whole metonymies allow representations of parts of the body to form signs such as BIRD, where the part is the beak; BULL, the shape of horns; CAT, whiskers, TIGER, stripes; GIRAFFE, long neck; and ELEPHANT, trunk. A similar metonymic relation is exploited for activities, where a part of an activity is highlighted to form a verb, as in DRIVE-CAR where the action of holding the steering wheel is generalised to the manifold activity of driving.

The pervasiveness of metonymy is reflected in the name signs used by members of the Deaf community. In Chapter 7 we described how signers identified each other by associated attributes, whether physical and therefore a part for whole metonymy such as PIGTAILS or RED-CHEEKS, or by activities associated with them, such as RUB-JAW, PLAY-PIANO or PUSH-GLASSES-UP-NOSE, which we could call an action for agent metonymy. These metonymic names support Kövecses and Radden's (1998) claim of a priority for experiential and in particular perceptual motivations in the selection of metonymic relations.

An extended figurative use of the terms DEAF and HEARING can be likened to metonymy: where the physical attributes can be used to refer to membership or otherwise of a culturally defined community. Thus a Deaf person may tell another Deaf person, 'YOU HEARING' as an insult to suggest that they are holding the values of the non-Deaf world above those of members of the Deaf community. In contrast, a Deaf person may tell a hearing person who is a fluent ISL user, 'YOU DEAF!' to compliment them on not only their signing skill, but also the positive views they hold towards Deaf culture, and perhaps the fact that they have embraced the values of the Deaf community.

Metaphor, which links different domains of knowledge, also plays an important role in the formation of lexical items. Some of these reflect metaphors in other languages, for example the metaphor described by Lakoff (1987: 384) for English as ANGER IS A HEATED FLUID IN A CONTAINER which is reflected in the ISL lexical metaphor that makes use of the HEATED FLUID IN A CONTAINER metaphor, with BOILING-IN-TORSO to mean 'really angry'. This takes the lexical sign BOIL which is normally articulated in neutral space and re-positions it at the signer's body to mean 'I was boiling (with anger)' This can be extended with the addition of BOIL+move-upwards-in-torso / STEAM-COME-OUT-OF-EARS to mean 'I boiled over and had steam coming out of my ears', a literal translation, or 'I was really angry'.[1] Other metaphors reflect the experience of Deaf signers. A particularly important metaphor is SEEING IS KNOWING, which reflects the importance of the visual field for Deaf signers, together with its corollary NOT SEEING IS NOT KNOWING. These metaphors have a grammatical reflex in the use of averted eyegaze to mark the lack of volition or control of a participant in an action, for example in passives constructions (Leeson 2001; Leeson and Saeed 2003). Shifting eyegaze away from an interlocutor is also a way of signalling a disengagement from dialogue, or interrupting.

ISL signers frequently employ ontological metaphors (Lakoff and Johnson 1980) where abstract concepts are conceptualised in concrete terms. An example is IDEAS ARE OBJECTS. The lexical sign for physically taking hold of an object, GRASP, is shown in Example 9.2 and this sign (on the dominant hand) has become the lexical sign for HAVE.[2] In Example 9.3 we see the same handshape used in a phrase GRASP (A DEER'S) ANTLERS.

Example 9.2

HAVE (tol hold/grasp something)
Senan (01) Personal Stories (Dublin)

Example 9.3

GRASPING ANTLERS
Fergus D. (06) Personal Stories (Dublin)

This sign is used metaphorically for REMEMBER when formed at the signer's head, as in Example 9.4.

Example 9.4

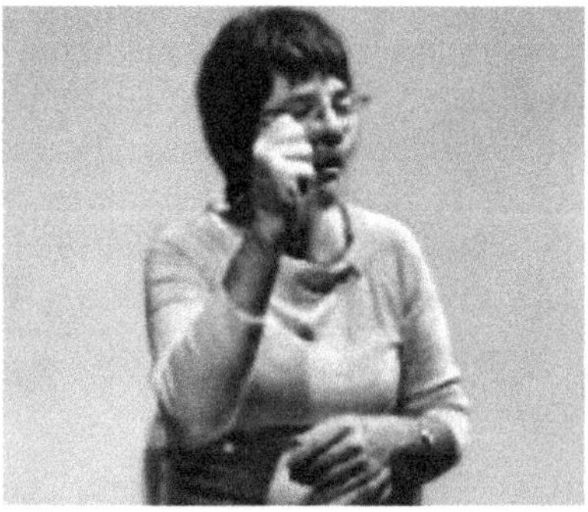

REMEMBER (GRASP-AT-HEAD)
Marion (08) Personal Stories (Dublin)

Similarly, the lexical sign THROW-AWAY, used for physical objects, shown in citation form in Example 9.5, can be used metaphorically at the signer's head to mean FORGET as in Example 9.6. This conception of ideas as objects in the signer's head also employs the BODY-AS-CONTAINER metaphor, discussed by Lakoff and Johnson (1980) and Lakoff and Kövecses (1987) amongst others.

Example 9.5

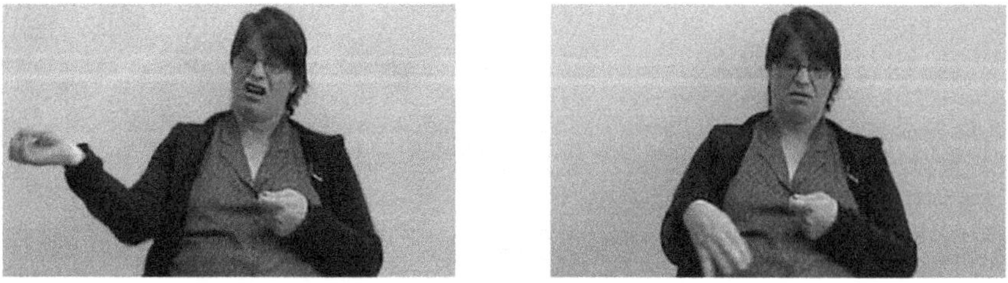

THROW-AWAY (physical entity)
Michelee (05) Personal Stories (Dublin)

In another metaphor, theories or opinions are conceptualised as a FLUID, so the same handshape used for WATER-FLOWS can, if made at the forehead, signify THEORY or PHILOSOPHY. This sign used as a double agreement verb can have the meaning HAVE-THE-SAME-OPINION or, to use an English metaphor, 'be on the same wavelength'.

A related metaphor employs a movement between CL-Bent-Index – CL-INDEX, which is used to represent physical items that are moving. This is particularly used to refer to something 'popping up' or, in context, splashes, for example when a raindrop hits the ground and bounces off the path; or a small entity appearing from nowhere.[3] This sign is used metaphorically,

Example 9.6

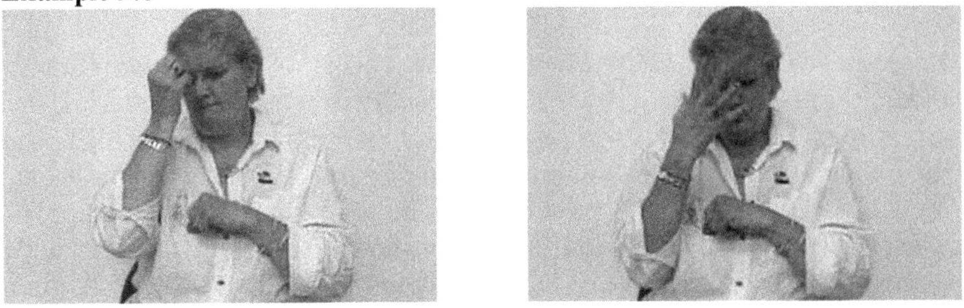

FORGET (THROW AWAY/LOSE – AT HEAD)
Catherine (31) Personal Stories (Cork)

articulated at the side of the signer's head, to mean 'an idea popped up in the mind', as shown in Example 9.7.

Example 9.7

IDEA-POP-UP (GET-IDEA)
Eric (32) Frog Story (Cork)

Such ontological metaphors are very common in ISL, so for example OPPRESSION is metaphorically conceptualised as shown in Example 9.8 as one dominant animate entity physically pressing down on a smaller entity; while people's behaviour can be handled like physical objects in the lexical verbs CONTROL, MANAGE, CO-ORDINATE and MANIPULATE.

Example 9.8

(a) OPPRESS (onset)
Senan (01) Personal Stories (Dublin)

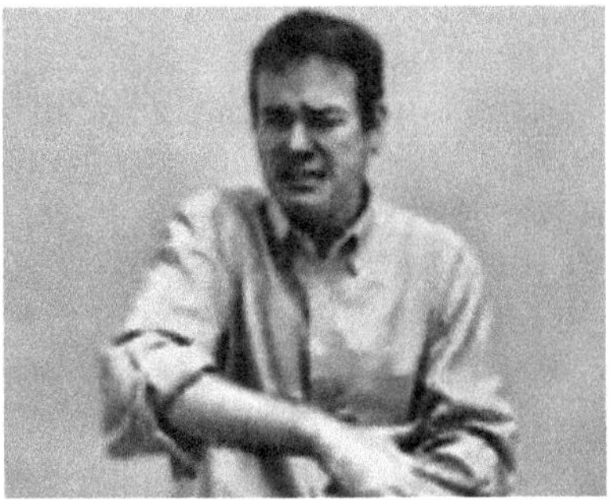

(b) OPPRESS (offset)
Senan (01) Personal Stories (Dublin)

9.5 Mental spaces

Fauconnier's (1985, 1997) Mental Space Theory is a cognitive semantic theory that began by describing the complexity of referential strategies, such as indirect reference, shifts of reference and referential opacity, which occur in ordinary spontaneous communication. It does this in terms of mental models, or spaces, that communicators mutually create and manipulate. These spaces contain representations of entities and relations currently under discussion. New spaces are created, for example, when speakers talk about hypothetical scenarios or events in the past. Such spaces have their internal coherence, but are also linked to other spaces, including a link to the present utterance space, by various linguistic devices. Although the referential strategies are triggered by language, Fauconnier identifies a range of cognitive processes that are used to 'flesh out' the under-represented meaning that the language input provides. The theory has been extended to describe a wide range of behaviour in spoken and signed languages. As the theory has developed, a number of cognitive processes have been identified in the use of such spaces, including partitioning, analogy, schema induction, structure projection and conceptual blending.

All of these processes take place within the general processes of meaning construction. Fauconnier argues that 'language expressions' (E) possess a 'meaning potential'. As discourse unfolds, complex cognitive processes are called into play. An expression thus generates meaning:

> when the grammatical information E contains is applied to an existing cognitive configuration, several new configurations will be possible in principle (i.e. comparable with the grammatical clues). One of them will be produced, yielding a new step in the construction underlying the discourse. (Fauconnier 1997: 38)

Fauconnier sees this as a process in which unfolding discourse is a 'succession of cognitive configurations' (ibid.). He argues that each successive cognitive configuration gives rise to the next under pressure from grammar and context, that is, both grammar and the unfolding context affect the interpretation of a linguistic event. Pragmatic factors may also affect the establishment of a new configuration. He argues that as discourse unfolds, the discourse participants metaphorically move through the 'space lattice', that is, the series of connected spaces that are established to represent the base viewpoint, conditional/hypothetical events, temporal variations, etc. referred to in discourse. Discourse participants' viewpoints and focus shift as they move through the space lattice while the base space remains accessible as a starting point for another construction. To allow discourse participants to find their way through this 'maze of mental spaces', and to use the partitioning of the spaces to draw appropriate inferences,

Fauconnier argues that three dynamic notions are crucial: Base, Viewpoint and Focus:

> At any point in the construction, one space is distinguished as Viewpoint, the space from which others are accessed and structured or set up; one space is distinguished as Focus, the space currently being structured internally, – the space, so to speak, upon which attention is currently focused; and one space is distinguished as the Base – a starting point for the construction of which it is always possible to return. Base, Viewpoint and Focus need not be distinct: more often than not, we find the same space serving as Viewpoint and Focus, or Base and Focus, or Base and Viewpoint, or all three: Base, Viewpoint and Focus. (49)

We have seen in the course of our description that ISL uses spatial locations as an integral part of its system of pronominal reference. Signers associate referent with points in the signing space that are termed 'loci'. Pronominal signs are directed to those loci to identify their referents. Liddell (2000) has argued that when ASL signers use a similar system they are directing the sign towards a token placed at the locus rather than the locus itself. This is supported by the fact that under certain conditions the token may move to another locus and still retain the referential link. It is also possible for two tokens to occupy the same locus. Also working on ASL, Van Hoek (1996) looks at the relationship that exists between mental spaces and referential loci, arguing that the most salient referents are accessed even where other loci have previously been used for pronominal reference for the same referent. She assumes that:

> loci may vary in their imagistic content; in one discourse (or at one moment in a particular discourse) a locus may be conceived as a detailed, highly specific mental image of the referent, and in another discourse (or at another point in time) may be a highly schematised, non-specific image – which includes the possibility that the image may consist of an association between the referent and the point in space, with no other visual-imagistic content. (234)

She goes on to develop her concept of the relationship between referents and loci by arguing that:

> these quasi-imagistic associations between referents and loci may involve much more than simply the establishment of the referent, as an isolated notion, with a particular point in space. Referential loci are frequently associated with the larger 'scenes' or spatial settings which the referent occupies. (234)

Van Hoek establishes that there is a relationship between mental spaces and referential loci. She provides evidence to support the view that the most salient referents in a discourse event are accessed even where other loci have previously been used for the same pronominal referent. She suggests that the principles of locus selection in ASL seem congruent with the general principles of accessibility that have been developed by Givón (1989) and Ariel (1988, 1990). Crucially, she notes that:

> Accessibility Theory holds that a particular nominal form is selected for reference in a given context to reflect the degree of accessibility (roughly 'retrievability') of the referent in that context. Cross-linguistically, full nominals (names and descriptive phrases) are markers of relatively low accessibility, used where the referent is not highly active in the addressee's awareness. Pronouns are markers of relatively high accessibility and null anaphora (i.e. no phonological marking of co-reference) marks still higher accessibility. (Van Hoek 1996: 337)

This may help explain the fact that fluent ISL signers can distinguish between c. locus as first person and c. locus as non-specified agent in discourse, as in passives (Leeson and Saeed 2004). As noted by Van Hoek, in passive constructions the patient is the most highly activated referent in both the signer's and the addressee's awareness, licensing the signer's use of constructions with little or no attention focused on the agent. Thus accessibility is determined by salience.

It seems, then, that mental space theory gives a useful tool to account for ISL signers' use of their pronominal system. The participants occupy the real space; the signer creates a further mental space by identify links between tokens and referents. The signer by pointing at loci then creates links between the two spaces. Pointing signs used deictically can indicate individuals present in the context of communication; mental space theory allows us to explain uses where the pointing sign indicates individuals who are part of the signer's mental representation.

9.6 Conceptual blending

Conceptual blending (Fauconnier and Turner 2002), or conceptual integration, is a development of mental space theory that seeks to describe how language users take knowledge from different domains of experience, viewed as mental spaces, and combine it to create new extended analogies. It has been applied to signed language narrative strategies such as those we saw in Chapter 8, where the signer integrates different elements, including his or her own body, into a composite representation of events. Dudis (2004) describes how ASL signers use simultaneous constructions involving the signer's hands and body, including eyegaze, to create and maintain grounded blends. He seeks to show how a signer's narrative goals interact with the physiological limits of a manually articulated language in the construction of a signed language narrative. Dudis reports how signers frequently establish simultaneous blends by assigning different body parts to separate spaces in order to overcome such constraints, leading to a range of narrative strategies on which signers can draw. One ASL example he gives (59) relates to a hunter's encounter with a deer, where the hunter and the deer are two elements that compose the base space, while use of the plain verb HUNT adds a hunting frame to the mental space. The narrator, by the shifted reference or surrogacy strategy we described in Chapter 8, may become the hunter during the narration while continuing the role of narrator. The signer's audience has no difficulty understanding the blended scene before them, for example when the signer's head tilt, eyegaze and hand configurations are the hunter's. Participants can also bring in and rely on knowledge from the relevant input spaces. Thus the audience can infer the use of a weapon in the hunting space without it being overtly mentioned.

Leeson and Saeed (2007) report on a range of conceptual blends in IS, using as an example the 'war in Iraq' narrative in Examples 5.2 and 8.14. They describe how the signer uses his body and the signing space to represent different views of the topography of Iraq and surrounding countries. They note that the signer establishes the discourse topic at the outset and establishes the historical context to this war, clearly establishing a base space for Iraq that is situated in neutral signing space. The signer then relates different sections of the country to security operations. For example, he discusses how the northern sector of Iraq was deemed a no-fly zone, as shown in Example 9.9. The signer uses a baby-C-handshape to point out parts of Iraq where planes are not allowed to fly. This baby-C is superimposed on the non-dominant CL-B-handshape which serves to represent the entire country of Iraq. In addition to being a structure that illustrates relative location, there is an iconic relation: the baby-C-handshape placed over the non-dominant hand, representing the aerial zone mapped out over the real-world geographical territory. However, the simultaneous construction here does not serve to mark the relative location of two elements but instead allows for a backgrounding–foregrounding contrast between the areas in Iraq which could be accessed by aircraft.

In this narrative the locations of the geographical areas in signing space and their mode of presentation shift as the narrator's viewpoint moves. In Examples 9.10–12 the narrator first sets the scene, presenting in 9.10 the geographical location of Kuwait relative to the location for Iraq, which is represented here on the non-dominant hand by the CL-C-handshape, holding Iraq's location firm. The signer explains that the invading forces wished to move on Iraq from the south, that is, troops would march northwards, from Kuwait, into Iraq. The signer goes on to note that the invading forces also wished to move simultaneously, from the north, through Turkey, moving

Example 9.9

(a) dh: CL:B 'THAT AREA')
ND: CL:B. ____________
Senan (01) Personal Stories (Dublin)

(b) dh: NOT ALLOW FLY-AIRPLANE
ND: CL:B ________________
Senan (01) Personal Stories (Dublin)

southwards into Iraq. The segments in bold indicate the relevant areas of text establishing these notions.

Example 9.10

SO PLAN FIRM WAR SHRUG
u.n. INSPECTOR EXAMINE++
INDEX+various-locations+sr WEAPONS EXAMINE SHRUG
HAVE-TO LEAVE FLY-OUT-OF i.r.a.q.
SAME TIME BEFORE-THAT-TIME AMERICA PLAN WANT WAR INDEX+sr
dh: AREA AROUND k.u.w.a.i.t. 2 / h CL-5+OPEN 'MANY-MOVE-NORTH'
nd: CL-C
SAME WANT
dh: TURKEY
nd: CL-B+MOVE-FROM-NORTH-TOWARDS-SOUTH
t.u.r.k.e.y.
dh:
nd: CL-B+MOVE-FROM-NORTH-TOWARDS-SOUTH
dh:
nd: CL-B-BENT 'MOVE-IN-FROM-NORTH'
ASK TURKEY PERMISSION ASK
'And so the war was planned. The UN inspectors who were in Iraq to search for weapons (of mass destruction) had to leave Iraq. At the same time, America was planning what they wanted in terms of a war plan. Specifically, they intended to move north from Kuwait and, at the same time, move south from Turkey, but in order to do this, they needed to get permission from the Turks'
(Senan (01) Personal Stories (Dublin))

The crucial instances can be seen in the illustrations below. In Example 9.11, the signer describes how the inspectors leave Iraq. What is interesting is how the event is framed. Here, Iraq, which has been at c. locus, is now moved to the left side of signing space, illustrating a shift in focus between the attention on what is happening in the country, and for now, the attention given to the inspectors' act of leaving Iraq. The fact that the signer, as narrator, is using NMFs associated with the plane's 'normal' departure ('mm') reinforces this, suggesting that more central focus, in this scene, is the controversial departure of the inspectors.

Example 9.11

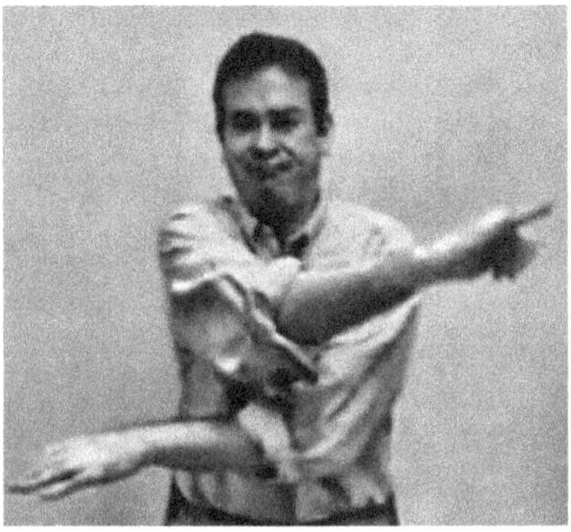

(U.N. inspectors) FLY-OUT-OF (i.r.a.q.)
'(The UN inspectors who were in Iraq to search for weapons (of mass destruction) had) to leave Iraq'
Senan (01) Personal Stories (Dublin)

Example 9.12 illustrates the backgrounding of the mental space for Iraq, which is gapped, or omitted, while the signer's dominant and non-dominant hand now represent the American army's intended path of invasion via Kuwait and Turkey. Both countries were previously established, and therefore, active referents for the viewer. Equally, the now invisible central space associated with IRAQ remains accessible while backgrounded, remaining the key concept across the narrative. In this detailed view of parts of this narrative we see a blending of spaces involving locations and entities in the real world, a projected map of these, and elements of the signer's real space. The signer uses parts of his body to represent entities moving around the war zone, while his eyegaze is directed towards the projected map, representing the viewpoint of the signer himself as narrator, inviting his audience to view the events.

Example 9.12

dh: CL:B+MOVE-FROM-NORTH-TOWARDS-SOUTH
nd: CL:B-BENT 'MOVE-IN-FROM-NORTH'................
'(America) intended to move north (from Kuwait) and, at the same time, move south (from Turkey)'
Senan (01) Personal Stories (Dublin)

9.7 Conclusion

We have briefly touched on some ideas from cognitive linguistics about how languages are constructed and used. In exploring the relationship between conceptual structures and language, this approach has shed light on such issues as the role of the body in linguistic concepts, iconicity, the role of metaphor and metonymy in lexicon and grammar, and the mental models used in managing referential links. These proposals seek to characterise all human languages but we hope to have shown in the course of this book how well they contribute to the understanding of sign languages, and Irish Sign Language in particular. Linguists have only started to investigate the complexity and richness of the grammatical structures and discourse practices of ISL. This book is presented in the hope of taking some early steps in what will be a long and exciting journey.

Notes

1. This metaphor is discussed by several writers, for example Lakoff and Kövecses (1987), as a combination of two more basic metaphors: EMOTION AS CONTAINED LIQUID and THE BODY AS CONTAINER FOR EMOTIONS.
2. The use of this handshape for HAVE seems to have emerged in the past twenty years or so, and may have been borrowed from BSL. Over the past two decades, this sign has moved from meaning 'to have a physical item in one's possession' (for example, HAVE BOOK, HAVE MONEY,

which literally can be held) to less concrete items like HAVE IDEA 'have an idea', HAVE VISION 'have a vision of something'.

3. This sign is also used as an established lexical item to mean OPPORTUNITY, that is something-good-pops-up, though this usage may have been borrowed from BSL in the 1990s, since it is not used widely in this way by older signers.

References

Aarons, D. and Reynolds, L. (2003), 'South African Sign Langauge: changing policies and practice', in L. Monaghan, C. Schmaling, K. Nakamura and G. H. Turner (eds), *Many Ways to be Deaf: International Variation in Deaf Communitites*, Washington, DC: Gallaudet University Press, pp. 194–210.

Aikhenvald, A. Y. (2000), *Classifiers: A Typology of Noun Categorization Devices*, Oxford: Oxford University Press.

Allan, K. (1977), 'Classifiers', *Language*, 53(2), 285–311.

Angry Silence, television documentary. Ireland: TG4/Irish Deaf Society, 1998.

Ariel, M. (1988), 'Referring and accessibility', *Journal of Linguistics*, 24, 65–87.

Ariel, M. (1990), *Accessing Noun-Phrase Antecedents*, London and New York: Routledge.

Armstrong, D. F. (1999), 'The gestural theory of language origins', *Sign Language Studies*, 8(3), 289–314.

Armstrong, D. F., Stokoe, W. C. and Wilcox, S. (1995), *Gesture and the Nature of Language*, Cambridge: Cambridge University Press.

Armstrong, D. F. and Wilcox, S. (2007), *The Gestural Origin of Language*, New York and Oxford: Oxford University Press.

Baker, C. and Padden, C. (1978), *American Sign Language: A Look at its Story, Structure and Community*, Silver Spring, MD: T. J. Publishers.

Baker, R. and Knight, P. (1988), '"Total communication": current policy and practice', in S. Gregory, P. Knight, W. McCracken, S. Powers and L. Watson (eds), *Issues in Deaf Education*, London: David Fulton, pp. 77–88.

Baker-Shenk, C. and Cokely, D. (1980), *American Sign Language: A Teacher's Resource Text on Grammar and Culture*, Silver Spring, MD: T. J. Publishers.

Battison, R. (1978), *Lexical Borrowing in American Sign Language*, Silver Spring, MD: Linstok Press.

Bergman, B. (1977), *Technad svenska. Utbildingsforskning*, (English translation: *Signed Swedish*, 1979), Stockholm: LiberLäromedel/Utbildningsförlaget.

Bergman, B. (1983), 'Verbs and Adjectives: Some Morphological Processes in Swedish Sign Language', in J. G. Kyle and B. Woll (eds), *Language in Sign: An International Perspective on Sign Language*, London: Croom Helm, pp. 3–9.

Bloomfield, L. (1926), 'A set of postulates for the science of language', *Language*, 2, 153–64.

Bloomfield, L. (1933), *Language*, New York: Henry Holt.

Boyes Braem, P. (2001), 'Functions of the mouthings in the signing of Deaf early and late learners of Swiss German Sign Language (DSGS)', in P. Boyes Braem and R. Sutton-Spence (eds), *The Hands are the Head of the Mouth: The Mouth as Articulator in Sign Languages*, Hamburg: Signum, pp. 99–132.

Brelje, H. W. (ed.) (1999), *Global Perspectives on the Education of the Deaf in Selected Countries*, Hillsboro, OR: Butte.

Brennan, M. (1983), 'The marking of time in British Sign Language', in J. G. Kyle and B. Woll (eds), *Language in Sign: An International Perspective on Sign Language*, London: Croom Helm, pp. 10–31.

Brennan, M. (1986), 'Linguistic perspectives', in B. T. Tervoort (ed.), *Signs of Life: Proceedings of the Second European Congress on Sign Language Research*, Amsterdam: Dutch Foundation for the Deaf and Hearing Impaired Child, Institute of General Linguistics, University of Amsterdam and Dutch Council of the Deaf, pp. 1–16.

Brennan, M. (1990), *Word Formation in British Sign Language*, Stockholm: University of Stockholm.

Brennan, M. (1992), 'The visual world of BSL: an introduction', in D. Brien (ed.), *Dictionary of British Sign Language/English*, London: Faber and Faber, pp. 1–134.

Brennan, M. (1994), 'Word order: introducing the issues', in M. Brennan and G. H. Turner (eds), *Word Order Issues in Sign Language*, Durham: International Sign Linguistics Association, pp. 9–46.

Brennan, M., Hughes, G. and Lawson, L. K. (1984), *Words in Hand: A Structural Analysis of the Signs of British Sign Language*, Edinburgh: Edinburgh BSL Research Project.

Brien, D. (ed.) (1992), *Dictionary of British Sign Language/English*, London: Faber and Faber.

Brisard, F. (2006), 'Logic, subjectivity and the semantics/pragmatics distinction', in A. Anthanasiadou, C. Canakis and B. Cornillie (eds), *Subjectification: Various Paths to Subjectivity*, Berlin: Mouton de Gruyter, pp. 41–74.

Brown, G. and Yule, G. (1983), *Discourse Analysis*, Cambridge: Cambridge University Press.

Bybee, J., Perkins, R. and Paglucia, W. (1994), *The Evolution of Grammar: Tense, Aspect and Modality in the Languages of the World*, Chicago: University of Chicago Press.

Byrne-Dunne, D. (2005), *Language Acquisition by Deaf Children in Ireland: Some Theoretical Considerations and Two Case Studies*, Dublin: Trinity College Dublin.

Catholic Institution for the Deaf and Dumb (1881), *Annual Report of the Catholic Institution for the Deaf and Dumb*, Dublin: Catholic Institution for the Deaf and Dumb.

Chafe, W. L. (1994), *Discourse, Consciousness and Time: Flow and Displacement of Conscious Experience in Speaking and Writing*, Chicago: University of Chicago Press.

Conama, J. B. (2008), *Evaluation of Signing Information Mid-West*, Limerick: PAUL Partnership.

Conama, J. B. and Grehan, C. (2002), *Is there Poverty in the Deaf Community?*, Dublin: Irish Deaf Society and Combat Poverty Agency.

Conrad, R. (1979), *The Deaf School Child: Language and Cognitive Function*, London: Harper and Row.

Conroy, P. (2006), *Signing In and Signing Out: The Education and Employment Experiences of Deaf People in Ireland. A Study of Inequality and Deaf People in Ireland*, Dublin: Irish Deaf Society.

Coogan, A. (2003), *Irish Deaf Women: The Appropriateness of their Education?*, Dublin: Trinity College Dublin.

Corker, M. (1996), *Deaf Transitions: Images and Origins of Deaf Families, Deaf Communities and Deaf Identities*, London: Jessica Kingsley.

Crasborn, O. (2001), *Phonetic Implementation of Phonological Categories in Sign Language of the Netherlands*, Utrecht: LOT.

Crean, E. J. (1997), *Breaking the Silence: The Education of the Deaf in Ireland 1816–1996*, Dublin: Irish Deaf Society.

Dahl, Ö. (1985), *Tense and Aspect Systems*, Oxford: Blackwell.

de Jorgio, A. (2000), *Gesture in Naples and Gesture in Classical Antiquity. A translation of La mimica degli antichi investigata nel gestire napoletano (Fibreno, Naples 1832) and with an introduction and notes by Adam Kendon*, Bloomington and Indianapolis: Indiana University Press.

De Smet, H. and Verstraete, J. C. (2006), 'Coming to terms with subjectivity', *Cognitive Linguistics*, 17(3), 365–92.

Department of Education (1972), *The Education of Children who are Handicapped by Impaired Hearing*, Dublin: Government Publications.

Department of Education and Science (1998), 'Education Act 1998', Dublin: Government Publications.

Deuchar, M. (1984), *British Sign Language*, London: Routledge and Keegan Paul.

Deuchar, M. (1987), 'Sign language research', in J. Lyons, R. Coates, M. Deuchar and G. Gazdar (eds), *New Horizons in Linguistics 2*, London: Penguin, pp. 311–55.

Dowty, D. R. (1991), 'Thematic proto-roles and argument selection', *Language*, 67, 574–619.

Dudis, P. (2002), 'Grounded blend maintenance as a discourse strategy', in C. Lucas (ed.), *Turntaking, Fingerspelling, and Contact in Signed Languages*, Washington, DC: Gallaudet University Press, pp. 53–72.

Dudis, P. (2004), 'Body partitioning and real-space blends', *Cognitive Linguistics*, 15(2), 223–38.

Engberg-Pedersen, E. (1993), *Space in Danish Sign Language: The Semantics and Morphosyntax of the Use of Space in a Visual Language*, Hamburg: Signum.

European Parliament (1988), 'Resolution on Sign Languages as Adopted by the European Parliament in Plenary Session on 17 June 1988', Doc. A2-302/87, Brussels: European Parliament.

European Parliament (1998), 'Resolution on Sign Languages as Adopted by the European Parliament in Plenary Session on 18 November 1998', Doc. B4-0985/98, Brussels European Parliament.

European Union of the Deaf (2010), Brussels Declaration on Sign Languages in the European Union, available at <eud.eu/uploads/brussels_declaration_English.pdf> (accessed 25 November 2011).

Evans, V., and Green, M. (2006), *Cognitive Linguistics: An Introduction*, Edinburgh: Edinburgh University Press.

Fass, D. C. (1991), 'met*: A method for discriminating metonymy and metaphor by computer', *Computational Linguistics*, 17(1), 49–90.

Fauconnier, G. (1985), *Mental Spaces: Aspects of Meaning Construction in Natural Language*, Cambridge, MA: MIT Press.

Fauconnier, G. (1997), *Mappings in Thought and Language*, Cambridge: Cambridge University Press.

Fauconnier, G., and Turner, M. (2002), *The Way We Think: Conceptual Blending and the Mind's Hidden Complexities*, New York: Basic Books.

Fitzgerald, A. (forthcoming), *A Cognitive Account of Mouthings and Mouth Gestures in Irish Sign Language*, Dublin: Trinity College Dublin.

Foley, W. A., and Van Valin, R. D. J. (1984), *Functional Syntax and Universal Grammar*, Cambridge: Cambridge University Press.

Foley-Cave, S. (2003), *Humour-Power-Identity: An Anthropological Exploration of Irish Deaf Humour*, Dublin: Dublin Business School.

Foran, Stanislus J. (1979), *Irish Sign Language*, Dublin: National Association for Deaf People.

Friedman, L. A. (ed.) (1977), *On the Other Hand: New Perspectives on American Sign Language*, New York: Academic Press.

Frishberg, N. (1975), 'Arbitrariness and iconicity: historical changes in American Sign Language', *Language*, 51, 676–710.

Garton, A. F. (1994), *Interacción social y desarrollo del lenguaje y la cognición*, Barcelona: Paidos.

Gascon-Ramos, M. (2008), 'Wellbeing in deaf children: A framework of understanding', *Educational and Child Psychology*, 25(2), 57–71.

Geeraerts, D. (2006), *Cognitive Linguistics: Basic Readings*, Berlin: Mouton de Gruyter.

Gillen, J. (2004), *You Have to Be Deaf to Understand: A Report Created by Deaf Ex-mainstream User Julianne Gillen on the Collective Experiences by a Group of Ex-mainstreamed Deaf in the Irish Education System from 1975–2001*, Dublin: Deaforward (Irish Deaf Society).

Givón, T. (1984), *Syntax: A Typological Functional Introduction*, Amsterdam and Philadelphia: John Benjamins.

Givón, T. (1989), *Mind, Code and Context: Essays in Pragmatics*, Hillsdale, NJ: Lawrence Erlbaum Associates.

Goldin-Meadow, S. (2003), *The Resilience of Language: What Gesture Creation in Deaf Children Can Tell Us about how all Children Learn Language*, New York: Psychology Press.

Goldin-Meadow, S. and Morford, M. (1994), 'Gesture in early child language', in V. Volterra and C. J. Erting (eds), *From Gesture to Language in Hearing and Deaf Children*, Washington, DC: Gallaudet University Press, pp. 249–62.

Goldin-Meadow, S. and Mylander, C. (1994), 'The development of morphology without a conventional language model', in V. Volterra and C. J. Erting (eds), *From Gesture to Language in Hearing and Deaf Children*, Washington, DC: Gallaudet University Press, pp. 165–77.

Gorbet, L. and Wilcox, P. (2010), 'Cross-linguistic conceptual schematization of "attention": American Sign Language (ASL) and Italian Sign Language (LIS)', paper presented at High Desert Linguistics Conference, Albuquerque, NM: University of New Mexico.

Grehan, C. (2008), *Communication Islands: The Impact of Segregation on Attitudes to ISL among a Sample of Graduates of St. Mary's School for Deaf Girls*, Dublin: Trinity College Dublin.
Griffey, N. (1994), *From Silence to Speech: Fifty Years with the Deaf*, Dublin: Dominican.
Grimes, J. E. (1975), *The Thread of Discourse*, The Hague: Mouton.
Haiman, J. (1998), 'The metalinguistics of ordinary language', *Evolution of Communication*, 2(1), 117–35.
Heiling, K. (ed.) (1999), *Global Perspectives on the Education of the Deaf in Selected Countries*, Hillsboro, OR: Butte, pp. 358–65.
Hockett, C. F. (1958), *A Course in Modern Linguistics*, New York: Macmillan.
Ingram, R. (2000), 'Foreword', in C. Roy (ed.), *Innovative Practices for Teaching Sign Language Interpreters*, Washington, DC: Gallaudet University Press.
Jacobowitz, E. L. and Stokoe, W. C. (1988), 'Signs of tense in ASL verbs', *Sign Language Studies*, 60, 331–40.
James, T., O'Neill, E. and Smyth, J. (1992), *Reading Achievements of Children with Hearing Impairments*, Dublin and Jordanstown: National Rehabilitation Board/ New University of Ulster, Jordanstown.
Janzen, T. (1998), *Topicality in ASL: Information Ordering, Constituent Structure, and the Function of Topic Marking*, PhD dissertation, Albuquerque, NM: University of New Mexico.
Janzen, T. (1999), 'The grammaticization of topics in American Sign Language', *Sign Language Studies*, 23(2), 271–306.
Janzen, T. (2005), *Perspective Shift Reflected in the Signer's Use of Space*, Dublin: Centre for Deaf Studies, School of Linguistic, Speech and Communication Sciences, Trinity College Dublin.
Janzen, T. (2010), 'Pragmatics as start point; discourse as end point', keynote paper presented at High Desert Linguistics Conference, Albuquerque, NM: University of New Mexico.
Janzen, T. D. and Shaffer, B. (2002), 'Gesture as the substrate in the process of ASL grammaticization', in R. Meier, D. Quinto and K. Cormier (eds), *Modality and Structure in Signed and Spoken Languages*, Cambridge: Cambridge University Press, pp. 199–223.
Johnson, M. (1987), *The Body in the Mind: The Bodily Basis of Meaning, Imagination, and Reason,* Chicago: University of Chicago Press.
Johnston, T. (1989), *Auslan: The Sign Language of the Australian Deaf Community*, Sydney: University of Sydney.
Johnston, T. (2001), 'The lexical database of Auslan (Australian Sign Language)', *Sign Language and Linguistics*, 4(1/2), 145–69.
Johnston, T. (2006), 'W(h)ither the Deaf Community: population, genetics, and the future of Austalian Sign Language', *Sign Language Studies*, 6(2), 137–73.
Johnston, T. and de Beuzeville, L. (n.d.), *Researching the Linguistic Use of Space in Auslan: Guidelines for Annotators Using the Auslan Corpus*, Sydney: Department of Linguistics, Macquarie University.
Johnston, T. and Schembri, A. (2007), *Australian Sign Language: An Introduction to Sign Language Linguistics*, Cambridge: Cambridge University Press.
Johnston, T., Vermeerbergen, M., Schembri, A. and Leeson, L. (2007), '"Real data

are messy": on the cross-linguistic analysis of constituent ordering in Australian Sign Language, Vlaamse Gebarentaal (Flemish Sign Language) and Irish Sign Language', in P. Perniss, R. Pfau and M. Steinbach (eds), *Sign Languages: A Cross-Linguistic Perspective*, Berlin: Mouton de Gruyter, pp. 163–205.

Karlsson, F. (1984), 'Structure and iconicity in sign language', in F. Loncke, P. Boyes-Braem and Y. Lebrun (eds), *Recent Research on European Sign Languages*, Lisse: Swets and Zeitlinger, pp. 149–55.

Kegl, J. A. and Wilbur, R. B. (1976), 'When does structure stop and style begin? Syntax, morphology and phonology vs. stylistic variation in American Sign Language', in C. Mufwene and S. Steever (eds), *Papers from the Twelfth Regional Meeting (Chicago Linguistics Society)*, Chicago: University of Chicago Press, pp. 376–96.

Kendon, A. (1980), 'Some uses of gesture', paper delivered to the New England Child Language Association, New London, CT.

Klima, E. S. and Bellugi, U. (1979), *The Signs of Language*, Cambridge, MA and London: Harvard University Press.

Knoors, H. (1999), 'The education of deaf children in the Netherlands', in H. W. Brelje (ed.), *Global Perspectives on the Education of the Deaf in Selected Countries*, Hillsboro, OR: Butte, pp. 249–60.

Kövecses, Z. and Radden, G. (1998), 'Metonymy: developing a cognitive linguistic view', *Cognitive Linguistics*, 9(1), 37–77.

Krausneker, V. (2001), 'Sign languages of Europe – future chances', in L. Leeson (ed.), *Looking Forward – EUD in the 3rd Millennium – The Deaf Citizen in the 21st Century*, Coleford: Douglas McLean, pp. 64–73.

Kyle, J. and Woll, B. (1985), *Sign Language: The Study of Deaf People and their Language*, Cambridge: Cambridge University Press.

Ladd, P. (2003), *Understanding Deaf Culture: In Search of Deafhood*, Clevedon: Multilingual Matters.

Ladefoged, P. (1993), *A Course in Phonetics*, Fort Worth and London: Harcourt Brace Jovanovich.

Lakoff, G. (1987), *Women, Fire, and Dangerous Things: What Categories Reveal about the Mind*, Chicago: University of Chicago Press.

Lakoff, G. and Johnson, M. (1980), *Metaphors We Live By*, Chicago and London: University of Chicago Press.

Lakoff, G. and Johnson, M. (1999), *Philosophy in the Flesh: The Embodied Mind and its Challenge to Western Thought*, New York: Basic Books.

Lakoff, G. and Johnson, M. (2003), *Metaphors We Live By*, new edn, Chicago and London: University of Chicago Press.

Lakoff, G. and Kövecses, Z. (1987), 'The cognitive model of anger inherent in American English', in D. Holland and N. Quinn (eds), *Cultural Models in Language and Thought*, Cambridge: Cambridge University Press, pp. 195–221.

Lane, H., Hoffmeister, R. and Bahan, B. (1996), *A Journey into the Deaf-World*, San Diego: Dawn Sign Press.

Langacker, R. (1987), *Foundations of Cognitive Grammar, Volume 1, Theoretical Foundations*, Stanford: Stanford University Press.

Lawson, L. K. (1983), 'Multi-channel signs', in B. Woll, J. G. Kyle and M. Deuchar (eds), *Language in Sign*, London: Croom Helm.

Leeson, L. (1996), *The Marking of Time in Signed Languages with Specific Reference to Irish Sign Language*, Dublin: Trinity College Dublin.
Leeson, L. (1997), *The ABC of Irish Sign Language: An Accompaniment to the Series of Programmes Shown on RTÉ*, Dublin: Irish Deaf Society and RTÉ.
Leeson, L. (2001), *Aspects of Verbal Valency in Irish Sign Language*, Doctoral thesis, Dublin: Trinity College Dublin.
Leeson, L. (2004), 'Signs of change in Europe: current European perspectives in the status of sign languages', in P. McDonnell (ed.), *Deaf Studies in Ireland: An Introduction*, Coleford: Douglas McLean, pp. 172–197.
Leeson, L. (2005), 'Vying with variation: interpreting language contact, gender variation and generational difference', in T. Janzen (ed.), *Topics in Signed Language Interpreting*, Amsterdam and Philadelphia: John Benjamins, pp. 251–92.
Leeson, L. (2006), *Signed Languages in Education in Europe – A Preliminary Exploration. (Preliminary Study. Languages of Education)*, Strasbourg: Council of Europe Language Policy Division.
Leeson, L. (2007), *Seeing is Learning: A Review of Education for Deaf and Hard of Hearing People in Ireland*, Trim: National Council for Special Education.
Leeson, L. (2010), 'Exploring discourse in Irish Sign Language', round table presentation, Winnipeg: Department of Linguistics, University of Manitoba.
Leeson, L. and Foley-Cave, S. (2007), 'Deep and meaningful conversation: challenging interpreter impartiality in the semantics and pragmatics classroom', in M. Metzger and E. Fleetwood (eds), *Translation, Sociolinguistic, and Consumer Issues in Interpreting*, Washington, DC: Gallaudet University Press, pp. 39–73.
Leeson, L. and Grehan, C. (2004), 'To the lexicon and beyond: the effect of gender on variation in Irish Sign Language', in M. Van Herreweghe and M. Vermeerbergen (eds), *To the Lexicon and Beyond: Sociolinguistics in European Deaf Communities*, Washington, DC: Gallaudet University Press, pp. 39–73.
Leeson, L. and Saeed, J. (2003), 'Exploring the cognitive underpinning in the construal of passive events in Irish Sign Language (ISL)', paper presented at *ICLC 8*, Logroño.
Leeson, L. and Saeed, J. (2004), 'The construal of passive events in Irish Sign Language (ISL)', paper presented at TISLR 8, Barcelona.
Leeson, L. and Saeed, J. (2007), 'Conceptual blending and the windowing of attention in Irish Sign Language', in M. Vermeerbergen, L. Leeson and O. A. Crasborn (eds), *Simultaneity in Signed Languages*, Amsterdam and Philadelphia: John Benjamins, pp. 55–73.
Leeson, L. and Saeed, J. I. (2010), 'Discourse markers in the Signs of Ireland corpus: the function of buoys', paper presented at High Desert Linguistics Society Conference, Albuquerque, NM: University of New Mexico.
Leeson, L., Saeed, J., Leonard, C., MacDuff, A. and Byrne-Dunne, D. (2006), 'Moving heads and moving hands: developing a digital corpus of Irish Sign Language. The 'Signs of Ireland' Corpus Development Project', *IT&T Annual Conference Proceedings 2006. October 25–26, 2006*, pp. 33–43.
Leeson, L. and Sheikh, H. (2010), *Experiencing Deafhood: Snapshots from Five Nations*, Dublin: Interesource Group Ireland.
LeMaster, B. (1990), *The Maintenance and Loss of Female and Male Signs in the Dublin Deaf Community*, Los Angeles: UCLA.

LeMaster, B. (1999–2000), 'Reappropriation of gendered Irish Sign Language in one family', *Visual Anthropology Review*, 15(2), 1–15.
LeMaster, B. (2002), 'What difference does difference make? Negotiating gender and generation in Irish Sign Language', in S. Benor, M. Rose, D. Sharma, J. Sweetland and Q. Zhang (eds), *Gendered Practices in Language*, Stanford: CSLI Publications, pp. 309–38.
LeMaster, B. and O'Dwyer, J. P. (1991), 'Knowing and using female and male signs in Dublin', *Sign Language Studies*, 73, 361–96.
Leonard, C. (2005), 'Signs of diversity: use and recognition of gendered signs among young Irish Deaf people', *Deaf Worlds*, 21(2), 62–77.
Liddell, S. K. (1978), 'Non-manual signals in ASL: a many layered system', in W. C. Stokoe (ed.), *Proceedings of the First National Symposium on Sign Language Research and Training, 1977*, Chicago: National Association of the Deaf, pp. 193–228.
Liddell, S. K. (1980), *American Sign Language Syntax*, The Hague and New York: Mouton.
Liddell, S. K. (1990), 'Four functions of a locus: reexamining the structure of space in ASL', in C. Lucas (ed.), *Sign Language Research: Theoretical Issues*, Washington, DC: Gallaudet University Press, pp. 176–98.
Liddell, S. K. (2000), 'Indicating verbs and pronouns: pointing away from agreement', in H. Lane and K. Emmorey (eds), *The Signs of Language Revisted: An Anthology to Honour Ursula Bellugi and Edward Klima*, Mahwah, NJ: LEA, pp. 303–20.
Liddell, S. K. (2003), *Grammar, Gesture, and Meaning in American Sign Language*, Cambridge: Cambridge University Press.
Liddell, S. K., Vogt-Svendsen, M. and Bergman, B. (2007), 'A crosslinguistic comparison of buoys. Evidence from American, Norwegian, and Swedish Sign Language', in M. Vermeerbergen, L. Leeson and O. Crasborn (eds), *Simultaneity in Signed Languages: Form and Function*, Amsterdam and Philadelphia: John Benjamins, pp. 187–215.
List, G., Wloka, M. and List, G. (1999), 'Education of the Deaf in Germany', in H. W. Brelje (ed.), *Global Perspectives on the Education of the Deaf in Selected Countries*, Hillsboro, OR: Butte, pp. 113–39.
Loncke, F., Quertinmont, S. and Ferreyra, P. (1990), 'Deaf children in schools: more or less native signers?', in S. Prillwitz and T. Vollhaber (eds), *Current Trends in European Sign Language Research. Proceedings of the 3rd European Congress on Sign Language Research, Hamburg, July 1989*, Seedorf: Signum, pp. 163–8.
MacSweeney, M. (1998), 'Cognition and deafness', in S. Gregory, P. Knight, W. McCracken, S. Powers and L. Watson (eds), *Issues in Deaf Education*, London: David Fulton, pp. 20–7.
Maguire, F. (1991), *A User's Guide for Irish Sign Language Research*, Dublin: Trinity College Dublin.
Mandel, M. (1977), 'Iconic devices in American Sign Language', in L. A. Friedman (ed.), *On the Other Hand: New Perspectives on American Sign Language*, New York: Academic Press, pp. 55–107.
Marschark, M. and Spencer, P. E. (2009), *Evidence of Best Practice Models and Outcomes in the Education of Deaf and Hard of Hearing Children: An International Review*, Trim: National Council for Special Education.

Mathews, E. (2007), 'Some statistics regarding the education of deaf and hard of Hearing children in Ireland: the current situation', in L. Leeson (ed.), *Seeing is Learning: A Review of Education for Deaf and Hard of Hearing People in Ireland*, Trim: National Council for Special Education, pp. 42–62.

Matthews, P. A. (1996a), 'Extending the lexicon of Irish Sign Language', *Teanga*, 16, 135–68.

Matthews, P. A. (1996b), *The Irish Deaf Community*, Baile Átha Cliath: Institiúid Teangeolaíochta Éireann.

Matthews, P. A. (2005), 'Practical phonology: what learners need to know about handshapes in Irish Sign Language', *Deaf Worlds*, 21(2), 32–61.

Matthews, P. A. and Foley-Cave, S. (2004), 'Village life: Deaf culture in contemporary Ireland', in P. McDonnell (ed.), *Deaf Studies in Ireland: An Introduction*, Coleford: Douglas McLean, pp. 65–84.

Mayberry, R. and Eichen, E. B. (1991), 'The long lasting advantage of learning sign language in childhood: another look at the critical period for language acquisition', *Journal of Memory and Language*, 30, 486–512.

McDonnell, J. (1997), 'The lexicon and vocabulary of signed English or manually coded English', *Teanga*, 17, 137–48.

McDonnell, P. (1979), 'The establishment and operation of institutions for the education of the Deaf in Ireland, 1816–1889', unpublished essay submitted in part-fulfilment of the requirements of the award of the Master in Education, University College Dublin, Dublin.

McDonnell, P. (1996), *Verb Categories in Irish Sign Language*, Dublin: Trinity College Dublin.

McDonnell, P. (2004), *Deaf Studies in Ireland – An Introduction*, Coleford: Douglas McLean.

McDonnell, P. (2010), 'Perspectives on deafness: history of the Irish Deaf community', in H. Sheikh (ed.), 'Perspectives on Deafness' elearning course, SIGNALL 3 (Leonardo da Vinci) Project, on restricted-access Moodle website.

McDonnell, P. and Saunders, H. (1993), 'Sit on your hands: strategies to prevent signing', in R. Fischer and H. Lane (eds), *Looking Back: A Reader on the History of Deaf Communities and their Sign Languages*, Hamburg: Signum, pp. 255–60.

McNeill, D. (1992), *Hand and Mind: What Gestures Reveal about Thought*, Chicago: University of Chicago Press.

McQueen, J. M. and Cutler, A. (1998), 'Morphology in word recognition', in A. Spencer and A. M. Zwicky (eds), *The Handbook of Morphology*, Oxford: Blackwell, pp. 406–27.

Meier, R. (1990), 'Person deixis in American Sign Language', in S. Fischer and P. Siple (eds), *Theoretical Issues in Sign Language Research, Vol. 1: Linguistics*, Chicago: University of Chicago Press, pp. 175–90.

Metzger, M. (1995), *The Paradox of Neutrality: A Comparison of Interpreters' Goals with the Reality of Interactive Discourse*, Washington, DC: Georgetown University.

Metzger, M. (1999), *Sign Language Interpreting: Deconstructing the Myth of Neutrality*, Washington, DC: Gallaudet University Press.

Militzer, S. (2009), 'The influence of oralism on mouth actions in Irish Sign Language (ISL)', paper presented at Boston University Conference on Language Development (BUCLD) 34, Boston.

Militzer, S. (2010), 'Puzzles of cross-modal language contact: code-mixing, mode-mixing, borrowing or language change? The case of Irish Sign Language', paper presented at High Desert Linguistics Society Conference, Albuquerque, NM: University of New Mexico.

Miller, C. (1994), 'Simultaneous constructions in Quebec Sign Language', in M. Brennan and G. H. Turner (eds), *Word Order Issues in Sign Language. Working Papers*, Durham: International Sign Linguistics Association, pp. 89–112.

Mindess, A. (1999), *Reading between the Signs: Intercultural Communication for Sign Language Interpreters*, Boston: Intercultural Press.

Morgan, G. (1998), *The Development of Discourse Cohesion in British Sign Language*, Bristol: Bristol University.

Morris, D., Collett, P., Marsh, P. and O'Shaughnessy, M. (1979), *Gestures: Their Origin and Distribution*, New York: Stein and Day.

National Institution for the Education of the Deaf and Dumb (1817), *Annual Report of the National Institution for the Education of Deaf and Dumb Children of the Poor in Ireland*, Dublin: National Institution for the Education of the Deaf and Dumb.

Nilsson, A.-L. (2007), 'The non-dominant hand in a Swedish Sign Language discourse', in M. Vermeerbergen, L. Leeson and O. Crasborn (eds), *Simultaneity in Signed Languages: Form and Function*, Amsterdam and Philadelphia: John Benjamins, pp. 163–85.

Nilsson, A.-L. (2008), *Spatial Strategies in Descriptive Discourse: Use of Signing Space in Swedish Sign Language*, Dublin: Centre for Deaf Studies, School of Linguistic, Speech and Communication Sciences, Trinity College Dublin.

Nilsson, A.-L. (2010), *Space in Swedish Sign Language: Reference, Real-Space Blending, and Interpretation*, Stockholm: Stockholm University Press.

Nonhebel, A., Crasborn, O. and van der Kooij, E. (2004), *Sign Language Transcription Conventions for the ECHO Project*, Nijmegen: University of Nijmegen.

Nunberg, G. (1995), 'Transfers of meaning', *Journal of Semantics*, 12(2), 109–32.

Ó Baoill , D. and Matthews, P. A. (2000), *The Irish Deaf Community Volume 2: The Structure of Irish Sign Language*, Dublin: ITE.

Orpen, C. E. H. (1836), *Anecdotes and Annals of the Deaf and Dumb*, London: Tims.

Padden, C. A. (1988), *The Interaction of Morphology and Syntax in American Sign Language*, New York: Garland.

Padden, C. A. (1990), 'The relation between space and grammar in ASL verbal morphology', in C. Lucas (ed.), *Sign Language Research: Theoretical Issues*, Washington, DC: Gallaudet University Press, pp. 118–32.

Pizzutto, E. and Pietrandrea, P. (2001), 'The notation of signed texts', *Sign Language and Linguistics*, 4(1/2), 29–45.

Pollard, R. (2006), *The Avenue*, Dublin: Denzille Press.

Poulin, C. and Miller, C. (1995), 'On narrative discourse and point of view in Quebec Sign Language', in K. Emmorey and J. Reilly (eds), *Language, Gesture and Space*, Hillside, NJ: Lawrence Erlbaum Associates, pp. 117–31.

Powers, S., Gregory, S. and Thoutenhoofd, E. D. (1998), *The Educational Achievements of Deaf Children: A Literature Review*, London: Department for Education and Employment.

Rainò, P. (2001), 'Mouthings and mouth gestures in Finnish Sign Language (FinSL)', in P. Boyes Braem and R. Sutton-Spence (eds), *The Hands are the Head of the*

Mouth: The Mouth as Articulator in Sign Languages, Hamburg: Signum, pp. 41–50.
Risler, A. (2007), 'A cognitive linguistic view of simultaneity in process signs in French Sign Language', in M. Vermeerbergen, L. Leeson and O. Crasborn (eds), *Simultaneity in Signed Languages: Form and Function*, Amsterdam and Philadelphia: John Benjamins, pp. 73–102.
Rosenstein, O. (2000), 'Is ISL (Israeli Sign Language) a Topic Prominent Language?', poster presented at TISLR 7, Amsterdam, 23–27 July 2000.
Roy, C. (1989), 'Features of discourse in an American Sign Language lecture', in C. Lucas (ed.), *The Sociolinguistics of the Deaf Community*, San Diego: Academic Press, pp. 231–51.
Rubino, C. (2001), 'Pangasinan', in J. Garry and C. Rubino (eds), *Encyclopedia of the World's Languages: Past and Present*, New York: Wilson Press, pp. 539–42.
Saeed, J. I. and Leeson, L. (2004), 'Windowing of attention in simultaneous constructions in Irish Sign Language (ISL)', paper presented at the Fifth Meeting of the High Desert Linguistics Society, Albuquerque, NM: University of New Mexico.
Sallandre, M.-A. (2007), 'Simultaneity in French Sign Language discourse', in M. Vermeerbergen, L. Leeson and O. Crasborn (eds), *Simultaneity in Signed Languages: Form and Function*, Amsterdam and Philadelphia: John Benjamins, pp. 103–26.
Sandler, W. and Lillo-Martin, D. (2006), *Sign Language and Linguistic Universals*, Cambridge: Cambridge University Press.
Sapir, E. (1921), *Language: An Introduction to the Study of Speech*, New York: Harcourt Brace.
Schembri, A. (2000), 'Rethinking "classifiers" in signed languages', paper presented at TISLR 7, Amsterdam.
Schembri, A. (2003), 'Rethinking "classifiers" in signed languages', in K. Emmorey (ed.), *Perspectives on Classifier Constructions in Sign Languages*, Mahwah, NJ: Lawrence Erlbaum, pp. 3–34.
Schembri, A., Jones, C. and Burnham, D. (2005), 'Comparing action gestures and classifier verbs of motion: evidence from Australian Sign Language, Taiwan Sign Language, and nonsigners' gestures without speech', *Journal of Deaf Studies and Deaf Education*, 10(3), 272–90.
Schick, B. (1990), 'Classifier predicates in American Sign Language', *International Journal of Sign Linguistics*, 1, 15–40.
Shaffer, B. (2000), *A Syntactic, Pragmatic Analysis of the Expression of Necessity and Possiibility in American Sign Language*, Albuquerque, NM: University of New Mexico.
Sign of the Times, television programme. Ireland: Mind the Gap Films for RTÉ, August 1995, June 1996.
Slobin, D. I. and Hoiting, N. (1994), 'Reference to movement in spoken and signed languages: typological considerations', paper presented at the Twentieth Annual Meeting of the Berkeley Linguistics Society, Berkeley.
Stalnaker, R. (1974), 'Pragmatic presuppositions', in M. Munitz and P. Unger (eds), *Semantics and Philosophy*, New York: New York University Press, pp. 197–213.
Stokoe, W. C. (1960), *Sign Language Structure: An Outline of the Visual Communication Systems of the American Deaf*, Silver Spring, MD: Linstok Press.

Stokoe, W. C. (1974), 'Classification and description of sign languages', in T. Sebeok (ed.), *Current Trends in Linguistics*, The Hague: Mouton, pp. 207–28.

Stokoe, W. C. (1978), *Sign Language Structure: The First Linguistic Analysis of American Sign Language*, Silver Spring: Linstok Press.

Studdert-Kennedy, M. (1987), 'The phoneme as a perceptuomotor structure', in D. A. Allport (ed.), *Language Perception and Production: Relationships between Listening, Speaking, Reading and Writing*, London: Academic Press, pp. 67–84.

Supalla, S. (1978), 'Morphology of verbs of motion and location in American Sign Language', in F. Caccamise and D. Hicks (eds), *American Sign Language in a Bilingual, Bicultural Context: Proceedings of the Second National Symposium on Sign Language Research and Teaching*, Coronado, CA: National Association of the Deaf, pp. 27–46.

Supalla, S. (1992), *The Book of Name Signs: Naming in American Sign Language*, San Diego: Dawn Sign Press.

Sutton-Spence, R. (2007), 'Mouthings and simultaneity in British Sign Language', in M. Vermeerbergen, L. Leeson and O. A. Crasborn (eds), *Simultaneity in Signed Languages: Form and Function*, Amsterdam: John Benjamins.

Sutton-Spence, R. and Boyes Braem, P. (2001), *The Hands Are the Head of the Mouth: The Mouth as Articulator in Sign Languages*, Hamburg: Signum.

Sutton-Spence, R., Ladd, P. and Rudd, G. (2005), *Analysing Sign Language Poetry*, Basingstoke: Palgrave Macmillan.

Sutton-Spence, R. and Woll, B. (1999), *The Linguistics of British Sign Language – An Introduction*, Cambridge: Cambridge University Press.

Talmy, L. (1985), 'Lexicalization patterns: semantic structure in lexical forms', in T. Shopen (ed.), *Language Typology and Syntactic Description*, Cambridge: Cambridge University Press, pp. 57–149.

Talmy, L. (1988), 'Force dynamics in language and cognition', *Cognitive Science*, 12, 49–100.

Talmy, L. (1996), ' The windowing of attention in language', in M. Shibitani and S. A. Thompson (eds), *Grammatical Constructions – Their Form and Meaning*, Oxford: Clarendon Press, pp. 235–87.

Tannen, D. (1989), *Talking Voices: Repetition, Dialogue, and Imagery in Conversational Discourse*, Cambridge: Cambridge University Press.

Taylor, J. (1985), *Linguistic Categorisation: Prototypes in Linguistic Theory*, Oxford: Clarendon Press.

Taylor, J. (1995), *Linguistic Categorisation. Prototypes in Linguistic Theory*, 2nd edn, Oxford: Clarendon Press.

The ABC of ISL (1997), television programme. Ireland: IDS and RTÉ.

Thorvaldsdottir, G. (2010), 'You get out what you put in: the beginnings of phonetic and phonological coding in the Signs of Ireland digital corpus', paper presented at LREC, Malta, 17–23 May 2010.

Timmermans, N. (2005), *The Status of Sign Languages in Europe*, Strasbourg: Council of Europe.

Traugott, E. (1989), 'On the rise of epistemic meanings in English', *Language*, 65(1), 31–55.

UNESCO (1994), *The Salamanca Statement and Framework for Action on Special Needs Education*, Salamanca: United Nations Educational, Scientific and Cultural Organisation (UNESCO) and Ministry of Education and Science, Spain.

United Nations (2006), *Convention on the Rights of Persons with Disabilities. Ad Hoc Committee on a Comprehensive and Integral International Convention on the Protection and Promotion of the Rights and Dignity of Persons with Disabilities*, New York: United Nations.

Valli, C. and Lucas, C. (1995), *Linguistics of American Sign Language*, 2nd edn, Washington, DC: Gallaudet University Press.

van der Kooij, E. (2002), *Reducing Phonological Categories in Sign Language of the Netherlands. Phonetic Implementation and Iconic Motivation*, Utrecht: LOT

Van Herreweghe, M. (2002), 'Turn-taking mechanisms and active participation in meetings with deaf and hearing participants in Flanders', in C. Lucas (ed.), *Turn-Taking, Fingerspelling, and Contact in Signed Languages*, Washington, DC: Gallaudet University Press, pp. 73–106.

Van Hoek, K. (1996), 'Conceptual locations for reference in American Sign Language', in G. Fauconnier and E. Sweetser (eds), *Spaces, Worlds and Grammar*, Chicago and London: University of Chicago Press.

Vermeerbergen, M. and Demey, E. (2007), 'Sign+gesture=speech+gesture? Comparing aspects of simultaneity in Flemish Sign Language to instances of concurrent speech and gesture', in M. Vermeerbergen, L. Leeson and O. Crasborn (eds), *Simultaneity in Signed Languages: Form and Function*, Amsterdam and Philadelphia: John Benjamins, pp. 257–82.

Vermeerbergen, M. and Leeson, L. (2011), 'European signed languages – towards a typological snapshot', in B. Kortmann and J. van der Auwera (eds), *The Field of Linguistics*, Berlin: Mouton de Gruyter, pp. 269–87.

Vestberg, P. (1999), 'Education of the Deaf in Denmark', in H. W. Brelje (ed.), *Global Perspectives on the Education of the Deaf in Selected Countries*, Hillsboro, OR: Butte, pp. 59–68.

Volterra, V. (1983), 'Gestures, signs and words at two years', in J. G. Kyle and B. Woll (eds), *Language in Sign*, London: Croom Helm, pp. 109–15.

Wallin, L. (1983), 'Compounds in Swedish Sign Language in historical perspective', in J. G. Kyle and B. Woll (eds), *Language in Sign*, London: Croom Helm, pp. 56–68.

Watson, L (1998), 'Oralism – current policy and practice', in S. Gregory, P. Knight, W. McCracken, S. Powers and L. Watson (eds), *Issues in Deaf Education*, London: David Fulton, pp. 69–76.

Watson, L. and Parsons, J. (1998), 'Supporting deaf pupils in mainstream settings', in S. Gregory, P. Knight, W. McCracken, S. Powers and L. Watson (eds), *Issues in Deaf Education*, London: David Fulton, pp. 135–42.

Wheatley, M. and Pabsch, A. (2010), *Sign Language Legislation in the European Union*, Brussels: European Union of the Deaf.

Wilbur, R. B. (1987), *American Sign Language: Linguistic and Applied Dimensions*, Boston: Little, Brown.

Wilbur, R. B. (1994), 'Foregrounding structures in American Sign Language', *Journal of Pragmatics*, 22, 674–72.

Wilcox, S. (2004a), 'Cognitive iconicity: conceptual spaces, meaning and gesture in signed languages', *Cognitive Linguistics*, 15(2), 119–47.

Wilcox, S. (2004b), 'Gesture and language: cross-linguistic and historical data from signed languages', *Gesture*, 4(1), 43–73.

Wilcox, S., Perrin-Wilcox, P. and Josep-Jarque, M. (2003), 'Mappings in conceptual space: metonymy, metaphor and iconicity in two signed languages', *Jezikoslovije*, 4(1), 139–56.

Woll, B. (1998), 'Development of signed and spoken languages', in S. Gregory, P. Knight, W. McCracken, S. Powers and L. Watson (eds), *Issues in Deaf Education*, London: David Fulton, pp. 58–68.

Woll, B. (2003), 'Modality, universality and the similarities across sign languages: an historical perspective', in A. Baker, B. van den Bogaerde and O. Crasborn (eds), *Cross-linguistic Perspectives in Sign Language Research. Selected Papers from TISLR 2000*, Hamburg: Signum, pp. 17–27.

Woll, B. and Sutton-Spence, R. (2007), 'Sign languages', in D. Britain (ed.), *Language in the British Isles*, Cambridge: Cambridge University Press.

Index of Names

General Index

n = note; f = figure